P. A. Lyons

Two Compoti

P. A. Lyons

Two Compoti

ISBN/EAN: 9783337018832

Printed in Europe, USA, Canada, Australia, Japan

Cover: Foto ©ninafisch / pixelio.de

More available books at **www.hansebooks.com**

REMAINS

HISTORICAL & LITERARY

CONNECTED WITH THE PALATINE COUNTIES OF

LANCASTER AND CHESTER.

PUBLISHED BY

THE CHETHAM SOCIETY.

VOL. CXII.

PRINTED FOR THE CHETHAM SOCIETY.
M.DCCC.LXXXIV.

Two "Compoti"

OF THE

LANCASHIRE AND CHESHIRE MANORS

OF

Henry de Lacy, Earl of Lincoln,

XXIV. AND XXXIII. EDWARD I.

TRANSCRIBED AND TRANSLATED BY THE
REV. P. A. LYONS, B.A.

PRINTED FOR THE CHETHAM SOCIETY.
M.DCCC.LXXXIV.

Printed by Charles E. Simms,
Manchester.

CONTENTS.

	PAGE
INTRODUCTION	v *seq.*
THE COMPOTUS, 12 December, 1294, to 30 September, 1296	1–56
The Translation	118–149
THE COMPOTUS, 30 September, 1304, to 30 September, 1305	57–117
The Translation	150–187
Notes and Corrections	188–192
Index	193 *seq.*

INTRODUCTION.

THE very interesting and valuable accounts here printed relate to the Lancashire and Cheshire estates of HENRY DE LACY, Earl of Lincoln,* one of the most conspicuous and powerful barons of the realm, whose influence on the history of the two counties Palatine was of high moment. He was Lord of the Honor of Clitheroe, Baron of Halton, and hereditary Constable of Chester; moreover, it was he who suggested to the monks of Stanlaw Abbey to remove into the valley of the Calder. He owned great estates in Yorkshire, Lincolnshire, and elsewhere; and it was in reference to him and his ancestors that Camden said that Lincolnshire "glorieth in the Earls which have borne title thereof."

His parentage and ancestry may be seen in the annexed pedigree. He was a Ward of Henry III., and was brought up at his Court. At the early age of six years he married Margaret, eldest daughter of William Longspee,

---

* He is often called in Norman-French deeds "le Compte de *Nichole*," the corrupt form for Lincoln. This title perplexed Mr. Ormerod (*Hist. Chesh.*, new ed., vol. i. p. 655, note *a*), who supposed that it was a clerical error for Lincolne. The Parliament of 1307 was summoned to meet at "Nicole." There was a Nichole Hall in Pontefract Castle.

Roger de Lacy, surnamed "Hell"; =Maud de Clare.
buried at Stanlaw, 1211.

John de Lacy, 1st *Earl of Lincoln* of =Alice, d. of =Margaret, eldest d. of
his line in right of his 2nd wife; bur.   Gilbert   Robert de Quincey and
at Stanlaw, 1240. *Cf.* the Compotus,   d'Aquila.   *Countess of Lincoln*;
pp. 15, 125; 97, 174.   d. 1232.

Edmond de Lacy; =Alice, d. of the Marquis de Saluces (Saluzzo),
died 5 June, 1258;   and cousin to Q. Eleanor of Eng.; mar. at
bur. at Stanlaw.   Woodstock, May, 1247; living 1294.

HENRY DE LACY, 2nd =Margaret, d. of Sir=Jane, d. of
and last *Earl of Lincoln*   Wm. Longspee;   Sir William
of this family, 1250-1311.   mar. 1256.   Martyn.

Alice,   = Thos. Plantagenet, son =   Sir   =   Sir   Edmund;   Margaret.
Countess of   and heir of Edmund,   Eubule   Hugh   John.
Lincoln,   Earl of Lancaster;   Lestrange.   Frenes.
b. *c.* 1283;   beheaded at Pon-   ob. vit. pat.
d. 1348.   tefract, 1322.

who was grandson of Henry II., and Rosamond Clifford. Hence de Lacy in the King's writs is frequently styled "our cousin." In 1268 he and his wife performed homage for, and obtained livery of, all the lands which descended to the latter on the death of William de Longspee, who was entitled to the earldom of Salisbury. De Lacy's early manhood was spent in warfare under Edward I., whom in many respects he resembled in character, and to whom he became a most devoted friend. He also lived on terms of amity with Edmund, Earl of Lancaster, the King's brother. On 8 March, 1272, de Lacy was knighted with Prince Edward and others, created Earl of Lincoln, and made governor of Knaresborough Castle. His chief Yorkshire barony was that of Pontefract, where he held his court; and that place is frequently named in the *Compotus*. Staincliff, another Yorkshire manor, is mentioned twice (pp. 14, 125). In the year last named, de Lacy, with the Earl of Lancaster, was engaged in the attack upon Robert de Ferrars at Chartley Castle, in Staffordshire, a rebel who would not surrender his stronghold; and a royal pardon for the slaughter of the garrison was subsequently obtained by the besiegers.

In 1276, de Lacy entered upon the first of many campaigns against the Welsh. In the following year he did homage for 7½ knights' fees. Numerous writs of summons for his attendance at Parliament were addressed to him from 1276 to 1309; he was also summoned to the King's councils; and during the same period he acquired the right of establishing many fairs upon his estates, including those in Lancashire. There are grants extant connected with Burnley, Congleton, Rochdale, Colne, Clitheroe, and other towns.* In 1279 he was one of the *locum tenentes* in England during the King's absence in France.

The Earl's great-grandfather had given Rochdale Church, an appendage of the Honor of Pontefract, to the Abbey of Stanlaw; and he himself, 1 January, 1283, made a grant of the Church of Whalley to the same Abbey. A later deed, dated Pontefract, the same year, granted the remainder of the advowson; and the donor expressed a wish that when the monks removed to

* Westminster, 6 June, 1294. Charter granting to Henry de Lacy, Earl of Lincoln, markets and fairs at his manors of Pontefract, Bradford, Campsall, Slaidburn and Almonbury in Yorkshire, Burnley in Lancashire, and places in other counties; and free warren in all his demesne lands of Knottingley, Owston, Campsall, &c., in the counties of York, Lancaster, Middlesex, Berks, Bucks and Oxford. (3 1*st Rept. Dep. Keeper*, p. 17.)

Whalley they would take with them the remains of his ancestors. (*Coucher Book*, p. 190.) He reserved to himself the right of hunting over the Whalley domains; and his love of the chase is also shown in many requests to the King for free warren over the different lands which he held. It was not without interest that he watched the progress of the enclosing of his park near Tottington in the year 1305; and the hawks (*esparvarii*) and cocks sent up to London in the same year may have been for presents to friends (pp. 115, 185).

In reward for his activity in the operations against the Welsh in 1282-3, one of the "Edwardian" castles was bestowed upon him. The royal grant of the Lordship of Denbigh is dated 1284; and the writs henceforth describe him as Lord of Ros and Rowynock. The quota of men from his lordship in 1287, towards the suppression of the Welsh rebellion, was 400 foot-soldiers. Leland ascribed to him the building of Denbigh, adding that his effigy was over the gateway.* At Conway, 12 May,

* Grants in fee from the Earl are dated at Denbigh, 8 June, 1283, to two of his clients, for their homage and service of certain acres of land of the waste of Congleton; and another of five acres of waste land in the foreign wood of Halton. In 1284 he held a license to grant lands in mortmain in his manor of Denbigh to the seven chaplains officiating in the chapel of that manor. (35*th Rep. Dep. Keeper*, p. 11; 31*st*, p. 14.) On 1 Sept., 1290, by a royal charter, all his men inhabiting, or who in future should inhabit, his town of Denbigh, should be free of toll, stallage, pavage, pannage, murage, pontage, and passage, in the counties of Chester, Salop, Stafford, Gloucester, Worcester and Hereford. Denbigh in this grant is misprinted *Dynelegh* (near Burnley) in Sir Peter Leycester, p. 274, and in Ormerod's *Cheshire*, vol. i. p. 699.

1283, de Lacy attested Bishop Burnell's charter granting a fair to Nantwich. He was with the King during his three years' absence in the French Provinces.

The foundation of Kirkstall Abbey, in 1152, was due to the benefaction of a de Lacy. In the year 1287 this convent had become so involved in debt to a Jew and other creditors that Abbot Hugh sold the Blackburnshire and other estates of the Abbey to de Lacy, at ten years' purchase. It does not appear whether the buyer was actuated by religion or interest. The transaction is noticeable from the fact that the Abbot has left an account of an interview with the Earl about the negociation. In a letter to his convent, dated 12 November, 1287, the Abbot describes his wearisome journey to Gascony in search of de Lacy. He set out on 18 September, and travelled thither through Burgundy. Arrived at St. Sever, called "the remotest part of Gascony," he says: "Here we found our patron, the Earl of Lincoln, with other great men of the Court, attending upon the King; and to him we explained fully and to the best of our ability the distresses of the House. He was touched with pity at our representation, and promised us all the information and assistance in his power." The sale of the land being arranged,* the wily ecclesiastic concluded

---

* St. Sever, Saturday next after the feast of St. Luke the Evangelist (25 October), 1287. Release and quitclaim from the Abbot and convent of Kirkestall to Henry de Lascy, Earl of Lincoln, and Constable of Chester, of all the Lands which they had and held of the said Earl in Accrington, Cliviger, and Hunscot, in the county of Lancaster, and

his letter by urging the monks to remove everything moveable from the land except the crops, and to labour day and night to that end, before the Earl's messenger, whom he was purposely detaining, arrived to take seizin! The Abbot added, " It will not be prudent to shew these letters to any one." (*Hist. Craven*, ed. 1878, pp. 81-2.)

"Infinite grants," says Sir Peter Leycester, "were made to and by this Henry Lacy;" and his statement is borne out by those printed in the *Histories* of Cheshire and Whalley, and in the Reports of the Keeper of the Public Records. The following are without date:

Henry de Lascy, Earl of Lincoln, to Sir Edmund Talebot and Jane his wife: the manor of Rishton in tail male special, to hold as fully as Adam de Rishton, a bastard, held the same. (35*th Report*, p. 11.)

Henry de Lascy, Earl of Lincoln, and Constable of Chester to the Monks of St. Mary of Rufford: all the lands which they held of him in Elmeton (Yorkshire). (*Ibid.*, p. 12.)

Henry de Lacy, Earl of Lincoln, and Constable of Chester, to the burghers of Congleton: a guild-merchant, housbote and haybote, and common of pasture, and privilege of grinding at the mill of Congleton. (*Cal. Inquis. p. m. Duch. Lanc.*, No. 47, pt. ii. vol. i.)

An Inquisition at Chester, 11 May, 1288, returned de Lacy as holding eight knights' fees. In 1290 he joined in the letter addressed to the Pope complaining of the attempt made to appropriate certain prebends of the Cathedrals of York and Lincoln to the Hospital of the Holy Ghost and the Basilica of St. Peter's at Rome. (*Parl. Writs;* and *cf. IV. Hist. MSS. Com.*, p. 396.)

in la Roundehay, Secroft, and Shadewelle, in the county of York. Attested by many bishops and knights, including Sir Otho de Grandison. (35*th Rept. Dep. Keeper*, pp. 11, 12.)

Introduction. xi

On 12 August, the same year, the king nominated him first commissioner for rectifying the abuses of Justice on the part of the Judges during the King's absence in France. In 1291-2 he accompanied the King in the expedition against Scotland, of which Edward claimed to be sovereign lord. In the latter year, de Lacy was called upon to establish his right for himself and vassals to be exempt from fines and amerciaments in the county of Lancaster. He proved that he had his free court at Clitheroe for the wapentake of Blackburnshire, where all his vassals had been wont to plead from time immemorial, as the sheriff pleads in other wapentakes. He also showed that he was free from fines and amerciaments of the county for all his lands and fees in Blackburnshire except two (Downham and Worston), and for his demesne lands in the hundreds of Leyland, Amounderness and West Derby, and to be free from suits of counties and wapentakes, except for his lands in Rochdale, for which he owed suit to the County Court of Lancaster and Wapentake of Salfordshire. (*Lanc. and Chesh. Records*, p. 358.)

The Earl was unfortunate in his offspring. His eldest son, Edmund, was drowned in a well at Denbigh Castle, and his son John was killed by falling through a window in Pontefract Castle. A tradition associates the latter catastrophe with the manor house of Ightenhill.

His daughter Alice, ultimately his heiress, born about 1283, was affianced at nine years of age (says Camden) to Thomas Plantagenet, son of Edmund (Crouchback)

Earl of Lancaster, on condition that if they died without heirs the Earl of Lincoln's property should go to Edmund Earl of Lancaster. The girl and her maid are introduced into the first of these two *Compoti* (pp. 16, 126). On 12 July, 1288, letters patent were granted to Alice de Lacy, of the Castle, town, manor, and Honor of Halton, in the county of Chester, for and during her life, with reversion after her decease to the King and his heirs. The marriage of his daughter seems to have turned the Earl's attention to the ultimate disposal of his property. He had evidently given up all hopes of an heir, and in 1292 surrendered his barony of Pontefract to the King. But soon afterwards the barony was re-granted with remainder to Edmund, Earl of Lancaster,* who about this time borrowed 4,000 marks from de Lacy.

* Westminster, 28 October, 1294. Charter granting to Henry de Lacy, Earl of Lincoln, and the heirs of his body, the estates surrendered by the said Earl to the King, viz., all the castles, lands, &c., which he held in the counties of Lancaster and Chester, the manor of Kingston in Dorset, and also the reversion of the manor of Slaidburn in Bouland, with the forest and chase, the manor and soke of Snaith, and all other lands and tenements held in dower by Alice de Lacy, mother of the said Earl, after the decease of the said Alice; and in failure of issue the premises are to remain to Edmund the King's brother, and his heirs for ever. (31*st Rept. Dep. Keeper*, p. 17.)

Westminster, same date. Charter granting the manor of Sutton [par. Prescot, co. Lanc.] to Henry de Lacy and Margaret his wife, Earl and Countess of Lincoln, for term of their lives; and after their decease to Thomas, son of Edmund the King's brother, and his wife Alice, daughter and heiress of the same Earl and Countess and the heirs of their bodies; with remainder in failure of issue to the right heirs of the said Thomas. (*Ibid.*)

Introduction.

From the year 1293 the Earl of Lincoln was employed in many embassies to France. On 11 November, 1294, the Welsh defeated the Earl at Denbigh, and soon afterwards they gained an advantage over Prince Edward. In the following year five Welsh hostages, including a chieftain, were conveyed through the Earl's territories to Pontefract. (*Comp.*, pp. 51, 147.)

The year to which the first *Compotus* belongs was one in which the kingdom was engaged in warfare in France, Wales and Scotland. Towards the expenses of the war with the latter country, 6*l.* is entered in the accounts (pp. 64, 154) for three knights' fees in Widnes. The Earl appears to have gone into Brittany with the army of the Earl of Lancaster, upon whose decease he succeeded as Commander, becoming also Viceroy of Aquitaine. The military affairs of the French provinces occupied the Earl's attention for a few years.

At the defeat of the Scots under Wallace at Falkirk, 22 July, 1298, de Lacy led the vanguard of the English army, which contained 1,000 men from Lancashire. Later in the same year he was entrusted with an enquiry into the conduct of the Justices of the Forests and other forest officers. The long-continued war with Scotland taxed Lancashire very heavily: in 1297 the Lancashire levies were 3,000 men, and the Yorkshire number was 4,000. In 1299 the quotas were 2,000 and 4,000 respectively from the same counties. The Earl was summoned, 18 November, 1298, to a Parliament to meet at Carlisle, 6 June, 1299, where musters were to assemble for punishing the rebellion of the Scots. Letters patent, dated Durham, 10 November, 1298, recite that the King had "lately" granted to de Lacy the stewardship, towns, castles, and all the lands and tenements of James, formerly steward of Scotland, the King's enemy and rebel, with some exceptions. (31*st Rept.*, p. 18.)

It was probably on his way to Scotland in 1300 that de Lacy, at Chester, did homage to the Prince of Wales for some of his lands. (*Hist. Chesh.*, vol. i. p. 232.) He was with the royal army when it assembled at Carlisle, 24 June, 1300, for the invasion of Scotland; and his scutage for this army in respect to the knights' fees for Widnes, Tottington, Penwortham, Blackburnshire, and Bowland, is entered in the *Compotus* (pp. 63, 101, 107, 112), amounting to the large sum of 25*l*. 8*s*. 7*d*.* His knights' fees in the year 1300 were nine in England and six in Wales.

The Earl participated in the capture of Carlaverock on the Nith, between 5th and 12th July, 1300. The siege of the Castle was the subject of a curious contemporary poem in Norman-French, which in lively verse sings the arms and the men engaged in the exploit. The characters of above one hundred noblemen and knights are sketched in the poem. The army, we learn, was divided

---

* Escuage, = Scutage, or Service of Shield, is thus noticed by Littleton: "When the King maketh a voyage royail into Scotland for to subdue the Scots, hee that holdeth by a fee of Knights service behooveth to be with the King by 40 dayes, well and convenably arrayed for the war." (Littleton's *Tenures*, ed. 1641.)

into four squadrons, commanded by the Earl of Lincoln, the Earl of Warren, the King himself, and Prince Edward of Carnarvon. The Earl of Lincoln is accordingly first noticed; he is termed the "good" Earl, and his military valour is pointed out as his chief characteristic; his banner was of yellow silk, bearing a lion rampant purple:

> Enris li bons Quens de Nicole,
> Ki provesté embrasce e acole,
> E son cuer le a soveraine,
> Menans le eschele premeraine,
> Banner ont de un cendal safrin
> O un lioun rampant purprin.

The poet then describes the retinue of "the good and well-beloved Earl," in which were John de Lancaster, John de Huddleston, &c.

The latter portion of the Earl's days was occupied in embassies to the Continent and in the Scotch wars. He was summoned to a Parliament to meet at Westminster, 28 February, 1305. In the year of the second *Compotus* he was in Lancashire, for his receiver at Clitheroe between May and September, 1305, paid 1*s*. 8*d*. for carrying the Earl's bed to Denbigh (pp. 115, 185). A succeeding entry seems to indicate that the Earl was staying at his Tottington manor. The same year he was despatched to Lyons, to be present at the inauguration of Clement V., and he presented him, in the King's name, with some vessels of pure gold. On 22 July, 1306, the King allowed him to give some advowsons to the scholars of Oxford in a certain house there. On 9 January, 1307, a royal commission empowered Walter, Bishop of Chester (*i.e.*, Coventry and Lichfield), treasurer of the exchequer, and de Lacy, to open the Parliament at Carlisle; and on the roll of that assembly in February, his name comes next after the Prince of Wales's. A commission of array for raising 1,000 foot-soldiers in Lancashire, attested at Carlisle, 19 March, gives 150 men as the quota from the liberty of Blackburnshire, and the rest formed the quota of the body of the county, the troops being needed to pursue Robert Bruce on the moors and marshes, where he was lurking. During this campaign de Lacy accompanied the ruthless King. The army left Carlisle 4 July, 1307; the King died at Burgh on the 7th. De Lacy was with the monarch in his last moments, and received his request to be faithful to his son. A letter written at the end of the month mentions the homage which had been done at Carlisle to the new King "by the Patriarch of Jerusalem, the Earl of Lincoln, and other great men." (35*th Rept.*, p. 25.) The Earl, at Edward II.'s coronation, bore one of the swords of state. About the same time he was made governor of Skipton Castle; and throughout the early part of the reign, he was prominent in the Scotch war and other events, acting on one occasion (1 Sept., 1310) as "Custos" of the kingdom.

His knights' fees in Lancashire were ultimately $14\tfrac{1}{3}$ in number. In 1303, in pursuit of the accumulation of property near his London house in Chancery Lane, he acquired from a barber named Richard de Munden, "a house with shops in Ironmonger Lane within the precincts of the Earl's mansion, lately belonging to Sir Otho de

Grandison, the same house having been of the gift of Aymer de Valence for term of life." The mansion, which was then in the suburbs, occupied a considerable portion of the present Inn of Court, called Lincoln's Inn, which, named after the Earl, bears his arms. In the records of the Duchy of Lancaster there is a *Compotus*, dated 1296, showing the receipts and expenditure in his garden at at Holborn, which he seems to have worked for profit as much as his Lancashire vaccaries.

Portions of the new buildings at Whalley had been completed in 1306; and on 12 June, 1308, the first stone of the conventual Church was laid by the Earl in person (*Whalley*, vol. i. p. 90). On 6 October, 1310, the King, by writ tested at "Byger," took the Earl into his protection, as well as all his lands in Chestershire.

The Earl died in London early in February, 1311; and he was buried with great pomp at St. Paul's, to which edifice he was a munificent contributor. A stately tomb was set up in his memory, which, though destroyed in the fire, has been preserved in a plate by Hollar. On 16 Feb., the Inquisition of his lands was taken; and on the 28th the King made a forced loan of 4,000 marks from his executors, N. de Reding, R. de Silkstone, J. de Sandale, the King's treasurer, and Sir H. le Scroop, knt., who proved the will 16 May (*Fasti Ebor*, vol. i. p. 381). Through the Plantagenets the estates came to the Duchy of Lancaster.*

---

* *Cf.* Camden's *Brit.*, ed. Holland, 1610, pp. 544-5; Brooke's *Catalogue*, pp. 124-5; Vincent, p. 320; Mills' *Catalogue of Honour*, p. 321; Dugdale's *Baronage*, vol. i. p. 103-6; Leycester's *Cheshire Antiqq.*, pp.

xviii *Introduction.*

There is not much in these rolls to afford an insight into the Earl's character. One or two instances seem to mark his generosity. His charities consist of a gift to the Black Friars of Chester, and of alms in the shape of cloth. His piety is more apparent. The lamp at Salley Abbey in memory of his grandfather was annually replenished. To the shrine of St. Edmund in that Abbey he gave costly articles, including a cup of silver-gilt which was said to have belonged to St. Edmund. The old cross in his market at Burnley was repaired and re-erected at his charges (p. 18), and still remains a relic of his days. (*Whalley*, vol. ii. p. 174.)

273-5; Orm. *Hist. Chesh.*, vol. i. pp. 693, 698; White Kennett's *Parochial Antiquities of Ambrosden*, vol. i. pp. 354 *seqq.*; Harland's *Clitheroe Charters*, pp. 8-11; Whitaker's *Whalley*, vol. i. p. 246; Gregson's *Fragments*, p. 100; Nicolas's *Siege of Carlaverock*, 1828, pp. 4-5, 93-8; Beamont's *Halton*, p. 27; Palgrave's *Parliamentary Writs*, passim; *Rolls of Parliament*, passim; 31*st and* 35*th Reports of Public Records; Chronicles of the Reigns Edwards I. and II.* (Rolls Series); Dodsworth's *MSS.* Mr. Selby has examined two curious and exhaustive Inventories of the muniments of Henry de Lacy, which appear, he says, to be of considerable interest. (*Lanc. and Chesh. Records*, p. 297.)—In 1292 the Earl, with other great men, was directed by letters patent to make certain provisions for the "due maintenance of arms." (31*st Report*, p. 16.) In 1306, in reply to a petition of the Parliament at Carlisle, Edward I. declared that after the grant which he had made to De Lacy for life of the Return of Writs in certain hundreds, he "would not grant a similar franchise, as long as he lived, to any one excepting his own children." (*Rot. Parl.*, p. 211 b.) The same King, by letter dated Lanercost, 18 February, 1306-7, addressed to Walter, Bp. of Chester, Henry de Lacy "nostre chier cousin," and others of the Council at Carlisle, referred to the appointment of Walter de Bedewynde as treasurer of York cathedral. (*Ibid.*, and *Le Neve*, vol. iii. p. 159.)

Introduction. xix

The two *Compoti* consist of the accounts for the years 1295-6 and 1304-5, of the Stewards, the Parkers, the Farm-bailiffs, the Cowherds, and other servants of the great Earl in the towns or granges of his Honor of Clitheroe and Barony of Halton.* The first large holding included the old parishes of Whalley and Blackburn, taking in Tottington and other places; and the second (called once "Haltonshire") comprised Widnes and Denton in Lancashire, with Congleton and other places in Cheshire extending from Mottram-in-Longdendale to Alderley and Little Peover.

CLITHEROE, the Lancashire stronghold and residence of the Earl, lying in the line of his journeys between Lancaster and Pontefract, here shews itself to be a place of importance as head of the Honor. It assumed an almost regal state when the Earl was present. There, annually, when his tenants appeared to offer him the three weeks' suit and service, the stewards from the neighbouring manors presented their exactly-balanced accounts to the auditors (*audientium*, p. 16). The revenue from that town was about £60 (equal to about £1,200 now), while Rochdale gave about £24, and Downham and Halton about £16 each. The Earl had manor-houses at Ightenhill, Colne, Accrington, and Tottington. Hard by were

---

* The originals are two large rolls, in very fine condition, now in the Record Office, London, forming Div. xxix., Bundle 1, of the "Ministers' Accounts," heretofore in the office of the Duchy of Lancaster. In the *Yorkshire Archæological Journal*, vol. viii. pp. 351-8, is printed the first part of the Compotus of the *Yorkshire* Estates of the Earl for A.D. 1295-6.

the forests, viz., Pendle, Accrington, Rossendale, and Trawden; and there were parks stocked with deer at Ightenhill and Musbirry. The Vaccaries, which formed a chief source of the Earl's revenue, were twenty-nine in number, producing annually about £3 each (pp. 111, 183). Whitaker's definition of *Vaccaria* as a breeding-farm is borne out by the accounts of what is called the *Instaurum*, or cattle-stock, of Blackburnshire (pp. 20-42, 129-142; 68-88, 156-168). Of the cattle, at that time small in size, the oxen were most valuable, for they were used with the wain and the plough. Edward I. more than once took the oxen of the Abbot of Bolton to carry the baggage of his armies towards Scotland. The average price of an ox in the years before us was about 9s.; a cow or heifer was about 7s., and a hide was worth about 2s. 6d.

At the head of each vaccary was an *Instaurator*, or bailiff in charge of the stock, who lived at the granges (*grangia*), while his assistant cowherds or herdsmen were sheltered in booths. Grange and Booth in many place-names still indicate the sites of these dwellings. The cattle, it is seen, were affected to some extent with the murrain; but they suffered more from the ravages of wolves.*

In a country thus infested sheep farming was at a dis-

---

* These animals infested the forests, particularly the forest of Rossendale, and were continually destroying the cattle. Dean Cutwulph of Whalley got his name from cutting off a wolf's tail while hunting; and some existing names, as Wolfendale, Wolfreden, Wolfenden, Wolfstones, Wolfstanclive, &c., are connected with the depredations or traditions of these animals.

advantage, and neither sheep nor wool are mentioned in the rolls.* The horses and charges for farriery in the Ightenhill accounts indicate the noted breeding establishment which was long kept up there. (*Whalley*, vol. i. p. 308.) A cart-horse was worth £2 or £3. Professor Rogers says that many of the horses bought for Merton College came from the North of England : he mentions one bought at Cockermouth in 1282 for £2 13s. 4d., and four bought at a place called the Park in 1285 for £5 6s. 8d. each. The horses and ponies in these accounts do not appear to have been of good breeds. The word *afer* was, in the time of Spelman, the common name in Northumberland for a poor horse.

Many facts of local interest may be derived from an examination of the two sets of entries under each place. The references to hay, oats, wheat, and corn-mills, show that the cultivation of waste lands was increasing near the towns, the example having been set by the monks. Enclosing was still going on with the favour of the Earl and his Stewards, for there are many entries relating to hedging and ditching, and to low rents, for the first year, of new enclosures, *terræ appruviatæ*, as they are called. The assarts (called in Lancashire *riddings*, and in Yorkshire *royds*), as well as the lawnds, or enclosures in parks,

* Sheep farms require good fences, and very few of the mountain slopes were at that time enclosed. When by an order of the King and Council, 30 July, 1297, 8,000 sacks of wool were ordered to be seized in 25 counties, Yorkshire alone of the northern counties is named. In that county the revenue of the Abbots from wool was very large, and the convent of Bolton gave rewards to those who killed wolves.

supply other signs of the development of agriculture under the hard conditions of the existing forest laws. There was an important fulling mill at Burnley, and another at Colne, pointing to a local woollen manufacture before the time of Queen Philippa. The fulling mill of Manchester is first named in 1322; and John Whitaker's assertion (*MS. Hist.*) that this mill was probably the earliest in all the north of the island is erroneous. Bradford fulling mill occurs in De Lacy's Inquisition of 1311. A few iron forges and workings on the Earl's estates are mentioned. There were also some very active operations in lead-mining and smelting in the neighbourhood of Haslingden, which were watched by the Earl with peculiar interest. Seven charres of lead were carried from Baxenden to Bradford (pp. 115-16, 185-6). No old lead workings have been recorded in this neighbourhood. John Webster, in his *Metallographia*, 4to., 1671, speaks of a former silver mine at Brunghill Moor, in the parish of Slaidburn, and of a lead mine at Rimmington, in the parish of Gisburn, belonging to Mr. Pudsey, of Bolton Hall, juxta-Bolland, whence the metal in Queen Elizabeth's days was obtained to coin "Pudsey's shillings" (pp. 20-1). Coals, called *sea*-coals, are noted as being sold at Trawden and Clivager. (*Cf. Whalley*, vol. i. 361, ii. 54.) In 1294, ten shillings' worth of coal was purchased by the convent of Bolton. The earliest notice of sea-coal met with by Prof. Rogers is at Dover, in 1278.

The rolls present an instructive picture of the country life of the uplands of Lancashire in feudal times, and indicate with minuteness the sources from which a great Baron condescended to take revenue. The amounts derived from markets, fairs, agistments or leys, fisheries, and the "merchats" of women,* are set down no less than old brushwood, penny rents, and the goods of dead villeins. The particulars of rents, produce, wages, and materials, supply valuable *data* for this part of the kingdom in the era preceding the Black Death. Had the accounts been more continuous they would have rivalled in value the household roll of Bp. de Swinfield.

That very excellent *History of Whalley*, which was based on cognate records of old date, lends a further value to these *Compoti*. Whitaker would have rejoiced to have speculated on the curious facts found in them, and to have drawn from them in picturesque and rhythmic language the important conclusions they present. He examined, it is true, the local portion of the Earl's great Inquisition *post mortem*, which is a condensed account of the property and its tenures, appraised under its real value; but the account in these *Compoti* is in some respects more exact, and deals with periods of fifteen and six years previously. The Inquisition was termed by Whitaker "one of the most valuable documents from which the history of Whalley has been compiled," and in recogni-

* The merchats (*marcheta* in Infim. Lat.) were the fines or cheats which a tenant paid his lord for the marriage of a daughter. One of these fines was, it seems, unjustly levied on Ellen de Rediker and Christiana de Wodehouses, who proved that they were not children of villeins (pp. 4, 119; 17, 127). *Cf.* Beaumont and Fletcher's play of *The Custom of the Country*.

xxiv　　　　*Introduction.*

tion of its value, the Chetham Society, in 1868, issued it in vol. lxxiv of the series, edited by Mr. John Harland. The copy printed was not, however, taken from the original Inquisition, which is extant (*Cal. Inquis. p. m.*, 1806, vol. i. p. 244; Gregson, p. 91), but from an old *MS.* translation in a book in the hands of the steward of the Honor of Clitheroe at Clitheroe Castle. The Inquisition and the *Compotus* admirably illustrate each other, and tend to make more complete the record of the *origines* of certain places.

The list of manors in the Barony of Halton (pp. 43, 142 *seq.*; 57, 150 *seq.*) is especially valuable. Some of these are not named as such in the Histories, and to those which are named important details may now be added.*

---

* Mottram-in-Longdendale is a case in point. The early history is given by Dr. Ormerod and Mr. Helsby (vol. iii. p. 851), and Mr. Earwaker (vol. ii. p. 112). Under the name of Langdendale the two *Compoti* clearly indicate its connection with the Barony, 1296–1305. The tenants in the valley were, we see, accustomed, according to an ancient tenure, to put in order the roads leading to Chester at the time of the Chester Fairs (pp. 46, 143; 60-1, 151). Longdendale does not occur in the Earl's Inquis. *post mortem.* But Sir Peter Leycester mentions it, though neither his editors nor Mr. Earwaker have availed themselves of the information. In the list of the places making up the Fee of the Lord of Halton, printed by Sir Peter (pp. 288 *seq.*, Orm., vol. i. p. 707), which, he says, "seems to be taken out of the records of *Halton* about *Edw.* 2," the manor of Longdendale is first named. This record says, "Dominus Robertus de Longdendale [probably Robert Holland] tenet Longdendale pro uno Feodo militis, & per Relevium cum acciderit, £5." It is added that "at the time when this Feodary was renewed, about *Hen.* 6," the tenant was Sir William Lovell. From a schedule amongst his own evidences, being an account

Introduction.

In these Cheshire accounts will be found the names of the officials of Halton Castle, and mayors of Congleton.

The *Senescalli* of Blackburnshire were persons of consequence, and the office was an object of ambition. The stewards who are introduced into these rolls founded some landed families in the county. *Robert de Heppale*, steward and chief "Instaurator" of Blackburnshire, occurs in Christopher Towneley's transcripts. He prepared the accounts, in conjunction with the *servientes* or *præpositi* Robert de Ryley and Peter de Ruddeby, for Accrington and several other manors and granges. He attested some of the Earl's local charters, and gave seizin of lands. In the Birch Feodary in Gregson's *Fragments* (p. 345), where the arms of the family are engraved, it is said that Robert, son of Robert de Heppale, held parts of several manors in the Wapentake of Leyland. In the second roll, *Edmund Talbot* is the steward. He belonged to the family of Talbot of Bashall (*Whalley*, vol. ii. p. 400), and was engaged to his patron for the repayment of a large loan (pp. 112, 183). Between Heppale and Talbot *Simon de Balderston* was steward, called in the second roll "Receiver of Lancaster" (p. 64). At pages 53, 148, *Nicholas de Leycester* is introduced. He was an ancestor of whom Sir Peter, the Cheshire historian, was proud. The latter calls him

of Hugh de Preston, Bailiff of Halton, 1359, Sir Peter cites the rent of 2s. 4d. (not 3s. 4d. as in the *Compotus*) "from a tenement [*qy.* the tenants] in Longdendale for the Ward of the Ways, which they used to keep at the time of *Chester*-Fair, *Termino Johannis Baptistæ*" (p. 284 ; Orm., vol. i. p. 704).

d

"Seneschal to Henry Lacy, Earl of Lincoln," adding that he finds him styled knight in 1292. He died in 1295, and his heir was Roger Leycester. (*Antiqq. of Cheshire*, p. 355; *Arley Charters*, p. xii; *Compotus*, pp. 65, 155.)

Gilbert de la Legh, of Hapton, the head stock-keeper of the Accrington vaccaries at a yearly salary of £2, was an ancestor of the Towneleys of Towneley. He is here occasionally called "Gilbert son of Michael;" and that the latter is the same person as the "Instaurator" is shewn by a charter granted by Henry de Lacy at Colne, 10 March, 1302, who confirmed to Gilbert, the son of Michael de la Leye, "nostre estorour de Blackburnshire," some lands in Clivager. (*Whalley*, vol. ii. pp. 190, 203.) At the date of the Earl's Inquisition he held 140 acres of land in Clivager. His assistant, *John de Paldene*, who was also associated with the steward, received the profits of the vaccaries, and attended to the sales of cattle at Bolton-le-Moors and Pontefract. Of the Under-bailiffs, without surnames, *Simon the Geldherd* was an important person in the vaccaries. He is once called *Custos Cromii* (p. 85; and *cf.* pp. 38, 39, and 40); but we do not identify the place, which was in Ightenhill manor. *John* the *Parker of Ightenhill* succeeded Peter de Ruddeby in that office, at an annual salary of 45s. 6d., with robes worth 13s. 4d.: these Parkers made the returns from their park and grange. *Thomas* "serviens" *of Standen*, whose wages were 1½d. per day, and a dress worth 6s. 8d., rendered the first account of that place, noticeable for corn and oats; and the second was rendered by *William de Brunlay*.

Introduction. xxvii

Of the auditors, high in the confidence of the Earl, *Sir William de Nony* was a cleric, being Rector of Slaidburn from 1295 to 1316, and chaplain of St. Michael's chapel in Clitheroe Castle (*Whalley*, vol. ii. p. 512; *Coucher Book*, p. 227). On 15 July, 1300, he brought from Scotland his master's will with seals attached, and delivered letters to Archbishop Corbridge at Thorp, begging that prelate to put his seal to it, which was done (*Fasti Ebor*, vol. i. p. 358). *Thomas de Fishburn*, who frequently attested the Earl's charters, was probably the Justice itinerant of that name, 1292–1317. *Robert de Silkstone*, who was one of the Earl's executors, was a cleric.

Oliver de Stansfeud, or *Stansfield*, Constable and Receiver of Pontefract Castle, was a great man with his master. His pedigree is in Watson's *Halifax*, p. 281, and in *Whalley*, vol. ii. p. 230. The Earl gave him the manor of Worsthorn, which he held by homage and service of one penny, and he lived at Hesandforth. His gravestone is in the Stansfield Chapel of Burnley Church, upon which is a sword referring to his office in the Castle. *Simon Noel* was Receiver of Clitheroe, as also was *Robert son of Adam;* both of whom drew up a good portion of the *Compoti*.

This volume, which has been several years in the press, was undertaken at the suggestion and at the expense of the late Mr. William Langton, who recognized the rare value of the subject. The connection of the Rev. P. A. Lyons with the last edition of the *History of Whalley*, 1876, seemed to point him out as a fitting editor, and Mr.

Langton committed the task to him. He is responsible for the transcript from the original rolls, and also for the translation up to page 184, which he saw through the press. His other engagements have prevented him from completing the work by an introduction, notes, and *corrigenda*. It is to be regretted that numerous errors have crept into both text and translation, which would no doubt have been corrected by Mr. Lyons had opportunity allowed. Some of the principal errors are pointed out on pp. 188 *seqq.*, but many other errors in figures and certain words could not be rectified without an examination of the rolls themselves. Some of the translations, too, are open to question; and those who use the volume for historical purposes are recommended in matters of doubt to refer to Ducange, Spelman, Cowell, and other authorities. The noticeable Latin words have been included in the Index, which has been made as helpful as possible. The Council of the Chetham Society regret to present to the members a book of so much value and interest in a somewhat unsatisfactory form; but the only alternative, that of further delay, would have involved the postponement of the general index and the completion of the first series of the publications.

J. E. BAILEY.

STRETFORD,
15 APRIL, 1884.

COMPOTUS TERRARUM HENRICI DE LACY COMITIS LENCOLNIE.

AKERINGTONE.
    Robertus de Heppehale Senescallus et Robertus de Reyleye serviens reddunt compotum suum apud Ichtenhille xxx⁰ die Januarii Anno Regni Regis Edwardi xxv^{to} Coram Eisdem [domino W. de Nony et Thome de Fisheburne] et de eodem Anno ut supra [videlicet ab incrastino Sancti Michaelis anno regni regis Edwardi xxiii usque incrastinum Sancti Michaelis anno regni regis Edwardi xxiiii].

De Liij s. vij d. ob. q^a.	de arreragiis ultimi compoti.
De iij d.	de quodam Curtilagio juxta vaccariam hoc anno.
De iiij s.	de herbagio vendito per loca.
De iiij li. xij s. iiij d.	de xxxvij quarteriis iij bussellis avene venditis.
De I d.	de una placea ad Linum seminandum.
De iiij d.	de uno veteri plaustro vendito.
De vj d.	de I veteri Cotagio apud Hoddesdene vendito.
De vj s. viij d.	de una placea que voccatur Rylayker posita ad firmam.
De L s. ij d.	de iiij^{xx} ij petris casei et xxvij petris butiri et dimidio petre utriusque venditis.
De Lv s.	de Simone Noel per I talliam.

    Summa Tocius Recepte xiij li. ij s. xi d. ob. q^a.

Mise et liberacio.
De quibus computant xxj d. In arrura et Herciatura.
Et iij s. ix d. ob. in ij plaustris et aliis ad plaustra cum ij securibus emptis.
Et xxv s. v d. ob. in cibo et stipendio I euntis ad plaustra et carrucam per annum et cariantis fenum et claustura.
Et vij s. in cibo et stipendio unius coadjuvantis ad plaustra et carucam.
Et xij s. iiij d. in domibus apud Akeringtone emendandis.
Et xiij d. In custu Molendini cum Molario et ferro empto.
Et xxij s. i d. ob. In haiis et pontibus faciendis.
Et iij s. ix d. in i tripoda sale et aliis neccessariis pro deyeria
Et vj d. In bladis sarclandis.
Et ix d. in ramis de parco colligendis et mundandis.
Et L s. v d. In pratis falcandis [herba] spargenda et feno levando et tassando.
Et v s. ix d. in xj acris et dimidio avene metendis.
Et iij s. x d. q^a In Liij quarteriis avene triturandis et ventandis.
Et iij s. vj d. In emundacione domus apud Hoddesden.
Et ij s. j d. In haiis emendandis ibidem.
Et vj d. in pratis mundandis.
Et xxix s. in pratis falcandis herba spargenda feno levando et tassando.
Et xix s. ob. q^a In j domo de novo construenda ibidem cum coopertura.
Et iij s. solutis Marie que fuit uxor Will'i de Bradeschac pro dote sua de libero tenemento quod fuit predicti Will'i viri sui in le Bradchevyd.
Et xxvj s. viij d. allocatis servienti pro servicio suo.
 Summa Tocius Mise et liberacionis xj li. ij s. iiij d. ob.
 Et sic debent Comiti xl s. vij d. q^a.

Grangia de Akerington.
Robertus de Ryleye reddit compotum suum de exitu grangie de fructibus autumpni anno Regni Regis Edwardi xxiij^o Coram eisdem die et loco supradictis.

Comitis Lencolnie.

Avena.
> Idem de Liiij quarteriis et iij bussellis de exitu.
> Summa Recepte Liiij quarteriis iij bussellis.
> De quibus computat xvj quarteriis in semine.
> Et j quarteria in prebenda affrorum et Boum.
> Et xxxvij quart. et iij bus. avene in vendicione ut supra.
> Est quietus.

Affri.
> Idem respondit de I Jumento et I pullo de rem. Et j pullo de exitu.
> Summa patet. Et remanent I Jumentum cum I pullo de exitu et J pullus secundi anni.

Boves
> Idem respondit de xij bobus de rem.
> Summa recepte patet.   Et remanent xij boves.

Deyeria.
> Idem respondit de CLvj caseis de exitu Deyerie cum xvj caseis factis post festum Sancti Michaelis. De quibus computat xvj caseis in decima. Et Cxl caseis ponderandis iiij^{xx} ij petras in vendicione ut supra.
> Est quietus.

Butirum.
> Idem respondet de xxvij petris et dimidio butiri de exitu Deyerie deducta decima. Summa patet. Et totum computat in vendicione ut supra. Est quietus.

COLNE.
> Robertus de Heppehale Senescallus et Simon Noel Receptor reddunt Compotum suum apud Ictenhille xxx° die Januarii Anno Regni Regis Edwardi xxv^{to} coram domino Will'o de Nony et Thome de Fisscheburne a festo Sancti Michaelis Anno Regni Regis Edwardi xxiij usque idem festum Anno Regni Regis Edwardi xxiiij^{to}.

Arreragia
De CCCCiiij^{xx} li. xxxi s. viij d. de arreragiis ultimi compoti.
De xxij li. xj s. viij d.   de firma de Kaune cum Membris et cum operibus arreragiis termino Egidii.
De xij li. xvj s.   de firma Molendini de Kaune et Walfredum decima deducta.
De xxxiij s. iiij d. ob.   de firma Molendini fulleretici de Kaune termino eodem.
De xi s.   de finibus terrarum Roberti Molendinarii Ade filii Ricardi Benedicti et Will'i fil. Ade de Alcancotes.
De xxix s. x d.   de minutis finibus terrarum de Kaune.
De xx s. viij d.   de perquisitis Hallemoti ibidem.
De xiij s. iiij d.   de Merchetis Elene filie Will. de Rediker et Christiane filie Ade de Wodehouses.
De xxij s. vj d.   de attachiamentis averiorum ibidem in Trochdene.
De x s.   de Carbonibus Marinis in Trochdene.
De xij s. ij d.   de averiis agistatis in Trochdene.
De iij s. vij d.   de feno vendito in Trochdene.
  Summa prima Recepte cum arreragiis D^{c}xxvj li. iiij s. ij d. ob.
Haselingdene.
De iij li. vj s. v d. ob.   de firma de Haselingdene termino Egidii.
De xiij s. iiij d.   de firma Molendini termino Michaelis.
De xxxiij s. x d.   de herbagio yemali in Roscyndale hoc anno.
De xiij s. iiij d.   de iiij^{xx} averiis de Abbate de Walley agistatis ibidem.
De xlix s. x d.   de averiis agistatis ibidem in estate hoc anno.
De xx s.   de herbagio de Derplaghe hoc anno.

Comitis Lencolnie. 5

De xxd.	de herbagio de primerolsyke hoc Anno.
De xiijs. iiijd.	de feno vendito ibidem Abbati de Walley hoc anno.
De iiijs. ijd.	de feno vendito ibidem aliis de patria.
De Lxs.	de i forgia ad ferrum posita ad firmam in Roscindale.

Summa Secunda Recepte xiiijli. xvs. xjd. ob.

Totingtone.

De xiijli. xijs. vjd. ob.	de firma de Totingtone terminis Pasche et Michaelis.
De iijs.	de firma Ricardi de Radeclive pro xx acris terre per cartam Comitis.
De xd.	de firma ejusdem pro ij acris et dimidio inclusis fossatis cum xx acris predictis quas duas acras et dimidium tenet ad voluntatem Comitis.
De xijd.	de domino de Byry pro terra de Shuttelesworthe.
De id. ob.	de firma Galfridi de Chadertone pro Shillingbothim pro I libra Cymini.
De xxvjs.	de firma Molendini de Totingtone deducta decima.
De vjs. viijd.	de stallagio ibidem.
De xiiijs.	de herbagio de Couhoppe hoc Anno.
De Cvjs. viijd.	de herbagio de [Couhope, *scored out*] Alvedene Musedene et Uggedene.
De xs.	de herbagio del Wythns.
De vjs. iiijd.	de aueriis agistatis in foresta de Totingtone.
	De quercubus Huccto et Minera nichil hoc anno.

Compotus Terrarum Henrici de Lacy

De xvs. vd.	de pannagio ibidem.
De xxxviijs. ijd.	de finibus terrarum ibidem.
De xliijs. xd.	de perquisitis Curie ibidem.
De xijs.	de Inparcamentis averiorum.

Summa Tercia Recepte xxvijli. xvijs. viijd

Rachedale.

De vjs.	de firma Burgencium de Rachedale termino Martini.
De xlixs. ijd.	de firma diversorum tenencium ibidem termino eodem.
De iijs.	de firma diversorum tenencium ibidem termino eodem.
De vijli. xixs. ixd. ob.	de firma Hugonis de Elaunde termino eodem.
De vs.	de viij^{va} parte Molendini ibidem.
De vjs.	de firma Abbatis de Stanlawe pro vj bovatis terre.
De xlijs. ixd. ob.	de firma tenencie quondam Johannis de Byrun.
De ijs.	de firma ejusdem pro tenemento in Butterworth.
De Liijs. viijd.	de Teolonio fori et Nundinarum et stallagio ibidem.
De xxvjs. viijd.	de herede Ade de Balghschae pro bedelria ibidem.
De xliijs. ijd.	de finibus terrarum ibidem.
De iiijli iiijs. iiijd.	de perquisitis Curie ibidem.
De viijd.	de Releuiis Henrici filii Ricardi filii Henrici pro terra patris.
De ijs.	de exitu terrarum quondam Henrici filii Patricii que est in manu Comitis per feloniam Ranulphi fratris et heredis ejusdem Henrici.

Summa quarta Recepte xxiiijli. xi den'.

Romesgreve.
    De xxs. iiijd.   de herbagio estivali ibidem vendito hoc anno.
                           De Cineribus Huceto et quercubus ibidem nichil hoc anno.

Hoddesdene.
    De iiijs. vjd.   de herbagio de Hoddesdene vendito hoc anno.
    De xiijs.   de veteri busca ad I forgiam per xiij Septimanas.

Worstone.
    De iiijli. vjs. id. ob.   de firma de Worstone termino Egidii.
    De ijd.   de firma Ade Wyot pro ij Colariis termino eodem.
    De xls.   de dominicis ibidem positis ad firmam.
    De xxiiiis.   de firma Molendini ibidem deducta decima.
    De xviijs. iiijd.   de finibus terrarum ibidem.
    De ixs. vjd.   de perquisitis Hallemoti ibidem.

Pennyltone.
    De vjli. iiijs. ijd.   de firma de Penniltone et Wymondeshouses termino Egidii.
    De Id.   de firma Henrici de Blakburne pro iiij^{xx} acris.
    De iiijs. vjd.   de perquisitis Hallemoti ibidem. De fine terre et inparcamento averiorum nichil hoc anno.

Ichtenhille.
    De Liijs. iiijd.   de firma de Ichtenhille termino Egidio.
    De lxxvs. vjd.   de finibus terrarum ibidem hoc anno.
    De Lixs. ijd.   de perquisitis Hallemoti ibidem.
    De ixs. iiijd.   de Letherwyte v Mulierum. De Merchato nichil.

De lxxjs. xd.   de Eschapiis Averiorum in foresta de Pennehille.
De ijs. vjd.   de Thisteltack Nativorum.
De Liijs.   de herbagio yemali in Pennehille.
De xlvs.   de herbagio estivali ibidem.
De xviijs. xd.   de feno vendito ibidem.
De vjs. viijd.   de fine Ade de Heley pro bonis puerorum suorum Comiti contingentibus.
De xs.   de xvij fraxinis venditis.
De vjs.   de veteri busca vendita.
De iijs.   de I Jumenta de vago vendito.
De Lxvjs. Id.   de iiij^{xx} porcis silvestribus.

Summa quinta Recepte xljli. iiijs. xj.d ob.

Habringeham.
De iiijli. xiiijs. iiijd.   de firma de Habringgeham termino Egidii.

Padingham.
De xjli. xijd.   de firma de Padingham termino Eodem.
De iiijli. xijs.   de firma Molendini de Padingham deducta decima.
De vjs. viijd.   de operibus remissis in Padingham.

Brunley.
De xiijli. viijs. vd. ob.   de firma de Brunley cum incremento xij anni preteriti.
De xijd.   de Incremento tofti quod Robertus faber tenet in Brunley.
De iijs. iiijd.   de operibus remissis ibidem.
De xli.   de firma Molendini de Brunley deducta decima.
De vjs. viijd.   de firma Molendini fulleretici ibidem hoc anno primo.
De Cvijs. ixd. ob.   de firma de Brereclive termino Egidii.

Merclesdene.
De Lxxixs. ob.	de firma de parva Merclesden termino Egidii.
De xiiijd.	de operibus remissis ibidem.
De vjs.	de firma de Chirche.
De xvijd ob.	de firma Ade de Simondestone termino Eodem.
De xiijs. iiijd.	de firma Thome de Hiltone.
De vs. vjd.	de firma de Berdeworthe et Ulvesboth.
De iijs. ixd.	de uno Mesuagio et vij acris terre que sunt in manu Comitis per feloniam Will'i de Berdworthe in Berdworthe.
De xviijd.	de Incremento ejusdem tenementi.
De xiiijs. iijd.	de firma Johannis de Blackburne pro xxviij acris terre et dimidio apud Berdworthgrene.

Summa Sexta Recepte lvjli. vijs. iiid.

Pennewortham.
De xliiijs. iiijd.	de firma Cotariorum et assartorum termino Michaelis.
De xxd.	de firma Hagonis Ploket.
De iijs.	de firma ejusdem pro I tofto et dimidia acra terre ad voluntatem.
De vijli. xiijs. iiijd.	de eodem pro pratis dominicis et piscariis ibidem termino eodem.
De Id.	de firma Prioris de Pennewortham pro I placea juxta prioratum.
De viijs. vd. qª	de warda Castri Lancastrie termino Johannis Baptiste.
De xvs.	de herbagio de Middelforde.
De xxiiijs.	de pannagio ibidem decima deducta.
De xxvjs viijd.	de piscaria de Northmeles termino Michaelis.

De viijs. Id.	de firma Roberti de Meles.
De xijd.	de firma de Galwaylandes.
De vjd.	de firma Rogeri de Walley pro dimidia libra piperis termino Egidii.
De Id.	de firma Roberti de Holande pro tenemento in Eukestone.
De iijs.	de firma de Adelingtone et Dokesbyry termino Martini.
De ijs.	de firma de Stanedisse et Langetre.
De ijs.	de firma de Northmeles termino Eodem.
De ixd.	de firma de Weltone termino Eodem.
De xviijd. Id. ob.	de sackefe termino Michaelis.
De Ls.	de firma domini Will'i de la Mere terminis Martini et Pentecostes.
De xvjs.	de firma tenementi quondam Johannis de Deyethalghe termino Michaelis.
De xxxs.	de Henrici Motoun pro bedelria.
De xxvs.	de finibus pro ingressu terrarum ibidem.
De iiijli. ixs. ijd.	de perquisitis Curie ibidem.
De vjd.	de bosco de Wrecko vendito.
De xvjd.	de Turbis venditis apud Pennewortham.
De vijs. viijd.	de custodia terre et heredis Ricardi de Stockport usque ad etatem.
De Liijs. iiijd.	de Warda terre et heredis Johannis de Neutone data Comiti ex concessione Ade de Frekiltone.

Summa Septima Recepte xxvijli. xs. ob. q Item Liijs. iiijd.
Dounum.

De iiijs.	de firmo cujusdam assarti in Dounum quod persona de Walley tenuit in eadem.

Comitis Lencolnie.

De viijli. xis. vd. ob.	de firma de Dounam cum incremento anni preteriti termino Egidii.
De Lxxiijs. iiijd.	de dominicis ibidem positis ad firmam termino Eodem.
De Liiijs.	de firma Molendini ibidem decima deducta.
De ijs. ob.	de turbis ibidem venditis.
De xs.	de firma Alexandri de Keuerdale termino Egidii.
De Id.	de firma Magistri Henrici de Claytone.
De xijd.	de firma Will. de Wadingtone termino Egidii.
De Id. ob.	de firma Ricardi clerici de Dounam pro I pari cyrotecarum.
De xs. vjd.	de finibus et perquisitis hallemoti ibidem.
De ijs.	de Inparcamento averiorum ibidem.

Summa Octava Recepte xvjli. viijs. vjd. ob.

Akerington.

De xxxjs. ixd.	de firma Lij acrarum et I Rode terre positis ad firmam.
De vijs.	de una placea que vocatur Pesecroft.
De iiijs.	de Aula Coquina et Grangia positis ad firmam.
De Ciijs. Id. ob. q^a	de iij vaccariis positis ibidem ad firmam termino Egidii.
De xxxvjs. viijd.	de firma Molendini ibidem decima deducta.
De ijs. vj'd.	de v acris vasti positis de novo ad firmam.
De xvijs. iiijd.	de finibus pro ingressu terrarum ibidem.
De xijd.	de perquisitis ibidem.
De vjs. vjd.	de Inparcamentis averiorum ibidem.

De xxxiiij s.   de busca et Minera venditis ad I forgiam ibidem pro xxvij Septimanis.
De vj s. viij d.   de herbagio de Brocholehurste.
Huncotes.
De C s. xj d.   de firma de Huncotes termino Egidii.
Clivacher.
De vj li. xiij s viij d.   de firma diversorum tenencium per Cartas in Clivacher termino Egidii.
De iiij li. vj s. iii d.   de firma Cotariorum et assartorum ibidem termino Eodem.
De vj d.   de firma Oliveri de Stanesfeud pro viij acris terre in Clivacher et vj acris terre in Brunley quas tenet per cartam Comitis.
De x d.   de dimidia libra piperis de redditu Ade filii Mathei.
De v d.   de ij paribus cirothecarum I pari calcariorum de redditu Mathei de Bercroft Johannis filii Mathei et Ade fabri termino Eodem.
De Lxxij s.   de firma Molendini ibidem decima deducta.
De xix d. ob.   de Releuio filii et heredis Iuonis de Clivacher.
De xviij d.   de perquisitis Hallemoti.
De xij d.   de Inparcamentis averiorum ibidem.
De iij d.   de carbonibus Marinis venditis ibidem.
De v s. iiij d.   de averiis agistatis in communi pastura de Clivacher.

Summa Nona Recepte xxxij li. xv s. x d. ob. q^a

Cliderhowe.
De xx s. iij d.   de firma de Baldwynhille terminis Martini et Pentecoste.

De ix li. vj d.	de firma Thaynorum ibidem termino Egidii.
De iij s. iiij d.	de Galfrido de Simondestone pro relaxacione secte Curie.
De iiij d.	de firma Dyote le Arrousmythe ad terminum vite sui et Dinarie Sororis ejus pro I Cotagio.
De ij s. vj d.	de Will. filii Henrici pro ij acris terre subtus Baldwynhille.
De iij s. viij d.	de firma Messuagii quondam Roberti li Arrousmythe.
De xviij d.	de herbagio fossatorum Castri.
De iij s.	de herbagio Gardini et I tofto adjacente.
De viij s.	de fructibus Gardini.
De vj li. xiij s. iiij d.	de firma burgensium ibidem termino Michaelis.
De viij li.	de Teolonio fori et Nundinarum ibidem.
De xij li.	de firma Molendini ibidem decima deducta.
De ij s.	de firma Walteri le Alblaster termino Michaelis.
De iiij s.	de firma de Sandwelle et Salewelle.
De vj s.	de firma Johannis de Danyscales.
De xij s.	de eadem firma pro ij annis preteritis unde Receptor non fuit carcatus.
De ij s.	de firma Randulphi de Mittone pro attachiamento Molendini ibidem.
De xlij s. viij d. ob.	de firma terre sub Salthille hoc anno.
De iiij li. xviij d.	de finibus pro ingressu terrarum ibidem hoc anno.
De xij li. xvj s. x d.	de perquisitis Curie ibidem hoc Anno.
De x s.	de Releuio heredum Ricardi de

Compotus Terrarum Henrici de Lacy

	Tounley pro tenementis in Touneley Coldecotes et Snoddesworthe.
De xviij s. v d.	de Relevio earundum pro tenement. in Brunschaghe.
De xxij s. vj d.	de Inparcamentis liberorum pro evasionibus in foresta.
De xl s.	de fine Ade de Dynley pro transgressione facta in foresta.
De xiij s. iiij d.	de fine Ricardi del Tyndehevyd quia non est prosecutus.
De Lx s.	de firma Henrici de Boltone pro Bedelria.
De xxxj s. v d.	de Warda Castri Lancastrie.
De xxiij li. vj s.	de firma Wapentak de Stainiclif.
De Lxxvij li. xviij s. iiij d.	receptis de Gilberti Instauratore ut in compoto.
De iiij^{xx} li. xx s.	de albo xxvij vaccariarum positarum ad firmam.
De xv li. x s.	receptis de Thome serviente de Standen ut in compoto.
De ix s. xj d.	de arreragiis Will'mi filii Margerie.
De vj li. x s.	de bonis Elie Thayn felonis decapitatis unde particule patentur in quadam cedula huic Rotulo appensa.
De ij s.	de Relevio heredis Ade de Tockholes pro tenemento in eadem.
De xlij s. vj d.	de exitibus cujusdam tenementi quod vocatur Snelleshowe in manu Comitis post decessum Petri de Cestria videlicet pro isto Anno et anno preterito.

Summa Decima Recepte CCLiij li. xiiij s. vj d. ob.

Summa Summarum Tocius Recepte $\overset{t}{\text{M}}$.xliij li. xiij s. iiij d.

Mise.
De quibus computat ijs. I d. ob. In aula et Grangia apud Kaune emendandis.

Et ij s. iiij d. ob. in iij acris prati falcandis herba spargenda feno levando cariando et tassando.

Et xiij s. I d. In custu Molendini aquatici de Kaune cum Rota exteriori emendanda.

Et xij s. viij d. In Molendino Fuleritico de Kaune emendando.

Et ij s. xj d. in Molendino de Worchestone emendando cum Rota exteriori emendanda.

Et xvj d. in Molendino de Dounum emendando.

Et xviij d. in Molendino de Totingtone emendando.

Et iij s. vij d. In Molendino de Brunley emendando cum ij Molariis de novo emptis.

Et iij s. vj d. In Molendino de Clivacher emendando.

Et xij s. x d. In Molendino de Padyngham emendand.

Et iij d. ob. In domibus infra Castrum emendandis.

Et ij s. In aula de Pennewortham et aula de Roscyndale emendandis.

Et xiij li. vj s. viij d. In feodo et Roba Senescalli per annum.

Et vij li. x s. In feodo et Roba Constabularii per annum.

Et xlv s. vj d. In vadiis parcarii de Ichtenhille per annum.

Et vj d. solutis Waltero de Wadingtone pro annua firma ei debita.

Et vj s. viij d. solutis Abbati de Salley pro I Lampade inveniendo pro anima Comitis Johannis.

Et l s. in Warda Castri Lancastrie.

Et xiiij s. viij d. in expensis Constabularii et Gilberti Instauratoris vendencium Instaurum Comitis In nundinis de Boltone et Sancti Egidii.

Et iiij s. ob. In expensis Senescalli Constabularii Instauratoris et aliorum pro visibus factis et pullanis signandis.

Et iiij li. xviij s. x d. In expensis tenencium Curias per patriam.

Et xxvj s. In vadiis unius Warrenarii custodientis Salthille Boscum de Dounum et Worstone.

Et lxxjs. iijd. ob. In expensis audientium Compotum ante hunc compotum.
Et xviijs. vd. In decasu firmarum ut patet cedula huic Rotula appensa.
Et vjs. viijd. in expensis capiencium porcos silvestres.
Et xlvs. vjd. In vadiis Janitoris per annum.
Et viijs. in cauancio et percameno pro isto anno et iij annis preteritis emptis.
Summa Prima Mise xliijli. xs. xjd. ob.

Mise forencie.
Idem computat xxvjs. In vadiis custodientis Marchias foreste de Rachedam et Bernolswyke hoc anno.
Et xxxijs. iiijd. In Centum quart. viginti et decem libris salvo ducendis de Cliderhowe usque Buckeby et denariis portandis per v vices usque Pontemfractum.
Et xijs. in v pullanis ducendis de Cliderhou usque Buckeby per preceptum Comitis feno, avena, litera cum expensis ducencium in redeundo.
Et lxviij's. datos de Huddelestone per litteram Comitis.
Et xs. condonatos Mabote Ancille Alesye de Lascy de herbagio unde Receptor carcatus est in compoto precedenti.
Et xs. [datos *dotted underneath*] condonatos Johanni del Barouforde de firma vaccarie quam tenuit.
Et lijs. vjd. ob. in uno Molendino fulleretico de novo constructo apud Brunley.
Summa secunda Mise xli. xjs. xjd. ob.

Liberacio.
Idem computat vjli. vijs. liberatis Petro Preposito de Ichtenhille per I talliam.
Et Lvs. liberatis preposito de Akerintone ut in compoto.
Et Ciiij^{xx} iijli. vjs. viijd. liberatos Thome de Raynevelle per I talliam scriptum per manum Roberti de Sulkestone clerici.
Et CCCLiiijli. liberatos Olivero de Stanesfeud ut in compoto.
Summa Tocius liberacionis D$_c$xlvjli. xiijs. viijd.

Summa Summarum Tocius Mise et Liberacionis D^cC li. xvj s.
vij d. Et sic debet Receptor Comiti CCCCxlij li. xvj s.
ix d. De quibus xiiij s. sunt de arreragiis Henrici de
Kyghley. Postea allocantur ei vj s. viij d. datis pro
decima porcorum silvestrium supra venditorum. Et
xiij s. iiij d. allocantur eidem de Merchetto ij Mulierum
unde injuste carcatus est supra in Kaune eo quod
Mulieres sunt libere condicionis.

ICTENHILLE.

Robertus de Heppehalle Senescallus et Petrus de Ruddeby
serviens reddunt compotum suum a iiij^{to} die Martii
Anno Regni Regis Edwardi xxiiij^{to} usque incrastinum
Sancti Michaelis Anno regni regis Edwardi xxiiij^{to}
Coram domino Will. de Nony et Thome de Fissheburne apud Ictenhille.

De vij s. ix d.	de uno affro et xvij bobus agistatis in Rohille.
De xxxvj s.	de iij bobus venditis.
De iiij s. xj d.	de coreo ix Jumentorum ij pullanorum in iij° anno et vij pullanorum in secundo anno.
De ix s.	de iiij quarteriis avene venditis.
De vj li. xij s.	receptis de Simone Noel ut in compoto.
De ix s. xj d. q^a.	de arreragiis Will. fil. Margerie super ultimum compotum.

Summa ix li. xix s. vij d. q^a.

Mise.

De quibus computat ij d. In custu Carucarum.

Et xxij d. In custu plaustrorum cum I plaustro de novo facto et uncto empto pro eisdem.

Et xx s. v d. in liberacionibus ij serviencium ad Carucas et plaustros.

Et ij d. ob. in cibo et stipendio unius herciatoris.

Et vij s. vj d. in liberacionibus ij hominum custodiencium pullanos in stabulo per x septimanas.
Et iij s. vj d. in stipendio eorundem per tempus Compoti.
Et vij s. xj d. q^a in domibus emendandis.
Et vij s. I d. in iiij quarteriis et dimidio avene emptis.
Et x d. in I tripoda I ferro pro pullanis signandis.
Et xx d. in focali prosternendo et cariando.
Et iiij s. vj d. in palicio emendando.
Et xviij s. x d. ob. in fossatis et haiis circa Hegham et in parco emendandis.
Et xvij s. vij d. ob. qr^a. In lx acris et dimidio prati falcandis.
Et xij s. vij d. in herba spargenda feno levando et tassando.
Et vj s. x d. ob. in xvj acris avene metendis colligendis et ligandis.
Et v s. ij d. ob. in Marchancia pullanorum capistris emptis pro eisdem et expensis coadjuvancium pro eisdem faldandis et capiendis.
Et xj s. iij d. in prebenda ij stallonum ferra pro eisdem et expensis garcionum custodiencium dictos stalones et ducencium de Ictenhille usque Pontemfractum.
Et viij s. vj d. In cursu aque de Kelder apud Whytacre divertendo pro palicio salvando.
Et xxv s. I d. in expensis Senescalli et aliorum capiencium xvj Cervos in foresta et v Damas in parco cum cariagio vj Cervorum et iiij Damarum de Ictenhille usque Pontemfractum.
Et xix d. ob. In palacio circa vivarium emendando et Claustura circa Rohille emendando.
Et ix s. xj d. q^a. liberatis Simoni Noel Receptori ut in compoto.
    Summa Tocius Mise et liberacionis viij li. xiij s. ij d. ob. q^a.
Et sic debet serviens Comiti xxvj s. iiij d. ob. Postea allocantur eidem vj s. viij d. pro Roba ejusdem hoc anno. Et ix s. I d. in I Cruce de novo faciendo et errigendo in Merkato de Brunley.

Grangia de Ictenhille.
Idem ut supra reddunt compotum suum de exitu grangie de fructibus Autumpni Anno xxiij⁰ coram eisdem ut supra.

Avena.
Idem respondet de xxvij qr^a receptis de Will'o filio Margerie de exitu.
Et de iiij qr^a et di. de empcione ut supra.
Summa recepte xxxj qr^a et di.
De quibus computat xv qr^a et ij bus. in semine. Et xj qr^a. vj bus. in prebenda pullanorum a iiij^{to} die Marcii usque ad festum Sancte Elene. Et iiij qr^a. in vendicione ut supra. Summa Mise ut supra.
Et est quietus.

Boves.
Idem respondet de xvii bobus receptis de Will'o filio Margerie ut in compoto.
Summa Recepte xvij boves.
De quibus computat iij in vendicione ut supra.
Et remanent xiiij boves.

Equicium.
Idem respondet de Lij Jumentis de rem.
Summa recepte patet.
De quibus computat ix in Morina de coriis responsum est supra.
Et I dato Will'o de Stopham per litteram Comitis. Et remanent xlij Jumenta.

Runcini.
Idem respendit de ij Runcinis de rem.
Summa recepte patet.
De quibus computat I liberatum preposito de Tanschelf ut in compoto. Et rem. I Runcinus.

Pullani.
Idem respondet de xxix pullanis in secundo anno de rem.
Summa recepte patet.

De quibus computat ij in Morina de coreis responsum est supra.
Et remanent xxvij pullani in iij anno quorum xiiij Masculi.
Pulli.
Idem respondit de xxij pullis I de exitu de rem.
Summa recepte patet.
De quibus computat vij in Morina de coriis responsum est supra. Et I in decima.
Et remanent xiiij pulli in secundo anno quorum vj Masculi.
Pulli de exitu.
Idem respondet de xxij pullis de exitu.
Summa recepte patet.
De quibus computat I in morina coreum nulliûs valoris.
Et remanent xxi pulli de exitu.

TROCHDENE.

Instaurator de Blakeburneschyre Robertus de Heppehale et Instauratores et vaccarii reddunt compotum suum apud Ictenhille xxvj die Januarii Anno Regni Regis Edwardi xxv° videlicet ab Incrastino Sancti Michaelis Anno Regni Regis Edwardi xxiij° usque ad festum Sancti Michaelis Anno Regni Regis Edwardi xxiiij° coram W. de Nony et Thome de Fissheburne.

Adam filius Johannis reddit compotum suum de xxxvj vaccis et ij Tauris de rem. Et de vj vaccis de addicione. Et de I vacca recepta de Instauratore. Summa recepte xliij vacce et ij tauri. De quibus computat I in morina pro carne et coreo xiiijd. Et ij liberantur Simone le Geldhirde. Et v liberantur instauratori cum I tauro. Et remanent xxxv vacce et I taurus. Idem respondit de iiij bobus de addicione et liberantur Galfrido parcario. Idem respondit de ix boviculis de rem. De quibus computat I strangulatum per lupum pro carne et coreo vjd. Et remanent v bovetti et iij Juvence. Idem Respondit de

Comitis Lencolnie.

xv vitulis de rem. De quibus computat ij in decima. Et remanent xiij boviculi quorum vj masculi. Idem respondet de xxv vitulis de exitu. De I recepto de Instauratore Summa recepte xxvj. De quibus computat ij in Morina pro carne et coreo ob. Et I in vendicione pro vjd. Et v liberantur Instauratori. Et

iijs. ijd. ob. I liberatur Simoni le Geldehirde. Et remanent xvij vituli de exitu.

Summa averiorum restancium in dicta vaccaria xxxv vacce, et I Taurus, v bovetti, iij Juvence, xiij boviculi quorum vj masculi et xvij vituli de exitu.

Matildis uxor Jordani del Bothe reddit compotum de xliij vaccis et I tauro de rem. Et de vij de addicione. Summa recepte L vacce et I taurus. De quibus computat I in Morina pro coreo et carne xxd. Et iij liberantur Simoni le Geldehirde. Et ij vacce liberantur Instauratori. Et remanent xliij vacce et I taurus. Idem respondet [de] v bobus de addicione et liberantur Galfrido parcario Idem respondet de ix boviculis de rem. De quibus computat I in Morina pro coreo ijd. Et remanent iij bovetti et v Juvence. Idem respondet de xvij vitulis de rem. De quibus computat I strangulatum per lupum pro carne et coreo xijd. Et I in decima. Et remanent xv boviculi quorum ix masculi. Idem respondet de xxiij vitulis de exitu. De quibus computat ij liberatos Simoni le Geldehirde. Et ij liberatos Instauratori. Et iij in

ijs. xjd. Morina pro coreis I d. Et remanent xvj vituli de exitu.

Summa averiorum restancium in dicta vaccaria xliiij vacce I taurus iij bovetti v Juvence xv boviculi quorum ix masculi. Et xvj vituli de exitu.

Emma del Munkerode reddit compotum suum de xlj vaccis

et I tauro de rem. et de iiij de addicione. Summa recepte xlv vacce et I taurus. De quibus computat iij liberatas Simoni le Geldehirde. Et iij liberatas Instauratori cum I tauro. Et remanent xxxix vacce. Idem respondet de v bobus de addicione et liberantur Galfrido le Parker. Idem respondet de xij boviculis de rem. Et remanent v bovetti et vij Juvence. Idem respondet de xv vitulis de rem. De quibus computat I in decima. Et remanent xiiij boviculi quorum vj masculi. Item I taurellus receptus de Instauratore. Idem respondet de xxij vitulis de exitu. De quibus computat I in Morina coreum nullius valoris. Et I liberatur Simoni le Geldhirde. Et iij liberantur Instauratori. Et remanent xvij vituli.

Summa· averiorum restancium in dicta vaccaria xxxix vacce v bovetti vij Juvence Item. I bovettus taurus receptus de Instauratore xiiij boviculi quorum vj masculi. Et xvij vituli de exitu.

Henricus de Emot loco Ade filii Maulke reddit compotum suum de xl vaccis et I tauro de rem. Et de vj de addicione. Summa recepte xlvj vacce et I taurus. De quibus computat J in morina pro coreo et carne ij s. Et ij liberantur Simoni le Geldehirde. Et iiij liberantur Instauratori. Et remanent xxxix vacce et J taurus. Idem respondet de iiij bobus de addi-
ij s. vj d. ob. cione et liberantur G. parcario. Idem respondet de xiiij boviculis de rem. Et remanent v bovetti et ix Juvence. Idem respondet de xxvj vitulis de exitu de quibus vj in Morina pro coreis et carne vj d. ob. Et J liberatur Simoni le Geldehirde. Et iiij liberantur instauratori. Et remanent xv vituli de exitu.

Summa averiorum restancium in dicta vaccaria xxxix vacce I taurus v bovetti ix Juvence viij boviculi iiij Juvencule et xv vitule de exitu.

Petrus del Fernyside reddit compotum suum de xxxviij vaccis et I tauro de rem. Et de vij de addicione. Et de iiij receptis de Instauratore. Summa recepte xlix vacce et I taurus. De quibus computat I strangulatam per lupum pro coreo et carne iiij d. Et I in morina pro coreo et carne xxij d. Et vij liberatas S. le Geldehirde. Et rem. xl vacce et I taurus. Idem respondet de vj bobus de addicione liberantur G. parcario. Idem respondet de xv boviculis de rem. De quibus I strangulatum per lupum pro coreo et carne ij s. xj d. ob. vj d. Et I in morina pro coreo iij d. Et remanent viij bovetti et v Juvence. Idem respondet de xvij boviculis de rem. De quibus computat ij in decima. Et rem. xv boviculi quorum ix masculi. Idem respondet de xvj vitulis de exitu. Et de iiij receptis de Instauratore. Summa recepte xx. De quibus computat ij in morina pro coreo ob. Et I liberatum Simoni le Geldehirde. Et remanent xvij vituli de exitu.

Summa averiorum restancium in dicta vaccaria xl vacce et I taurus viij[to] bovetti v Juvence xv boviculi quorum ix mascnli et xvij vituli de exitu.
Summa denariorum in foresta de Trochden x s. vij d. ob.

PENNEHILLE.

Ricardus de Byrchenleye reddit compotum suum de xliiij vaccis et I tauro de rem. Et de iij de addicione. Summa recepte xlvij vacce et I taurus, et de quibus computat iij liberatas Simoni le Geldehirde. Et viij liberatas Instauratori. Et remanent xxxvj vacce et I taurus. Idem respondet de I bove de rem. Et de iiij de addicione et liberantur G. parcario. Idem respondit de xiij boviculis de rem̄. Et rem̄ vj bovetti et vij Juvence. Idem respondet [de] xv vitulis de rem̄. De quibus computat ij in decima. Et I liberatur ij d.

Instauratori. Et remanent xij boviculi quorum ix masculi. Idem respondet de xxiiij vitulis de exitu. De quibus computat iiij in Morina pro carne et coreis ij d. Et vij liberantur Instauratori. Et remanent xiij vituli de exitu.

Summa averiorum restancium in dicta vaccaria xxxij vacce et I taurus vj bovetti vj Juvence xij boviculi quorum ix masculi et xiij vituli de exitu.

vs. x d.

Ricardus filius Benedicti reddit compotum suum de xlij vaccis et I tauro de reṁ. Et de v de addicione. Et de iiij receptis de Instauratore. Summa recepte lj vacce et I taurus. De quibus ij in Morina pro coreis et carne iiij s. v d. Et iij liberantur S. le Geldhirde. Et I liberatur Instauratori. Et remanent xlv vacce et I taurus. Idem respondet de iiij bobus de addicione et liberantur G. parcario. Idem respondet de xiij boviculis de reṁ. De quibus I in Morina pro coreo et carne xij d. Et remanent vj bovetti et vj Juvence. Idem respondet de xvj vitulis de reṁ. De quibus I in decima. Et remanent xv boviculis quorum vj masculi. Idem respondet de xv vitulis de exitu. Et de iiij receptis de Instauratore. Summa xix. De quibus computat I in morina coreum nullius valoris. Et I liberatum S. le Geldehirde. Et ij in vendicione v d. Et reṁ xvj vituli.

Summa averiorum restancium in dicta vaccaria xlv vacce I taurus vj bovetti vj Juvence xv boviculi quorum vj masculi et xvj vituli de exitu.

Henricus filius Kitte reddit compotum suum de xlij vaccis et I tauro de reṁ. Et de vj de addicione. Et de I recepta de Instauratore. Summa recepte xlix vacce et I taurus. Item I tauro de addicione. De quibus computat iij liberatas S. le Geldehirde. Et II libera-

Comitis Lencolnie.

Id.

tas Instauratori. Et remanent xliiij vacce et jj tauri. Idem respondet de I bove de addicione et liberatur G. parcario. Idem respondet de x boviculis de rem̄. Et remanent iij bovetti et vij Juvence. Idem respondet de xiij vitulis de rem̄. De quibus I in decima. Et remanent xij boviculi quorum v masculi. Idem respondet de xix vitulis de exitu. Et de I recepto de Instauratore. Summa recepte xx. De quibus iij in Morina pro coreis Id. Et ij liberatos Instauratori. Et remanent x vituli de exitu.

Summa averiorum restancium in dicta vaccaria xliiij vacce et ij tauri iij bovetti vij Juvence xij boviculi quorum v masculi et xv vituli de exitu. Postea allocatur eidem una vacca quia ablata fuit per latrones, condonatur per Comitem.

ijs. iijd.

Will's de Penniltone reddit compotum suum de xxxvj vaccis et ij tauris de rem̄. Et de vij de addicione. Summa recepte xliij vacce et ij tauri. De quibus I in morina pro coreo et carne xxijd. Et ij liberantur S. le Geldehirde. Et I liberatur Instauratori. Et remanent xxxix vacce et ij tauri. Idem respondet de ij bobus de addicione et liberantur G. parcario. Idem respondet de xiiij boviculis de rem̄. Et remanent ix bovette et v Juvence. Idem respondet de xiiij vitulis de rem̄. De quibus ij in morina pro coreo et carne iiijd. Et I in decima. Et remanent xi bovicùli quorum v masculi. Idem respondet de xxiij vitulis de exitu. De quibus computat ij in morina pro coreis Id. Et I liberatur S. le Geldhirde. Et ij liberantur Instauratori. Et rem̄ xviij vituli de exitu.

Summa averiorum restancium in dicta vaccaria xxxix vacce et ij tauri ix bovetti v Juvence xj boviculi quorum v masculi et xviij vituli.

E

Benne de Holcoumbe reddit compotum suum de xlvj vaccis et I tauro de rem. Et de iiij de addicione. Et I recepta de Instauratore. Summa recepte L j vacce et I taurus. De quibus computat iij in Morina pro coreis et carne iijs. viijd. Et I liberatur S. le Geldhirde. Et v liberantur Instauratori. Et remanent xlij vacce et I taurus. Idem respondet de v bobus de addicione et liberantur G. parcario. Idem respondet de x boviculis de rem. Et remanent viij^to bovetti et ij Juvence. Idem respondet de xiij vitulis de rem. De quibus I in decima. Et remanent xij boviculi quorum v masculi. Idem respondet de xxij vitulis de exitu. Et de ij receptis de Instauratore. Summa
iij s. xj deñ. recepte xxiiij. De quibus computat iiij in Morina pro coreis iijd. Et v liberantur Instauratori. Et remanent xiiij vituli de exitu.

Summa averiorum restancium in dicta vaccaria xlij vacce et I taurus viij^to bovetti ij Juvence xij boviculi quorum v masculi et xiiij vituli de exitu.

Johannes del Haregreves loco Will. filii Hauwysie reddit compotum suum de xlj vacce et I tauro de rem. Et de vj de addicione. Et de vj receptis de Instauratori. Summa recepte liij vacce et I taurus. De quibus computat I liberata S. le Geldhirde. Et remanent Lij vacce et I taurus. Idem respondet de ij bobus de addicione et liberantur G. parcario. Idem respondet de ix boviculis de rem. De quibus I in vendicione pro xvjd. Et remanent iij bovetti masculi et v Juvence. Idem respondet de xv vitulis de rem. De quibus I in morina pro coreo iijd. Et I in decima. Et remanent xiij boviculi quorum vij masculi. Idem
xxd. respondet de xij vitulis de exitu. Et de vj receptis de Instauratore. Summa xviij. De quibus computat iij in morina pro coreis I d. Et remanent xv vituli de exitu.

Comitis Lencolnie. 27

Summa averiorum restancium in dicta vaccaria Lij vacce et I taurus iij bovetti et v Juvence xiij boviculi quorum vij masculi et xv vituli de exitu.

Will. filius Gryffry reddit compotum suum de xlj vaccis et I tauro de rem̄. Et de vj de addicione. Et de iij receptis de Instauratore. Summa recepte L vacce et I taurus. De quibus computat I in vendicione pro iijs. vjd. Et ij liberantur S. le Geldhirde. Et remanent xlvij vacce et I taurus. Idem respondet de iij bobus et I tauro de addicione. De quibus iij liberantur G. parcario. Et remanet I taurus. Idem respondet de x boviculis de rem̄. Et remanent vij bovetti et iij Juvence. Idem respondet de xvj vitulis de rem̄. De quibus computat ij in decima. Et remanent xiiij boviculi quorum v masculi. Idem respondet
iijs. vjd. de xv vitulis de exitu. Et de iij receptis de Instauratore. Summa xviij. De quibus computat ij in Morina pro coreis ob. Et remanent xvj vituli de exitu.

Summa averiorum restancium in dicta vaccaria xlvij vacce et ij tauri vij bovette iij Juvence xiij boviculi quorum v masculi et xvj vituli de exitu.

Johannes del Barouford loco cujus Thomas filius Alani reddit compotum suum de xxxvj vacce et I tauro de rem̄. Et de ix addicione. Et de I recepta de Instauratore. Summa recepte xlvj vacce et I taurus. De quibus computat ij liberantur S. le Geldhirde. Et iiij liberantur Instauratori. Et remanent xl vacce
N et I taurus. [Item J vacca additur de boviculis ut inferius — *scored out.*] Idem respondet de ix bobus de addicione et liberantur G. parcario. Idem respondet de xiij boviculi de rem̄. [De quibus I additur cum vaccis — *scored out.*] Et remanent v bovetti et viij^{to} Juvence. Idem respondet de viij vitulis de rem̄.

Et de I recepto de Instauratore. De quibus computat I in decima. Et remanent xiij boviculi quorum vij masculi. Idem respondet xxiij vitulis de exitu. De quibus computat I in Morina coreum nullius valoris. Et ij liberantur S. le Geldhirde. Et iiij liberantur Instauratori. Et remanent xvj vituli de exitu.

Summa averiorum restancium in dicta vaccaria xl vacce et I taurus v bovetti viij Juvence xiij boviculi quorum vij masculi et xvj vituli de exitu.

Adam filius Nicolai reddit compotum suum de xl vaccis et I tauro de rem. Et de ij de addicione. Et de iij receptis de Instauratore. Summa recepte xlv vacce et I taurus. De quibus computat ij liberatas S. le Geldhirde. Et ij in Morina pro coreis et carne pro iijs. vjd. Et remanent xlj vacce et I taurus. Idem respondet de v bobus de addicione et liberantur G. parcario. Idem respondet de xij boviculis de rem. [De quibus viij^{to} liberatas — *scored out.*] Et remanent viij bovetti et iiij Juvence. Idem respondet de xiiij vitulis de rem. De quibus I in Morina pro coreo iiijd. Et I in decima. Et remanent xij bo-

iiijs. xjd. viculi quorum iiij masculi. Idem respondet de xvj vitulis de exitu. Et de iij receptis de Instauratore. Summa xix. De quibus computat ij in Morina pro coreis I d. Et remanent xvij vituli de exitu. Item debet xijd. pro vitulis minus bene custoditis.

Summa averiorum restancium in dicta vaccaria xlj vacce et I taurus viij bovetti iiij Juvence xij boviculi quorum iiij masculi et xvij vitulis de redditu.

Will. Gougge loco Ricardi de Bercroft reddit compotum suum de xlj vaccis et I tauro de rem. Et de iiij de addicione. Et de ij de Instauratore. Summa recepte xlvij vacce et I taurus. De quibus computat I in

Morina pro carne et coreo pro ij s. iiij d. ob. Et iiij liberantur S. le Geldhirde. Et ij liberantur Instauratori. Et remanent xl vacce et I taurus. Idem respondet de iij bobus de addicione et liberantur G. parcario. Idem respondet de xij boviculi de rem. De quibus computat I strangulatum per Lupum pro coreo et carne xij d. Et remanent vij bovetti et iiij Juvence. Idem respondet de xiiij vitulis de rem. De

iij s. v d. ob. quibus ij in decima. Et rem. xij boviculi quorum vj masculi. Idem respondet de xix vitulis de exitu. Et de ij receptis de Instauratore. Summa xxi. De quibus computat iij in Morina pro coreo I d. Et ij liberantur Instauratori. Et remanent xvj vituli de exitu.

Summa averiorum restancium in dicta vaccaria xl vacce et I taurus vij bovetti iiij Juvence xij boviculi quorum vj masculi et xvj vituli de exitu.

Robertus Attebrigge reddit compotum suum de xxxix vaccis et I tauro de rem. Et de v de addicione. Summa recepte xliij vacce et I taurus. De quibus computat I in Morina pro coreo et carne xviij d. Et ij liberantur Simoni le Geldhirde. Et remanent xlj vacce et I taurus. Idem respondet de iij bobus de addicione et liberantur G. parcario. Idem respondet de iij boviculis de rem. De quibus computat I in Morina pro coreo et carne I d. ob. Et remanent iiij bovetti et v Juvence. Idem respondet de xiiij vitulis de rem. De quibus ij in Morina pro coreis et carne ij d. Et

xxij d. ob. remanent xij boviculi quorum iiij masculi. Idem respondet de xvij vitulis de exitu. Et ij de exitu vaccarum que fuerint in dubio. Summa xix. De quibus ij in Morina pro coreo I d. Et I liberatur S. le Geldhirde. Et remanent xvj vituli de exitu.

Summa averiorum restancium in dicta vaccaria xlj

vacce et I taurus iiij bovetti v Juvence xij boviculi quorum iiij masculi et xvj vituli de exitu.
Summa denariorum in foresto de Pennehille xxvij s. viij d. ob.

Roscyndale.
    Henricus del Estock reddit compotum suum de xxxv vaccis et I tauro de rem. Et de iij de addicione. Et de ij de Instauratore. Summa recepte xlj vacce et I taurus. De quibus computat ij liberatas Simoni le Geldhirde. Et v liberatas Instauratori. Et remanent xxxix vacce et I taurus. Idem respondet de v bobus de addicione et liberantur G. parcario. Idem respondet de xv boviculis de rem. Et remanent x bovetti et v Juvence. Idem respondet de xij vitulis de rem. ʻEt I de Instauratore Summa xiij. De quibus I in decima. Et rem. xij boviculi quorum vij masculi. Idem respondet de xxiiij vitulis de exitu. Et de I recepto de Instauratore. Summa xxv. De

Id.   quibus ij in Morina pro coreo Id. Et iiij liberantur Instauratori. Et remanent xix vituli de exitu.

    Summa averiorum Restancium in dicta vaccaria xxxix vacce et I taurus x bovetti v Juvence xij boviculi quorum vij masculi et xix vituli de exitu. Postea allocatur eidem Henrico I vacca de qua testificatum fuit super compotum quod ablata fuit per latrones.

Henricus de Hoghton loco ejus Johannes de Pycoppe reddit compotum suum de xxxviij vaccis et I tauro de rem. Et de v de addicione. Et de iij de Instauratore. Summa recepte xlvj vacce et I taurus. De quibus computat I strangulatam per Lupum pro coreo et carne iij s. Et ij liberantur Instauratori. Et remanent xliij vacce et I taurus. Idem respondet de vj bobus de addicione et liberantur G. parcario. Idem

Comitis Lencolnie. 31

respondet de xij boviculis de rem. Et remanent viij bovetti quorum I taurellus et iiij Juvence. Idem respondet de xviij vitulis de rem. De quibus computat ij in decima. Et I in Morina pro coreo I d. Et remanent xv boviculi quorum x masculi. Idem

iij s. ix d. ob. respondet de xvj vitulis de exitu. Et de iij receptis de Instauratore. Summa xix. De quibus computat iiij in morina pro coreo et carne viij d. ob. Et remanent xv vituli de exitu.

Summa averiorum restancium in dicta vaccaria xliij vacce et I taurus viij bovetti quorum I taurellus iiij Juvence xv boviculi quorum x masculi et xv vituli de exitu.

Johannes filius Odouse loco Ade de Wordhille reddit compotum suum de xxxvij vacce et I taurus de rem. Et de vj de addicione. Et de vj receptis de Instauratore. Summa recepte xlix vacce et I taurus. De quibus computat ij in morina pro coreis et carne jj s. x d. Et ij liberantur S. le Geldhirde. Et ij liberantur Instauratori. Et remanent xliij vacce et I taurus. Idem respondet de vj bobus de addicione et liberantur G. parcario. Idem respondet de ix boviculis de rem. De quibus computat I strangulatum per Lupum pro coreo et carne xvj d. Et remanent iiij bovetti et iiij

v s. Juvence. Idem respondet de xv vitulis de rem. De quibus computat iiij in Morina pro coreis et carne ix d. Et I in decima. Et remanent xj boviculi quorum vj masculi. Idem respondet de xv vitulis de exitu. Et de v de Instauratore. Summa recepte xx. De quibus computat iij in Morina pro coreis I d. Et remanent xvij vituli de exitu.

Summa averiorum restancium in dicta vaccaria xliij vacce et I taurus iiij bovetti iiij Juvence xj boviculi quorum vj masculi et xvij vituli de exitu.

Compotus Terrarum Henrici de Lacy

Robertus de Couhoppe loco Cecilie de Heleye reddit compotum suum de xxxvij vaccis et I tauro de rem. Et de iiij de addicione. Et v receptis de Instauratore. Summa recepte xlvj vacce et I taurus. De quibus computat I in morina pro coreo et carne xijd. Et iij liberantur S. le Geldhirde. Et I liberatur Instauratori, Et remanent xlj vacce et I taurus. Idem respondet de v bobus de addicione et liberantur G. parcario. Idem respondet de ix boviculis de rem. De quibus computat I in vendicione pro xd. Et remanent vij bovetti et I Juvenca. Idem respondet de xiij vitulis de rem. De quibus computat I in

xxijd. ob. decima. Et remanent xij boviculi quorum vij masculi.
Item xs.   Idem respondet de xij vitulis de exitu. Et de vj receptis de Instauratore. Summa recepte xviij. De quibus computat iiij in Morina pro coreis ob. Et remanent xiiij vituli de exitu. Ricardus filius Cecilie de Heley fecit finem xs. pro iiij vitulis perditis per defectum custodie ejusdem Cecilie.

Summa averiorum restancium in dicta vaccaria xlj vacce et I taurus vij bovetti I Juvenca xij boviculi quorum vij masculi et xiiij vituli de exitu. Plegii dictorum x solidorum Henricus del Estocke et Ricardus de Heley.

Roscyndale.

Ricardus de Dunnockschae reddit compotum suum de xxxv vaccis et I tauro de rem. Et de I de addicione. Et de I recepta de Instauratore. Summa recepte xxxvij vacce et I taurus. De quibus computat I strangulatam per Lupum pro coreo et carne vjs. Et I liberatur S. le Geldhirde. Et iij vacce et I taurus liberantur Instauratori. Et rem̄ xxxij vacce. Idem respondet de viij bobus de addicione et liberantur G. parcario. Idem respondet xij boviculis de rem. Et rem. vj

bovetti quorum I taurellus et vj Juvence. Idem respondet de xij vitulis de rem. De quibus I strangulatum per Lupum pro coreo et carne ix d. Et I in
vj s. x d. decima. Et remanent x boviculi quorum v masculi. Idem respondet de xxj vitulis de exitu. Et I recepto de Instauratore. Summa recepte xxij. De quibus computat ij in Morina pro coreis I d. Et I liberatur S. le Geldhirde. Et iij liberantur Instauratori. Et remanent xvj vituli de exitu.

Summa averiorum restancium in dicta vaccaria xxxij vacce vj bovetti quorum I taurellus vj Juvence x boviculi quorum v masculi et xvj vituli de exitu.

Ricardus de Bercroft loco Roberti de Couhoppe reddit compotum suum de xxxv vaccis et ij tauris de rem. Et de iij de addicione. Summa recepte xxxviij vacce et ij tauri. De quibus computat iiij liberatas Instauratori. Et remanent xxxiiij vacce et ij tauri. Idem respondet de v bobus de addicione et liberantur G.
xij d. ob. parcario. Idem respondet de xj boviculis de rem.
Item v s. Et remanent iij bovetti et viij Juvence. Idem
viij d. respondet de xiiij vitulis de rem. De quibus ij in Morina pro coreis xviij d. Et remanent xiij boviculi quorum vj masculi. Idem respondet de xx vitulis de exitu. De quibus computat v in Morina pro coreis ij d. ob. Et ij liberantur instauratori. Et remanent xiij vituli de exitu.

Summa averiorum restancium in dicta vaccaria xxxiij vacce et ij tauri iij bovetti viij Juvence xij boviculi quorum vj masculi et xiij vituli de exitu. Postea venditur I vacca super compotum pro v s.

Thomas del Estocke reddit compotum suum de xxxij vaccis et I tauro de rem. Et de ix de addicione. Et de iiij receptis de Instauratore. Summa recepte xlv

F

vacce et I taurus. De quibus computat ij liberatas
Instauratori. Et iiij liberantur S. le Geldhirde. Et
I strangulatur per Lupum pro coreo et carne iiijs. xd.
Et remanent xxxix vacce et I taurus. Idem respondet de ij bobus de addicione et liberantur G.
parcario. Idem respondet de xj boviculis de rem.
Et remanent vj bovetti et v Juvence. Idem respondet
vs. xd. de xij vitulis de rem. De quibus computat I strangulatum per lupum pro corio et carne ixd. Et I in
decima. Et remanent x boviculi quorum vj masculi.
Idem respondet de xiiij vituli de exitu. Et iiij receptis de Instauratore. Summa xviij. De quibus
iij in Morina pro coreo et carne iijd. Et remanent
xv vituli de exitu.

Summa averiorum restancium in dicta vaccaria
xxxix vacce et I taurus vj bovetti v Juvence x boviculi quorum x masculi et xv vituli de exitu.

Henricus de Hoghtone loco Henrici de Berdeshille reddit
compotum suum de xxiiij vacce et I tauro de rem.
et de ix de addicione. Et de iij receptis de Instauratore. Summa recepte xlvj vacce et I taurus. De
quibus computat I in morina pro coreo et carne
iiijs. iiijd. Et I liberatur Simoni le Geldhirde. Et
remanent xliiij vacce· et I taurus. Idem respondet
de ij bobus de addicione et liberantur G. parcario.
Idem respondet de x boviculis de rem. Et de I
recepto de Instauratore. Et de I invento per examinacionem visus Senescalli. Summa xij. Et re-
iiijs. xjd. manent viij bovetti quorum I taurellus et iiij Juvence.
Idem respondet de xvj vitulis de rem. De quibus
computat ij in morina pro coreis vjd. Et I in decima.
Et remanent xiij boviculi quorum v masculi. Idem
respondet de xx vitulis de exitu. Et de ij receptis
de Instauratore. Summa xxij. De quibus computat

ij in morina pro coreo Id. Et I liberatur Instauratori. Et I liberatur S. le Geldhirde. Et remanent xviij vituli de exitu.

Summa averiorum restancium in dicta vaccaria xliiij vacce et I taurus viij bovetti quorum I taurellus iiij Juvence xiij boviculi quorum v masculi et xvij vitulis de exitu.

Will. de Dynley loco Cristiane de Dynley reddit compotum suum de xli vaccis et I tauro de rem. Et de iiij de addicione. Summa recepte xlv vacce et I taurus. De quibus computat I in morina pro corio et carne iiijs. Et ij liberantur Instauratori. Et ij liberantur S. le Geldhirde. Et remanent xl vacce et I taurus. Idem respondet de iiij bobus de addicione et liberantur G. parcario. Idem Respondet de x boviculis de rem. Et remanent v bovetti et v Juvence. Idem respondet de xviij vitulis de rem. De quibus computat ij in decima. Et I liberatur Instauratori. Et
iiijs. Id. remanent xv boviculi quorum v masculi. Idem re-
Item iiijs. spondet de xxj vitulis de exitu. De quibus computat iij [in]morina pro carne et coreis Id. Et I liberatur S. le Geldhyrde. Et I liberatur Instauratori. Et remanent xvj vituli de exitu.

Summa averiorum restancium in dicta vaccaria xl vacce et I taurus v bovetti v Juvence xv boviculi quorum v masculi et xv vituli de exitu. Postea venduntur super compotum I vacca et I vitulus pro iiij solidis.

Alanus de Roclif reddit compotum suum de xxix vaccis de rem. Et de I de addicione. Et de vj receptis de Instauratore. Summa recepte xxxvj vacce. De quibus computat I strangulatam per lupum pro carne et coreo vs. Et remanent xxxv vacce. Idem re-

36 *Compotus Terrarum Henrici de Lacy*

spondet de ix bobus de addicione et liberantur G. parcario. Idem respondet de xiiij boviculis de rem. De quibus I in morina pro coreo et carne xij d. Et remanent vij bovetti quorum I taurellus. Et vj Ju-
vj s. xj d.ob. vence. Idem respondet de xviij vitulis de rem. De quibus I in decima. Et I in morina pro coreo xd. ob. Et remanent xvj boviculi quorum vij masculi. Idem respondet de xij vitulis de exitu. Et de vj receptis de Instauratore. Summa xviij. De quibus computat iij in morina pro coreo I d. Et remanent xv vituli de exitu.

Summa averiorum restancium in dicta vaccaria xxxv vacce vij bovetti quorum I taurellus vj Juvence xvj boviculi quorum vij masculi et xv vituli de exitu.

Will. filius Andree loco Roberti de Anteley reddit compotum suum de xxxix vaccis et I tauro de rem. Et de vij de addicione. Et de iiij vaccis de Instauratore. Summa recepte L vacce et I taurus. De quibus computat I in morina pro coreo et carne ij s. vj d. Et I liberatur S. le Geldhirde. Et ij liberantur Instauratori. Et remanent xlvj vacce et I taurus. Idem respondet de vj bobus de addicione et liberantur G. parcario. Idem respondet de ix boviculis de rem. De quibus I in morina pro coreo xvj d. Et remanent v bovetti et iij Juvence. Idem Respondet de xvij vitulis de rem. De quibus I in morina pro coreo I d. Et I in decima. Et remanent xv boviculi quorum
iiij s. I d. vij masculi. Idem respondet de xv vitulis de exitu. Et de iiij receptis de Instauratore. Summa xix. De
Idem iiij s. quibus computat v in morina pro coreo ij d. Et remanent xiiij vituli de exitu.

Summa averiorum restancium in dicta vaccaria xlvj vacce et I taurus v bovetti et iij Juvence xv boviculi quorum vij masculi. Et xiiij vituli de exitu. Postea venditur I vacca super compotum pro iiij solidis.
Summa denariorum foreste de Trochdene lxvij s. ij d.

Comitis Lencolnie.

VACCARIA DE AKERINGTONE.
Makocke de Anteley reddit compotum suum de C vaccis et I tauro de rem. Et de xiiij de addicione, cum iij tauris. Summa recepte Cxiiij vacce et iiij tauri. De quibus computat iij liberatas S. le Geldhirde. Et iij liberantur Instauratori. Et ij in morina pro carne et coreis iiij s. ix d. Et I taurus liberatur Instauratori. Et remanent Cvj vacce et iij tauri. Idem respondet de xviij bobus de addicione. Et vj bobus de rem. Summa recepte xxiiij. De quibus computat vj liberatos Will. de Anteleye. Et xviij liberantur G. parcario. Est quietus. Idem respondet de Lvj boviculis de rem. De quibus computat ij in morina pro coreis et carne ij s. Et I in vendicione pro xv d. Et I liberatur Instauratori. Et remanent Lij bovetti quorum xxviij masculi et xxiiij feminei. Idem respendet de xxxvj vitulis de rem. De quibus computat ij in decima. Et iij strangulatos per Lupum, pro coreis et carne xx d. Et remanent xxxj boviculi quorum xix masculi. Idem respondet de xlviij vitulis de exitu. Et de ij receptis de Instauratore. Summa recepte L. De quibus computat iiij in morina pro coreit iiij d. Et remanent xlvj vituli de exitu.

x s.

Summa averiorum restancium in dicta vaccaria Cvj vacce et iij tauri xxviij bovetti et xxiiij Juvence xxxj boviculi quorum xix masculi et remanent xlvj vituli de exitu.

Galfridus parcarius reddit compotum suum de iij bobus de rem. Et de Cxxxvij bobus receptis de vaccariis ut supra. Summa recepte Cxl boves. De quibus computat ij strangulatos per Lupem pro coreis et carne iiij s. Et iij liberantur Gilberto Instauratori. Et iiij s. Cxxxv liberantur Simoni le Geldhirde.
Summa mise ut supra. Et est quietus

Simon le Geldhirde reddit compotum suum de Cxxxv bobus receptis de Galfrido parcario ut supra. Et remanent Cxxxv boves. Idem respondet de Lx vaccis receptis de vaccariis. Summa Lx. De quibus computat iij in iijs. iiijd. ob. Morina pro coreis et carne iijs. iiijd. Et xxxj vacce liberantur G. Instauratori. Et remanent xxvj vacce. Idem respondet de xij vitulis receptis de vaccariis ut supra. Et de ij de exitu vaccarum de Croin' in custodia ejusdem. Summa xiiij. De quibus computat I in morina pro coreo ob. Et xiij liberantur Instauratori. Et est quietus.

Summa averiorum restancium in custodia dicti Simonis Cxxxv boves xxvj vacce.

Will's de Anteley reddit compotum suum de Cxxij bobus xiiijs. de rem.' Et de vj receptis de vaccario de Akeryngtone. Summa Cxxviij. De quibus computat ij in morina pro coreis et carne xiijd. Et Cxxvj liberantur G. Instauratori. Et est quietus.

Summa denariorum de Akeryngtone et custodiencium Boum et Averiorum de Crom xviijs. vd.

Gilbertus filius Michaelis Instaurator tocius Instauri, Petrus de Bradeleye Ricardus clericus Instaurator de Pennehille, Henricus del Estocke Instaurator de Roscyndale Will's de Rocheleye Instaurator de Trochdene reddunt compotum suum de xlij vaccis de rem. Et de $\overset{xx}{iiij}$. xiiij vaccis et iiij Tauris receptis de vaccariis ut in Compoto. Summa recepte Cxxxvj vacce et iiij tauri. De quibus computat lx liberatas vaccariis ut in compoto. Et lxxij vaccas et iiij tauris in vendicione ut inferius. Et remanent iiij vacce. Idem respondet de Liiij bobus de rem. Et de Cxxix bobus receptis de custodiente averiorum de Crom' Summa recepte $C\overset{xx}{iiij}$. iij boves. De quibus computat Cxxxvij boves in vendicione ut inferius. Et remanent xlvj boves.

Comitis Lencolnie.

Idem respondet de I boviculo de rem. Et de I bovetto recepto de vaccario de Akeringtone. De quibus computat I bovettun liberatum vaccario de Roscyndale ut in compoto. Et remanet I bovettus Taurellus. Idem respondet de ij boviculis receptis de vaccario de Roscindale et liberantur aliis vaccariis de eisdem ferestis. Est quietus. Idem respondet de lx vitulis receptis de vaccariis. Et de ix vitulis receptis de Juvencis de Hoddesdene. Summa recepte Lix vituli. De quibus computat lix liberatos vaccariis ut in compato. Et xj in vendicione ut inferius.

Est quietus.

Summa averiorum restancium in custodia dicti G. iiij vacce xlvj boves I Bovettus taurellus. Postea venduntur iij boves ut inferius.

Denarii recepti — Gilbertus filius Michaelis respondet de vjli. iijs. xi den. receptis de correis et carnibus animalium mortuorum in foresta de Trochdene, Pennehille et Roscyndale et aliis ut in compoto dictorum vaccariorum. Et de Lvijli. xiiijs. vjd. receptis de Cxxxvij bobus venditis. Et de xs. receptis de iij bobus venditis ut supra. Et de xxiiijs. receptis de iiij tauris venditis ut supra. Et de xxiiijli. ixs. xd. receptis de lxxij vaccis et xj vitulis venditis ut supra.

Summa tocius Recepte $\overset{xx}{iiij}$.xli. ijs. iijden.

Mise.

De quibus computat xlviijs. Id. ob. In liberacione duorum Custodiencium boum et I custodientis vaccarum apud Hoddesdene et Akeringtone.

Et viijs. in stipendiis eorundem per annum.

Et vs. vjd. in cibo et stipendio I coadjuvantis predictorum per vices.

Et ixs. iijden. In cibo et stipendio I custodientis vaccarum de Croym. in Hegham per xxj Septimanas in estate et I custodientis boviculos apud Standene per xij Septimanas tempore yeme.

Et. vs. xd. In I domo pro boviculis in Sapedene removenda et ibidem iterum construenda.

Et xixs. ixd. ob. In I boveria removenda apud Rughley et iterum ibidem construenda.

Et xxijs. Id. ob. In una grangia de novo construenda apud Wynewelle in feresta de Trochdene.

Et iijs. vjd. In reparacione I domus prostrate per I quercum ibidem.

Et xxd. In reparacione vaccariarum in foresta de Roscyndale.

Et vs. iiijd. In haiis faciendis circa prata apud novam aulam in Rosendale et Blakay.

Et vs. ixd. In stipendio prosternendi houcetum et Ramos pro averiis sterilibus.

Et ixden. In averiis fugandis per diversa loca.

Et ijd. In I ferro empto pro averiis signandis.

Et xiiijd. In stipendio I hominis custodientis vitulos pro Lupo.

Et iijs. condonatis Matilde del Bothe pro una vacca ablata per latrones.

Et xls. in feodo Gilberti Instauratoris per annum.

Et viijs. allocatis Instauratori forestarum pro vitulis signandis et stipendio clericorum suorum.

Et xxs. viijd. q^a. allocatis dicto Gilberto in quibus Comes ei tenebatur super ultimum compotum.

Et Lxxvijli. xviijs. iiijd. liberatis Simoni Noel presens recognovit.

Summa Tocius Mise et liberacionis $\overline{iiij}$.viijli. vjs. xjd. ob. Et sic debet domino Comiti dictus Gilbertus xxxvs. iijd. ob. Postea allocantur eidem Gilberto viijs. soluti Ade de Shippewelbothym quos solvit pro meremio prosternendo et carpentando quod captum fuit de eadem ad opus Comitis pro I grangia construenda apud Blakay. Et sic debet de claro xxvijs. iijd. ob.

STANDENE.

Robertus de Heppehale senescallus et Thomas serviens ibidem reddunt compotum suum apud Ichtenhille xxx° die Januarii Anno Regni Regis Edwardi xxiiij coram eisdem et de eodem Anno ut supra.

De xiiijli. xviijs. vijd. ob. de arreragiis ultimi Compoti.
De xxs. de liberacione prati de Grenelache vendito hoc anno.
De xxs. de liberacione prati vendito per diversa loca hoc Anno.
De xxxjs. vjd. de lxvj averiis agistatis ibidem per capita hoc anno.
De vs. vd. de v bussellis frumenti venditis.
De xli. xvijs. vijd. ob. de lxx quarteriis vj bussellis et dimidio avene venditis.
De xxxiijs. xd. de faldagio ibidem hoc anno.
Summa Tocius Recepte xxxjli. vijs.

Mise.
De quibus computat iijs. iijd. ob. In custu unius caruce per annum cum stipendio fabri.
Et iijd. in iij haiis faciendis pro bobus.
Et ijs. viijd. in ij plaustris de novo faciendis.
Et xls. iiijd. In liberacionibus ij Carucariorum per annum.
Et viijs in stipendio eorundem per annum.
Et xs. vjd. In cibo et stipendio I custodientis Boum in estate et averiorum agistatorum.
Et xld. In cibo et stipendio unius herciatoris tempore seminis.
Et ijs. vjd. in cibo et stipendio ejusdem auxiliantis boum custodiendum in estate et averia agistata.
Et xxijd. in domibus cooperiendis.

Et xij d. in bladis sarclandis.

Et xvj s. ob. q^a. In falcacione xxxv acrarum et dimidii prati falcandi apud Standene et novum pratum de Cliderhowe.

Et xvij s. vij d. ob. In stipendio Cix hominum metencium bladum quasi per unum diem.

Et xiij s. ix d. In I qr^a et v bus. frumenti emptis ad semen.

Et vj s. iij d. ob. in Cj qr^a vj bus. avene triturandis et ventandis.

Et xlv s. vj d. In vadiis Servientis per annum, qui capit in die I d. ob.

Et vj s. viij d. In Roba ejusdem.

Et xv li. x s. liberatos Simoni Noel presens recognovit.

Summa Tocius Mise et liberacionis xxiiij li. ix s. vij d. q^a.

Et sic debet Comiti vj li. xvij s. iiij d. ob. q^a. De quibus lxxv s. vij d. ob. q^a. sunt de arreragiis Radulfi filii Lucke quondam propositi. Et xxxvij s. I d. ob. q^a. sunt de arreragiis Jordani quondam propositi. Et sic debet dictus Thomas de claro xxiiij s. vij d. ō. q^a.

Grangia de Standen.

Idem ut supra reddunt compotum suum de exitu grangie de fructibus Autumpni Anno Regni Regis Edwardi xxiij Coram eosdem die et loco ut supra.

Frumentum.

Idem respondet de v bussellis frumenti de exitu. Et de I qr^a v bus. de exitu grangie. Summa Recepte ij qr^a I bus. De quibus computat I qr^a et v bus. in semine. Et v bus. in vendicione. Est quietus.

Avena.

Idem respondet de Cxxj qr^a. vj bus. et dimidii avene de exitu grangie. Summa Recepte Cxxj qr^a vj bus. et dimidium. De quibus computat Lj qr^a in semine Et lxx qr^a vj bus. et dimidium in vendicione.

Est quietus.

Comitis Lencolnie. 43

Boves.
Idem respondet de xviij bobus de rem. Summa Recepte
xviij boves.   Et remanent xviij boves.

Halton.

Willielmus de Wambwelle Receptor reddit compotum suum apud Haltone xv die Novembris coram Willielmo de Nony et Thome de Fisseburne videlicet ab Incrastino Sancti Michaelis anno Regni Regis Edwardi xxiij usque Incrastinum Sancti Michaelis anno regni regis Edwardi xxiiij°

De iiij^{xx} li. ix s. vi d.	de arreragiis ultimi compoti.
De Cviij s. v d.	de firma de Haltone termino Martini.
De I d.	de firma Johannis Boydel pro I placea ad torale.
De vij li. ij s. ix d. ô.	de firma de Runcouer superiori et inferiori cum sex denariis de firma Thome parcarii ut in compoto precedente terminis Martini et Johannis Baptiste.
De xiij d.	de Incremento firme Roberti dolle pro J acra terre invento per mensuracionem quinque acrarum terre quas emit de Ricardo clerico.
De ij s.	de firma Roberti parcarii pro I placea vasti in Haltone.
De xxiij d.	de firma Gilberti fabri pro I placea vasti ad fab. hoc anno primo.
De iij s.	de bovaria Comitis posita ad firmam hoc anno primo.
De Cxv s. iij d. ô.	de Cxv acris iij rodis dimidio et I placea in Bondeth et Chyrchefeld termino Michaelis.

De xxxvs. ixd.	de xxxv acris iij rodis et dimidio terre et iij placeis terre in bosco de Haltone positis ad firmam termino Michaelis.
De vs.	de firma cujusdam Molendini equicii hoc anno primo et in anno sequenti reddet decem solidos.
De xxs.	de piscaria de Runcouer terminis Purificacionis et Michaelis.
De xijd.	de piscaria per cepes termino Michaelis.
De xviijd.	de alia piscaria ibidem hoc anno.
De xijd.	de piscaria de Bodeworhe.
De Cvjs. xjd. ò.	de firma de Whyteley cum breda terminis Martini et Johannis Baptiste.
De xxijs.	de firma Thome de Bartone pro dominicis de Anderbuske termino Martini.
De xxxiijs. xd.	de firma de Anderbuske terminis Martini et Johannis Baptiste.
De xs.	de x acris terre quas Johannes Segersteyn tenet ibidem terminis eisdem.
De iijs. iijd.	de firma de Cronleycroft terminis eisdem.
De xs.	de iij acris J roda vasti positis ad firmam terminis eisdem.
De xjs. xjd. ò.	de firma de Northcotes termino Martini.
De vjs. viijd.	de firma de Penre termino Martini.
De vs.	de firma de Aldredley termino eodem.
De xiijs. iiijd.	de firma de Lysenker termino eodem.

Comitis Lencolnie.

De xij s.	de firma de Byrcheles termino eodem.
De xij d.	de firma Thome de Makelesfelde in eodem termino eodem.
De vij s.	de firma de Toft termino eodem.
De iij s. i d.	de firma de Hulle et Walmefelde termino eodem.
De vij s. xj d.	de firma de Coten termino eodem.
De xl s.	de firma Endesbyre et Pexhille termino eodem.
De iiij d.	de firma de Gropenehalle termino Johannis Baptiste.
De xij s. vj d.	de firma diversorum tenencium in Cestria terminis Martini et Johannis Baptiste.
De ô. qᵃ.	de J libra Cymini de redditu Ranulphi de Deresbyre pro uno burgagio in Cestria termino Johannis Baptiste.
De xx s.	de firma I saline in Northwico terminis eisdem.
De iiij li. ix s. ô.	de firma de mora terminis eisdem.
De xx d.	de J. libra piperis de redditu Simonis Le Buter termino Johannis Baptiste.
De xij d.	de uno pari Cerotecarum de redditu de Felewelle.
De Cvj s. viij d.	de Stallagio de Felewelle et quarta parte piscarie ejusdem termino Michaelis.
De ij s.	de piscaria de Waletone inferiori termino Baptiste.
De iij s. iiij d.	de tenentibus de Langdendale pro custodia viarum versus Nundinas Cestrie.

De Liij s. ij d.   de Liiij acris dimidio terre de dominicis de Haltone positis ad firmam deductis decima et redecima termino Michaelis.

Summa prima Recepte cum arreragiis Cxxxiiij li. xj s. viij d. q^a

De vj s. viij d.   de I placea pasture in Marisco tradita bondis ad firmam hoc anno primo.

De v s.   de herbagio vendito per loca.

De xx s. ij d.   de xiiij bobus xv bovettis et boviculis agistatis in parco.

De pannagio parci nichil.

De xxx s.   de albo x vaccarum positarum ad firmam deducta decima.

De Lxxiij s. ij d.   de averiis agistatis in Northewode.

De xix s. viij d.   de veteri busca vendita in eadem.

De x s. iij d. ô.   de pannagio de Whytteley in diversis[?] deducta decima et redecima.

De ix s.   de pannagio bosci forinseci ob Hautone.

De xi s. vj d. q^a   de pannagio de Haltone et Runcouer deductis decima et redecima.

De lxxij s.   de xxxij porcis de pannagio de Haltone Runcouer Whitteley venditis deductis decima et redecima.

De C s.   de operibus autumpni arura et streteward.

De xvij s. v d. ô.   de finibus diversarum villarum pro Marketgalt hoc anno.

De xiiij li. xvj s.   de finibus et perquisitis libere Curie de Haltone. De releviis nichil.

Comitis Lencolnie. 47

De xij s.	de Merchetto Margarete filie Alani de Haltone et Margerie filie Ade de Cliftone.
De Lxviij s. ij d.	de perquisitis Halimoti de Haltone et finibus pro ingressu terre.

De bonis Nativorum Mortuorum nichil hoc anno.

De xxvj s. viij d.	de Merchetto Margerie filie Ade Lenke, Amabilie filie Ricardi de Whitteley, et Alicie filie Ricardi de la Grene de eadem.
De xxxviij s. iiij d.	de perquisitis halimoti de Whitteley et finibus pro ingressii terre.

De bonis Nativorum Mortuorum nichil hoc anno.

De xs.	de tallagio bondorum de Haltone.
De Liij s. viij d.	de tallagio bondorum de Runcoure superiori et Inferiori.
De Liij s. iiij d.	de tallagio bondorum de Whitteley, et debent predicti bondi dare tallagium quolibet tercio anno.
De xvj li. xj s. vj d.	de teoloneo Nundini de Haltone hoc anno.
De vj s. ix d.	de teoloneo cervisie ibidem.
De xxiiij s.	de firma Molendini de Whitteley terminis Martini et Johannis Baptiste.
De xvj s.	de warda averiorum in falda Castri de Haltone.
De xxj li.	de serjancia liberi Hundredi de Haltone hoc anno.
De C s.	de advocacionibus hoc anno.
De xlv s.	de iij forestariis de Norhtwode pro balliva forestarie.

De mele silvestri nichil hoc anno.

De viij s.   de uno pullano I pultrella venditis de vago.

De xiiij s.   de veteri feno vendito.

De xvij s. v d. ô.   de warda de Endesbyre et Pexhille usque ad etatem heredis.

De viij li.   de fine Roberti filii et heredis Roberti de Mascy infra etatem qui abductus fuit et maritatus per Ricardum de Mustone cujus heredis maritagium pertinebat ab Comitem pro eo quod Idem heres tenuit tenementa sua in Waletone et Sale de herede Ranulphi Starky per servicium Militare qui. quidem heres Ranulphi Starky fuit infra etatem et in custodia Comitis et predictus Robertus de Mascy est plene etatis. Ideo nichil de exitibus custodie terrarum ejusdem.

De Lxxiij s. viij d.   de custodia terre et heredis Radulphi Starky in Fettone.

De xxv s.   de custodia terre et heredis Thome de Waleton in Hattone.

De vj li. xx d. q^a.   de custodia terre et heredis Galfridi Chedel in Cliftone.

De xx s.   de custodia terre et heredis Ricardi de Whittely et non plus quia v solidi assignantur matri pro custodia heredis.

De xxij s. I d. ô.   de custodia terre et heredis Hugonis de Duttone in Bekewycke de termino Johannis Baptiste.

De xvj s.   de pipere et aliis venditis super compotum ut Inferius.

Comitis Lencolnie. 49

De vs. vjd. de perquisitis Halimoti tenencium varde de Fettone.
Summa secunda Recepte Cxvijli. xiijs. ixd. ô.

WYDENESSE.

De viijli. xixs. Id. qª.   de firma de Wydenesse Apeltone cum breda terminis Natalis et Johannis Baptiste.

De xlixs. ô. qª.   de firma de Uptone termino Michaelis.

De lxxs.   de dominicis ibidem positis ad firmam terminis Natalis et Johannis Baptiste.

De xxxs. Id.   de firma iij Molendinorum ibidem terminis eisdem.

De vijs.   de firma Henrici Le Waleys pro I roda terre et uno Molendino equicio ubi prius fuit Molendinum manuale.

De ijs.   de hominibus de Runcouer pro turbis habendis.

De xxvjs. Id.   de firma que vocatur Sacfe terminis predictis.

De vjs. viijd.   de Repesilver termino Michaelis.

De ijs. viijd.   de firma Ricardi de Donigtone termino Nativitatis beate virginis.

De Oxsegalte nichil hoc anno quia nihil nisi tercio anno, quod erit in proximo anno.

De xxvjs. viijd.   de Medietate bonorum Ricardi de Dentone Nativi comitis defuncti.

De Cvjs. viijd.   de fine Ricardi filii Ricardi de Dentone pro terra patris sui tenenda in Dentone.

De Liijs. iiijd.   de fine Philippi de la Leghe qui

	disponsavit filiam Rogeri de Wydenesse Nativi Comitis pro terra ejusdem Rogeri tenenda in Wydenesse.
De Liij s. iiij d.	de fine Willielmi filii Dobbe de Uptone pro tenemento quod Johannes Magge Nativus Comitis tenuit.
De xviij s.	de Merchetto Amabille filie Willielmi de Upton, Margerie filie Ricardi de Dentone, Alicie filie Willielmi filii Edde, et Margerie filie W. de Assebroke.
De Lij s. ix d.	de perquisitis Halimoti et minutis finibus.
De ix s.	de relevio Ricardi filii Henricis pro medietate Molendini de Dentone.
De xxxv s.	de Minutis finibus liberorum hominum pro Ingressu terre.
De Lxv s. viij d.	de perquisitis libere Curie de Wydenesse.
De xv d.	de chenagio xv hominum.
De vj s. viij d.	de chenagio Ranulphi de Wydeness.
De ix s. ð. q^a.	de pannagio de Wydenesse deducta decima et redecima.
De xx s.	de fine forestarii de Wydenesse pro balliva forestarie.
De Lx s.	de Roberto Le Noreys pro seriancia libere Curie de Wydenesse.
De xiij li. vj s. viij d.	de tallagio bondorum de Wydenesse hoc anno qui non dant

tallagium nisi quolibet tercio anno.
Summa tercia Recepte Lvijli. xvjs. iiijd. ô. q^a.

De xiijli. vijs.   de Nicholao Frodesham de arreragiis suis per ij tallias que remanent penes Receptorem.
De xxijli. iijs. iiijd.   de preposito de Congletone per ij tallias.
Summa quarta recepte xxxvli. xs. iiijd.
Summa Summarum totius Recepte CCCxlvli. xiijs. ijd. ô.

Mise Manerii.
    De quibus computat xvs. xd. In domibus Infra Castrum et seldis In mercato cooperiendis et emendandis.
    Et vijs. vijd. In ij molaribus emptis pro Molendino equicio.
    Et xixs. In cibo et stipendium J carcttari et ferramento affrorum per annum.
    Et vijs. vijd. In pratis falcandis et feno levando.
    Et xxxijs. viijd. In vadiis et roba parcarii per annum.
    Et xijs. xd. In expensis custodiencium Nundinam hoc anno.
    Et xxxixs. ixd. In vj vaccis cum vj vitulis emptis.
    Et vjli. xiijs. iiijd. In feodo Senescalli per annum.
    Et vijli. xs. In feodo et roba Constabularii per annum.
    Et vs. iiijd. In litteris portandis per loca.
    Et xxvjs. vjd. In expensis ducencium Tuder abcarwar et iiij socios suos obsides de Haltone usque Pontemfractam.
    Et xxxIs. In expensis Thome de Fisseburne per suos adventus et Johannis de Blakeburne pro J adventu.
    Et xxijs. datos narratoribus et clericis in Comitatu Cestrie pro negociis Comitis.
    Et xvli. solutos executoribus domini Walthivi Darderne in parte solucionis Lxli. in quibus Comes ei tenebatur per scriptum suum obligatorium pro quieta clamacione

dotis Manerii de Congleton quam Margeria mater predicti Walthivi petiit versus Comitem ut dotem suam unde littere acquietancie remanent penes receptorem.

Et viij s. vj d. In decasu firm tenencium heredis Ranulphi de Starky In Stretton hoc anno.

Et xij s. x d. In Cxlj rodis et dimidio veteris palicii removendis et Item plantandi xiij rodas novi palicii facti et xxvij rodas haye facte circa parcum.

Et vj s. vj d. In Centum et sexaginta tribus libris portandis bis usque Pontem fractem.

Et C$^{xx}_{iiij}$vj li. x s. liberatis Olivero de Stanefeld Constabulario Pontisfractis ut in compoto.

Summa tocius mise et liberacionis CCxxviij li. xiiij s. Et sic debet receptor Comiti Cxvij li. xij s. ồ.

Affri.
Idem respondet de ij affri de rem. Summa recepte patet.
Et remanent ij affri masculi.

Boves.
Idem respondet de J bove de rem. Et de J de addicione.
Summa recepte ij.
Et remanent ij boves.

Vacce.
Idem respondet de viij vaccis et J tauro. Et de ij de addicione. Et de vj de empcione ut supra.
Summa recepte xvj vacce J taurus.
Et remanent xvj vacce, J taurus.

Bovetti.
Idem respondet de ij boviculis de rem. Summa recepte ij.
Et remanent ij bovetti quorum J masculus.

Boviculi.
Idem respondet de vj vitulis de rem. Summa recepte vj.
Et remanent vj boviculi quorum v masculi.

Vituli.
Idem respondet de vij vitulis de exitu. Et de vj de empcione

Comitis Lencolnie. 53

ut supra. Summa recepte xiij. De quibus computat
I In decima. Et remanent xij vituli quorum vij masculi.

Piper, cymen, Cerotoce, Sagitte, Cultelle, lancee.

Idem respondet de ij lanceis et xij sagittis barbatis de rem. de I libra piperis I libra Cyminis de redditu Prioris de Norton in Aston, de I libra piperis de redditu Cestrie. de J libra piperis de redditu Simonis le Roter pro tenemento in More.

Et de I pari cerotecarum furratarum de redditu de Thellewelle, de vj saggittis barbatis de redditu de Sproscroft.

Et de J pari calcarium de redditu de Penre.

Et de J cultello de redditu Aydropi Mylingtone.

Et de J lancea de redditu heredis Nicholai de Leycestria.

Et de ix libris piperis, iij libris Cyminis de supradicta firma de tribus annis proximis precedentibus unde receptor non fuit carcatus.

Et de tribus paribus cerotecarum furratarum, xviij sagitte, iij paribus calcarium, iij cultellis, iij lanceis de supradicta firma de tribus annis proximis precedentibus unde receptor non fuit carcatus.

De quibus còmputat iiij paria cerotecarum iiij libras piperis
xvj s.   In vendicione ut in isto compoto et in tribus compotis. precedentibus et tatum residuum in vendicione super compotum.   Est quietus.

CONGLETONE.

Willielmus de Wambwelle constabularius Castri de Haltone et Alexander Mercer prepositus reddunt compotum suum apud Haltone xvj die Novembris regni regis Edwardi xxv coram domino W. de Nony et T. de Fisseburne videlicet a die dominico proximo post festum Sancti Nicholai anno regni regis Edwardi xxiij° usque Incrastinum Sancti Michaelis anni ejusdem.

Compotus Terrarum Henrici de Lacy

De xiiij li. vs. viij d. ó.   de redditibus et firmis ibidem de termino Johannis Baptiste.
De xxv s. viij d. ó.   de dominicis ibidem positis ad firmam termino eodem.
De x s.   de firma rupe Molarium posita ad firmam eadem termino.
De viij li. vj s. viii d.   de furno communi posito ad firmam.
De viij li. vj s. viij d.   de firma Molendini hoc anno.
De vj s. viij d.   de teoloneo fori ibidem et Nundini.
De ij s.   de herbagio gardini.
De ij s.   de herbagio del flaskes.
De ij s. vj d.   de herbagio vendito per loca.
De xj d.   de pomis venditis.
De xlviij s.   de finibus et perquisitis Curie.
Summa tocius Recepte xxvj li. xviij s. ij d.

Mise Manerii et liberacio.
De quibus computat viij d. In emendacione domorum.
Et vj s. ij d. In iiij acris prati falcandis, herba spargenda, feno levando et tassando et cariando.
Et xxj li. xij s. liberatos Willielmo de Wambewelle ut in compoto.
Et v s. allocantur preposito pro servicio suo.
Et vj s. vj d. In decasu firmarum hoc anno.
    Summa Summarum tocius Misa et liberacionis xxij li. x s. v d. Et sic debet prepositus Comiti iiij li. vij s. ix d.

CONGLETONE.
Willielmus de Hesketh Senescallus et Alexander Mercer prepositus reddit compotum suum loco et die et coram eisdem ut supra videlicet ab Incrastino Sancti Michaelis anno regni regis Edwardi xxiij usque Incrastinum sancti Michaelis anno regni regis Edwardi xxiiij°.

Comitis Lencolnie. 55

De iiij li. vij s. ix d.   de arreragiis compoti ut supra.
De xxviij li. xj s. v d.   de redditibus et firmis liberorum et burgencium ibidem terminis Martini et Johannis Baptiste.
De L j s. v d.   de xxvij acris dimidio de dominicis positis ad firmam.
De xx s.   de firma Rupis Molarium posite ad firmam hoc anno.
De viij s.   de furno communi posito ad firmam hoc anno.
De viij li.   de firma Molendini hoc anno.
De x s.   de teoloneo fori et Nundini.
De iij s. iiij d.   de herbagio et fructu gardini.
De ij s.   de herbagio de flaskes.
De xvj d.   de herbagio vendito de terris vastis.
De iij s. iiij d.   de columbello vendito.
De xxv s. iij d.   de finibus et perquisitis Curie.
De x s. vj d.   de iiij acris prati de dominicis positis ad firmam.
De xvij s.   de feno ejusdem prati de anno preterito vendito.
     Summa tocius Recepte xlviij li. xj s. iiij d.

Mise Manerij et liberacio.
    De quibus computat iiij d. In haiis circa gardinum factis.
    Et vj s. viij d. allocatos preposito pro servicio suo per annum.
    Et C s. solutos domino Nicholao de Leyburne de termino Johannis Baptiste quas Comes eidem concessit ad terminum vite sue per cartam et de cetero habebit idem dominus Nicholaus ad terminum vite sue decem libras de Manerio de Congletone per predictam cartam solvendas eodem terminis Martini et J Baptiste.
    Et C s. solutos domino Roberto fratri ejusdem domini

Compotus Terrarum Henrici de Lacy

Nicholai de termino Johannis Baptiste per cartam Comitis in fema peditta [*i.e.*, forma predicta?] per manus Willielmi de Wambewelle.

Et xxijli. iijs. iiijd. liberatos Willielmo di Wambwelle presens recognovit.

Et xiijs. In decasu permarum hoc anno.

    Summa Summarum tocius mise et liberacionis xxxiijli. iijs. iiijd. Et sic debet prepositus Comiti xvli. viijs.

COMPOTUS TERRARUM HENRICI DE LACY COMITIS LINCOLNIE DE ANNO REGNI REGIS EDWARDI XXXIII.

HALTONE.
Willielmus de Heskeyth Senescallus, et Willielmus de Wambwelle Receptor de Haltone reddunt compotum suum apud Haltone, xxj die Februarii Anno regni regis Edwardi xxxv coram domino Willielmo de Nony et Roberto de Silkestone videlicet ab incrastino sancti Michaelis Anno regni regis Edwardi xxxij usque incrastinum sancti Michaelis Anno regni regis Edwardi xxxiij.
De Cxxxijli. iijs. viijd. ob. q^a de arreragiis ultimi compoti.
Summa arreragiorum Cxxxijli. iijs. viijd. ob. q^a.

De Cxiijs. ixd.	de firma de Haltone termino Martini.
De iijs.	de bovaria Comitis posita ad firmam.
De vijli. iijs. xd. ob.	de redditu de Runcoure Inferiore et superiore terminis Martini et Johannis Baptiste.
De Id.	de J placea vasti appruviata ibidem hoc anno primo.
De Cxvs. ixd.	de Cxv acris iij rodis in Bondheth et Chirchefelde.
De xxxvs. ixd.	de xxxv acris iij rodis terre in bosco de Haltone.
De vjd.	de Thome parcario pro J. cotagio in Runcoure.
De iiijli.	de firma iiij Molendinorum terminis Purificacionis et Michaelis.

De xx s.	de piscaria de Runcoure.
De xx d.	de piscaria per retia ibidem. De piscaria per cepes nihil.
De vj s. viij d.	de quadam piscaria inter Haltone et Runcoure hoc anno primo.
De xij d.	de piscaria de Budwurthe.
De Cxvj s. xj d. ob.	de firma de Whitlay cum breda terminis Martini et Johannis Baptiste.
De x s.	de Johanne le Segerstayn per x acris ibidem terminis predictis.
De xxij s. iij d.	de xxij acris J roda terre ibidem terminis predictis.
De v s.	de v acris terre ibidem positis ad firmam.
De xvj s.	de iiij placeis ibidem appruviatis hoc anno primo.
De xxij s.	de firma Thome de Bartone pro dominicis de Andrebusk.
De xxxiij s.	de redditu de Andrebuske terminis predictis.
De iiij s.	de Incremento firme Rogeri fabri in eadem hoc anno primo.
De x s.	de firma de Cornleycroft terminis predictis.
De xj s. xj d. ob.	de redditu de Norhcote termino Martini.
De vj s. viij d.	de redditu de Penre termino Martini.
De v s.	de redditu de Aldredelay terminis predictis.
De xiij s. iiij d.	de redditu de Lesynker termino Martini.
De xij s.	de redditu de Byrchels termino eodem.

Comitis Lencolnie. 59

De xij d.	de redditu Thome de Macklesfelde termino eodem.
De xl s.	de redditu de Endesbyre et Pexhille termino eodem.
De vij s.	de redditu de Toftes termino predicto.
De iij s. J d.	de redditu de Hulm termino eadem.
De vij s. xj d.	de redditu de Cotum termino eadem.
De iiij d.	de redditu de Gropenhale termino Johannis Baptiste.
De xiij s. vj d.	de redditu diversorum tenencium in Cestria terminis predictis.
De J d.	de J libra Cyminis de redditu Ranulphi de Deresbyre in eodem.
De xij d.	de J libra piperis de redditu Ranulphi le Roter in eodem.
De xij d.	de J pari cirotecarum de redditu de Thellewelle termino Michaelis.
De xx s.	de firma cujusdam saline in Northwyco terminis predictis.
De iij li. xiij s. iij d. ob.	de redditu de More terminis predictis.
De J d.	de J placea appruviata ibidem hoc anno primo.
De xvij d.	de xvij averiis agistatis in communi pastura ibidem.
De Cvj s. viij d.	de stallagio et quarta parte piscarie de Thellewelle.
De ij s.	de piscaria de Nether Waltone termino Johannis Baptiste.
De iij s. iiij d.	de tenentibus de Langdendale

	pro Warda viarum quam facere consueverunt versus Nundinas Cestrie. De passagio Batelli nihil.
De Lxjs. iijd. ob. q^a.	de Liij acris dimidio de dominicis de Haltone redecima deducta.
De vjs. viijd.	de una placea pasture posita ad firmam bondorum de Haltone.
De xxiiijs.	de firma Molendini aquatici in Whytlay decima deducta.

Summa secunda Recepte Lxli. iiijs. viijd. ob. q^a.

De vijli. xs.	de x bobus vj vaccis ante fetum venditis.
	De albo vaccarum, herbagio parci, herbagio per loca nihil.
De Lvijs. ijd.	de finibus villatarum de Strettone, Combebache, Coggishil et Aldewyke cum fine Willielmi de Wyrisbanke pro averiis agistatis in Northwode.
De xijs. xjd.	de CLv averiis agistatis ibidem per capita.
De xxs. vjd.	de veteri busca vendita ibidem per caractatas.
De xlvs.	de Balliva Forestarie ibidem.
De xxixs. xd.	de Thisteltacke de Northwode hoc anno.
De xiiijs. ixd.	de Thisteltacke de Runcoure, Helton et More.
De ixs.	de Haltone et Runcoure pro evasoribus in Astmore.
De Cxiijs. iiijd.	de operibus autumpnalibus aura[?] et stretewarde.
De xvjs. ixd. ob.	de Markethgalt de Haltone.

Comitis Lencolnie.

De ixli. xixs.   de perquisitis libere Curie de Haltone.
De iijs.   de Merchetto Alicie Lille.
De Liiijs. viijd.   de Minutis finibus et perquisitis Halmoti.
De xxiiijs.   de fine Henricis de Troforde pro Ingressu terre W. fratris sui.
De ixs. ijd.   de catallis Ricardi le Mercer Fugitivi.
De xxxiijs. iijd.   de perquisitis halmoti de Whytlay.
De xls.   de fine Johannis de Bartone pro ingressu tenementi quod vicarius de Budwurthe tenuit.
De xxvjs. viijd.   de fine Thome del Strete pro ingressu ij acrarum terre appruvatarum de vasto.
De vs. ijd.   de Warda averiorum in falda.
De vjs.   de uno bove de vago vendito.
De xixs. ijs.   de tallagio bondorum de Haltone.
De iiijli. viijs. ixd.   de tallagio bondorum de Runcoure.
De iiijli. xiijs. iiijd.   de tallagio bondorum de Whitlay.
De ixs. vjd.   de tallagio bondorum de More.
De viijs. ixd.   de Melle et cera Silvestri vendita.
De xvijli. xd.   de teoloneo Nundinarum de Haltone.
De ixs. ijd.   de teoloneo cervisie in dictis Nundinis.
De iiijs. ixd.   de teoloneo Nundinarum Sancte Katerine.
De xxiijli.   de Willielmo Danyel pro serjancia Hundredi de Haltone.
De vijli. vjs. viijd.   de Ricardo Starky pro advocacionibus.

De x s. de custodia terre et heredis domine de Hul super Daneno[?]
De xvj s. vj d. de ij affris venditis et J pullo.
Summa Tercia Recepte Ciij li. xvij s. vij d. ob.

Wedenes.
De ix li. iij s. ix d. q^a. de redditu de Wedenes, Apeltone et Dentone cum breda de Apeltone terminis Martini et Johannis Baptiste.
De L s. ob. q^a. de redditu de Uptone termino Michaelis.
De ij s. de J cotagio et iij acris terre ibidem.
De Lxx s. de dominicis de Wydenes terminis Nativitatis et Johannis Baptiste.
De xxxvj s. ix d. de firma iij Molendinorum ibidem terminis predictis.
De vij s. de Alano de More pro J roda terre et J Molendino equicio.
De ij s. de Nativis de Runcoure pro turba habenda.
De xxvj s. J d. de redditu qui vocatur Sakefe. De Oxgalt nihil.
De vj s. viij d. de Repe silure termino Michaelis.
De ij s. viij d. de Redditu Ricardi de Doningtone termino Nativitatis Marie.
De xiiij d. de redditu Ricardi de Molyneus pro xiiij acris terre in Baynel.
De ij d. de Alans Wulnet et Willielmo de Holford pro dimidia acra terre.
De xxj s. viij d. de fine Willielmi de Uptone et sociis suis pro ingressu unius acre terre vaste appruviate hoc anno primo.

Comitis Lencolnie. 63

De xl s.	de fine Johannis filii Andrei de Dentone pro ingressu terre quam Johannes de Dentone avus suus tenuit.
De iiij s.	de Mercheto Matillidis filie Willielmi de Uptone.
De vj li.	de perquisitis Halmoti de Wedenes.
De iiij li. ix s. ij d.	de perquisitis Libere Curie de Wedenes.
De vj s. viij d.	de chenagio Ranulphi de Wedenes.
De ij s. ij d.	de chenagio xxvj nativorum hominum.
De xij s.	de Thisteltake de Wedenes.
De Lx s.	de serjancia Libere Curie de Wedenes.
De xx s.	de fine Forestarii de Wedenes pro Balliva.
De xx li.	de tallagio bondorum de Wedenes qui dant quolibet tercio anno.
De Cx s.	de Alexandro preposito de Congletone per J talliam.
De xxij li. v s.	de Johanne preposito de Congletone per ij tallias.
De xxvj li. xiij s. iiij d.	de Nicholao de Frodesham in parte solucionis arreragiorum suorum.
De vj li. vj s.	de iij feodis Militum et viij parte et xl parte J feodis in Wydenes pro exercitu Scocie de anno regni regis Edwardi xxviij.

Summa Quarta Recepte Cxviij li. xviij s. iiij d.
Summa Summarum tocius Recepte $\frac{C}{iiij}$.xvli. iiij s. v d.

De quibus computat iij s. vij d. In domibus infra Castrum cooperiendis et emendandis.

Et xv s. In aula placitorum cooperienda cum bordis factis et clavis emptis.

Et iiij s. In una domo removenda et iterim reficienda juxta grangiam pro bouettis.

Et xiiij s. x d. In xvj acris prati falcandis, herba spargenda, et feno levando cariando et tassando.

Et vij s. vj d. In foragio empto pro averiis Comitis.

Et x s. viij d. In stipendio custodientis eosdem in yeme et prostruentis buscam pro Castro et ramos pro feris.

Et vj s. In palicio parci emendando per loca.

Et xij s. iij d. In expensis custodiendi Nundinas.

Et iiij s. In redecima Molendini de Haltone.

Et vj li. xiij s. iiij d. In feodo Willielmi de Heskeythe Senescalli per annum.

Et L s. In robis ejusdem.

Et vij li. x s. In feodo et robis Receptoris per annum.

Et xiij s. iiij d. In feodo Janitoris per annum.

Et xxxij s. viij d. In vadiis et stipendiis parcarii per annum.

Et xiij s. iiij d. In feodo Will'i de Midgelay narratoris per annum.

Summa prima Mise xxiij li. x s. vj d.

Idem computat viij d. In litteris portandis per loca.

Et v s. In denariis salvo ducendis per tres vicis usque Pontem fractam.

Et xx s. datos fratribus predicatoribus Cestrie per litteram Comitis.

Et xvj s. condonatos Ricardo filio Ricardi de Dentone per Comitem de fine facto pro ingressu terre patris sui, de quibus Receptor onerabatur in compoto precedenti.

Et vj li. solutas Comiti Lancastrie per Manus Simonis de Baldrestone Receptoris sui Lancastrie pro iij feodis Militum in Wedenes pro exercitu Scocie de anno regni regis Edwardi xxiiij.

Comitis Lencolnie.

Et C$^{xx}_{iiij}$·vij li. liberatos Olivero Receptori Pontisfracte ut in compoto.

Et xliiij li. xvij s. ij liberatos domino Nicholao de Readinge Receptori hospicii Comitis ut in compoto.

Summa Secunda Mise et liberacionis CCxxxix li. xvij s. x d·

Summa Summorum tocius Mise et Liberacionis CCLxiij li. ix s. iiij d.

Et debet Receptor Comiti CLij li. xv s. J d.

Piper, Cym., Cirotece, Sagitte lancea, cultelli, calcaria.

Idem respondet de ij li. piperis, ij li Cyminis, xij sagittis, ij paribus calcarium, ij cultellis, ij Lanceis.

Et de J li. piperis, J li. Cyminis de redditu Prioris de Nortone.

Et de J li. piperis J li. Cyminis de redditu in Cestria.

Et de J li. piperis de redditu Simonis le Roter pro xxiiij acris terre in More.

Et de J pari cirotecarum furratarum de redditu de Thellewelle.

Et de vj sagittis barbatis de redditu de Spronthescrofte.

Et de J pari alborum calcarium de redditu de Penre.

Et de J cultello de redditu Endrope de Milington.

Et de J Lancea de redditu Rogeri de Leycestria.

De quibus computat J li. piperis, J li. Cyminis, J par cirotecarum furratarum in vendicione ut supra.

Et remanent iiij li. piperis, iij li. Cyminis, xviij sagitte barbate iij paria calcarium alborum iij cultelle et iij Lancee.

Affri.

Idem respondet de iiij affris de rem. Et de J de addicione.

Summa Recepte v affri.

De quibus computat ij in vendicione ut supra.

Et remanent iij affri quorum J Jumentum cum J pullo de exitu.

Pulli.

Idem respondet de J pullo de rem. in secundo anno.

Summe Recepte patet.

Et remanet J pullus Masculus in tercio anno.

K

Pulli.
  Idem respondet de J pullo de rem. Summa Recepte patet.
  Quam computat in vendicione ut supra.
                                            Et quietus est.
Boves.
  Idem respondet de xij bobus de rem. Et de v de addicione.
                                Summa Recepte xvij boves.
  De quibus computat x in vendicione ut supra.
                                         Et remanent vij boves.
Vacce.
  Idem respondet de xlvj vaccis ij tauris de rem.
  Et de x vaccis J tauro de addicione.
      Summa Recepte Lvj, iij tauri.
  De quibus computat vj in vendicione ut supra.
              .   Et remanent L vacce, iij tauri.
Bovetti.
  Idem respondet de xx boviculis de rem.
                                Summa Recepte patet.
          Et remanent vij bovetti et xiij Juvence.
Boviculi.
  Idem respondet de xxxv vitulis de rem.
                                Summa Recepte patet.
          Et remanent xxxv boviculi quorum.
Vituli.
  Idem respondet de xij vitulis de exitu.
                                Summa Recepte patet.
  De quibus computat ij in decima et redecima.
                                      Et remanent x vituli.

CONGLETON.
  Willielmus de Heskeythe Senescallus et Alexander Le
      Mercer et Johannes de Bradake prepositi de
      Congletone reddunt compotum suum loco et die,
      coram eisdem et de eadem tempore ut supra.
  De xli. xjs.   de arreragiis ultimi compoti.

Comitis Lencolnie. 67

De xxxli. ixs. iijd. ob. q^a. de redditu et firmis liberorum bondorum et cotariorium ij terminis.
De xxxvs. viijd. de xxvj acris iij rodis terre de dominicis.
De xxvjs. viijd. de Rupe Molarium posita ad firmam.
De xs. de communi furno posito ad firmam.
De viijli. de firma Molendini deducta decima.
De xxxs. de teoloneo fori et Nundinarum.
De vjs. viijd. de herba et fructu gardini et colubare positis ad firmam.
De xs. vjd. de vestura iiij acrarum prati vendita.
De ijs. de pastura que vocatur Flaskes vendita.
De xxxvijs. iijd. de perquisitis Curie.
Summa tocius Recepte Lvjli. xixs. ob. q^a.

De quibus computat vjs. viijd. allocatos prepositi pro serviciis suis.
Et xli. solutas domino Nicholao de Leyburne terminis Martini et Johannis Baptiste pro annua firma ei debita ad terminum vite per scriptum Comitis.
Et xli. in solucione domino Roberto fratri suo in forma predicta.
Et iiijs. ixd. In expensis vj hominum de Haltoneschyre pro Metis vasti de Congletone faciendis.
Et xxvijli. xvs. liberatos Willielm Receptori di Haltone ut in compoto.
Summa tocius Mise et liberacionis xlviijli. vjs. vd.
Et sic debentur Comiti viijli. xijs. vijd. ob. q^a.

Instaurum de Blakeburneschyre. Edmundus Talbot Senescallus et Johannes de Paledene Instaurarius cum aliis Instarariis et vaccariis reddunt compotum suum apud Ichtenhil ix die Maii Anno regni regis Edwardi xxxiiij coram domino Will'o de Nony videlicet ab incrastino Sancti Michaelis Anno regni regis Edwardi xxxij usque incrastinum Sancti Michaelis Anno regni regis Edwardi xxxiij.

Troudene. Johannes del Bothe reddit compotum suum de xxxix vaccis I tauro de rem̄: Et de v vaccis de addicione. Summa Recepte xliiij vacce I taurus De quibus computat, [*Interlineation* Computat I taurus in Morina pro coreo et carne iijs. xjd.] ij liber. S. le Geldhirde. Et iiij liberantur Instaurario. Et remanent xxxviij vacce I taurus. Idem respondet de I bove de addicione. Et liberatur Henrico Hare custodienti boum. Idem respondet de xij boviculis de rem̄. Et remanent vj bovetti et vj Juvence. Idem respondet de xv vitulis de rem̄. De quibus computat I Masculum in decima. Et remanent xiiij boviculi quorum viij Masculi. Idem respondet de xx vitulis de exitu. De quibus computat I in Morina pro coreo
iijs. xjd. ō. ob. Et liberatur S. le Geldhirde. Et iij liberantur Instaurario. Et remanent xv vituli.

Summa averiorum restancium in dicta vaccaria xxxviij vacce vj bovetti quorum I taurellus et vj Juvence xiiij boviculi quorum viij Masculi et xv vituli.

Adam filius Jurdani reddit compotum suum de xl vaccis I tauro de rem̄. Et de viij vaccis de addicione. Et de I vacca recepta de Instaurario. Summa recepte xlix vacce I taurus. De quibus computat ij in Morina, pro coreis iijs. ij ob. Et I liberatur S. le Geldhirde. Et iiij liberantur Instaurario remanent xlij vacce I taurus. Idem respondet de iiij bobus de

Comitis Lencolnie. 69

addicione. Et liberantur Henrico Hare. Idem respondet de xiij boviculis de rem̄. Et rem̄ vj bovetti et vij Juvence. Idem respondet de xiiij vitulis de rem̄. De computat ij Masculos in decima. Et rem̄ xij boviculi quorum vj Masculi. Idem respondet de xv vitulis de exitu. Et de I recepto de Instaurario. Summa recepte xvj. De quibus computat ij in
iijs. iijd. Morina pro coreis jd. Et remanent xiiij vituli.

 Summa averiorum restancium in dicta vaccaria xlij vacce I taurus vj bovetti et vij Juvence xij boviculi quorum vj Masculi, et xiiij vituli.

Robertus filius Johannis reddit compotum suum de xxxiij vaccis I tauro de rem̄. Et de I vacca de addicione. Et de v receptis de Instaurario. Summa recepte xxxix vacce I taurus. De quibus computat ij vaccas I taurum liberantur Instaurario. Et remanent xxxvij vacce. Idem respondet de x boviculis de rem̄. De quibus computat I in vendicione pro ijs. Et remanent vj bovetti et eorum I taurellus et iij Juvence. Idem respondet de xiij vitulis de rem̄. De quibus computat I in Morina pro coreo ijd. Et I femineam in decima. Et remanent xj boviculi quorum iiij Masculi. Idem respondet de xj vitulis de exitu. Et de v receptis de Instaurario. Summa Recepte xvj. De quibus computat I in Morina pro coreo ob. Et
ijs. ijd. ob. remanent xv vituli.

 Summa averiorum restancium in dicta vaccaria xxxvij vacce vj bovetti et eorum I taurellus et iij Juvence, xj boviculi quorum iiij Masculi et xv vituli.

Juliana de Bothe reddit compotum suum de xxxviij vacce I tauro de rem̄. Et de iiij de addicione. Et de ij tauris receptis de Instaurario. Summa recepte xlij vacce iij tauri. De quibus computat I taurum et I

vaccam in Morina pro coreis et carne viijs. 10d. Et v vacce I taurus liberantur Instaurario. Et ij liberantur S. de Geldhirde. Et remanent xxxiiij vacce I taurus. Idem respondet de v bobus de addicione. Et liberantur Henrico Hare. Idem respondet de ix boviculis de rem̄. Et remanent iiij bovetti et v Juvence. Idem respondet de xvj vitulis de rem̄. De quibus computat I Masculum et I femineam in decima. Et remanent xiiij boviculi, quorum viij
viijs. xd. ō. Masculi. Idem respondet de xxj vitulis de exitu. De quibus computat I in Morina pro coreo ob. Et v liberantur Instaurario. Et remanent xv vituli.

Summa averiorum restancium in dicta vaccaria, xxxiiij vacce, I taurus, iiij bovetti, v Juvence, xiiij boviculi quorum viij Masculi et xv vituli.

Ranulphus de Fernyside loco Godefride de Lothresdene reddit compotum suum de xl vaccis I tauro de rem̄. Et de ij de addicione. Et de iiij receptis de Instaurario. Summa Recepte xlv vacce I taurus. De quibus computat I in Morina pro coreo et carne ijs. vjd. Et ij liberantur S. le Geldhirde. Et iiij liberantur Instaurario. Et remanent xxxviij vacce, I taurus. Idem respondet de iiij bobus de addicione. Et liberantur Henrico Hare. Idem respondet de xiiij boviculis de rem̄. Et remanent vj bovetti et viij Juvence. Idem respondet de xiiij vitulis de rem̄. De quibus computat I Masculum in decima. Et remanent xiij boviculi quorum viij Masculi. Item, idem debet xviijd. pro vitulis male custoditis. Idem respondet de xiiij
iiijs. vitulis de exitu. Et de iij receptis de Instaurario. Summa recepte xvij. De quibus computat ij in Morina pro coreis Id. Et remanent xv vituli.

Summa averiorum restancium in dicta vaccaria xxxviij vacce I taurus, vj bovetti, viij Juvence, xiij boviculi quorum viij Masculi et xv vituli.

Comitis Lencolnie. 71

Penhul.
Ricardus filius Benedicti reddit compotum suum de xxxviij vaccis de reṁ. Et de iij de addicione. Et de vij vaccis I tauro receptis de Instaurario. Summa Recepte xlviij vacce I taurus. De quibus computat v liberatas S. le Geldhirde. Et remanent xliij vacce I taurus. Idem respondet de ij bobus de addicione. Et liberantur Henrico Hare. Idem respondet de xj boviculis de reṁ. Et remanent v bovetti et vj Juvence. Idem respondet de xvij vitulis de reṁ. De quibus computat ij in Morina pro coreis vijd. Et I Masculum et I femineam in decima. Et remanent xiij boviculi,
vijd. ob. quorum ix Masculi. Idem respondet de xij vitulis de exitu. Et de vij receptis de Instaurario. Summa Recepte xix. De quibus computat I in Morina, pro coreo ob. Et remanent xviij vituli.

Summa averiorum restancium in dicta vaccaria xliii vacce I taurus v bovetti vj Juvence, xiij boviculi quorum ix Masculi et xviij vituli.

Robertus de Holecombe reddit compotum suum de xlj vaccis I tauro de reṁ. Et vij de addicione. Et de vij vaccis receptis de Instaurario. Summa Recepte lv vacce I taurus. De quibus computat I in Morina, pro coreo ijs. ijd. Et iiij liberantur S. le Geldhirde. Et ij liberantur Instaurario. Et remanent xlviij vacce I taurus. Idem respondet de vj bobus de addicione. Et liberantur Henrico Hare. Idem respondet de ix boviculis de reṁ. Et remanent iiij bovetti et v Juvence. Idem respondet de xvj vitulis de reṁ. De quibus computat I femineam in decima. Et remanent xv boviculi quorum vj Masculi. Idem respondet de xj vitulis de exitu. Et de vij de Instaurario.
ijs. iijd. Summa Recepte xviij. De quibus computat ij in Morina pro coreis Id. Et remanent xvj vituli.

Compotus Terrarum Henrici de Lacy

Summa averiorum restancium in dicta vaccaria xlviij vacce, I taurus iiij bovetti v Juvence xv boviculi quorum vj Masculi et xvj vituli.

Will's filius Hauwysie reddit compotum suum de xxxviij vaccis I tauro de rem̄. Et de v de addicione. Et de vij receptis de Instaurario. Summa Recepte L vacce I taurus. De quibus computat ij liberatas S. le Geldhird. Et iij liberantur Instaurario. Et remanent xlv vacce I taurus. Idem respondet de vj bobus de addicione. Et liberantur Henrico Hare. Idem respondet de xiij boviculis de rem̄. Et remanent vij bovetti et vj Juvence. Idem respondet de xvij vitulis de rem̄. De quibus computat ij in Morina, pro coreis iiij d. Et I Masculum I femineam in decima. Et remanent xiij boviculi quorum ix Masculi. Et idem debet ij s. vj d. pro emendacione boviculorum. Idem
ij s. x d. respondet de xiiij vitulis de exitu. Et de vij receptis de Instaurario. Summa Recepte xxj. De quibus computat iij liberatos Instaurario. Et remanent xviij vituli.

Summa averiorum restancium in dicta vaccaria xlv vacce, I taurus, vij bovetti, vj Juvence, xiij boviculi quorum ix Masculi et xviij vituli.

Adam filius Nicholai loco Ade de Grangie reddit compotum suum de xxxiiij vaccis I tauro de rem̄. Et de viij de addicione. Et de iij receptis de Instaurario. Summa Recepte xlv vacce I taurus. De quibus computat I in Morina pro coreo ij s. ij d. Et ij liberantur Instaurario. Et remanent xlij vacce I taurus. Idem respondet de iij bobus de addicione. Et liberantur Henrico Hare. Idem respondet de xij boviculis de rem̄. De quibus computat I in Morina, pro coreo xj d. Et remanent vj bovetti et eorum I taurellus et v

Comitis Lencolnie.

Juvence. Idem respondet de xv vitulis de rem. De quibus computat I Masculum in decima. Et remanent xiij boviculi quorum vj Masculi. Idem respondet de xij vitulis de exitu. Et de iij receptis de Instaurario. Summa Recepte xv. De quibus computat iij in
iijs. I d. ō   Morina pro coreis ob. Et remanent xij vituli.

Summa averiorum restancium in dicta vaccaria xlij vacce, I taurus, vj bovetti, et eorum I taurellus, v Juvence, xiiij boviculi quorum vj Masculi, et xij vituli.

Robertus de Merkelesdene reddit compotum suum de xlvj vaccis I tauro de rem. Et de ij de addicione. Summa Recepte xlviij vacce I taurus. De quibus computat I in Morina pro coreo ijs. ij d. Et ij liberantur S. le Geldhirde. Et iij liberantur Instaurario. Et remanent xlj vacce I taurus. Idem respondet de iij bobus de addicione. Et liberantur taurellus Henrico Hare. Idem respondet de xiij boviculis de rem. De quibus computat I bovettum taurellum liberatum Instaurario. Et remanent viij bovetti et eorum I taurellus et iiij Juvence. Idem respondet de xv vitulis de rem. De quibus computat I Masculum et I femineam in decima. Et remanent xiij boviculi quorum v Masculi. Idem
ijs. iijd.   respondet de xx vitulis de exitu. De quibus computat ij in Morina pro coreis I d. Et I liberatur Instaurario. Et remanent xvij vituli.

Summa averiorum restancium in dicta vaccaria xlj vacce, I taurus, viij bovetti et eorum I taurellus et iiij Juvence xiij boviculi quorum v Masculi et xvij vituli.

Henricus filius Christiane reddit compotum suum de xlvj vaccis I tauro de rem. Et de v de addicione. Et de iij receptis de Instaurario. Summa Recepte Liij vacce

L

I taurus. De quibus computat I in Morina pro coreo et carne ijs. xd. Et ij liberantur S. le Geldhirde. Et remanent L vacce I taurus. Idem respondet de ij bobus de addicione. Et liberantur Henrico Hare. Idem respondet de xiij boviculis de reɱ. De quibus computat I in Morina pro coreo vjd. Et remanent xij boviculi quorum vij Masculi. Idem respondet de xiij vitulis de reɱ. De quibus computat I Masculum in decima. Et remanent xij boviculi quorum vij Mas-
iijs. iiijd. ō. culi. Idem respondet de xiij vitulis de exitu. Et de iij receptis de Instaurario. Summa Recepte xv. De quibus computat I Masculum in decima. Et remanent xij boviculi quorum iiij Masculi. Idem respondet de xij vitulis de exitu. Et de iij receptis de Instaurario. Summa Recepte xv. De quibus I in Morina pro coreo ō. Et remanent xiiij vituli.

Summa averiorum restancium in dicta vaccaria L vacce I taurus, vij bovetti, v Juvence, xij boviculi quorum iiij Masculi et xiiij vituli.

Ricardus de Bradelay loco Ade filii Petri reddit compotum suum de xlvj vaccis ij tauris de reɱ. Et de v de addicione. Et de iiij receptis de Instaurario. Summa Recepte Lv vacce ij tauri. De quibus computat viij liberatas S. le Geldhirde. Et iiij vacce I taurus liberantur Instaurario. Et remanent xliij vacce I taurus. Idem respondet de I bove de addicione. Et liberatur Henrico Hare. Idem respondet de xiij boviculis de reɱ. De quibus computat I in Morina pro coreo vjd. Et remanent vij bovetti v Juvence. Idem respondet de xvj vitulis de reɱ. De quibus computat I in Morina pro coreo iiijd. Et I Masculum in decima. Et remanent xiiij boviculi, quorum vij Masculi. Idem respondet de xv vitulis de exitu. Et de iiij receptis
xijd. de Instaurario. Summa Recepte xix. De quibus

computat iiij in Morina pro coreis ij d. Et remanent xv vituli.

Summa averiorum restancium in dicta vaccaria xliij vacce I taurus vij bovetti v Juvence xiiij boviculi quorum vij Masculi et xv vituli. De quibus dictus Adam respondet de I vitulo.

Will's del Wode loco Will'i de Penhiltone reddit compotum suum de xiij vaccis ij tauris de rem̄. Et de iij de addicione. Summa Recepte xlv vacce ij tauri. De quibus computat I vacca in Morina pro coreo ij s. ij d. Et viij vacce I taurus liberantur Instaurario. Et remanent xxxvj vacce I taurus. Idem respondet de vj bobus de addicione. Et liberantur Henrico Hare. Idem respondet de xiij boviculis de rem̄. Et de I invento super visum. Et remanent v bovetti et ix Juvence. Idem respondet de xv vitulis de rem̄. De quibus computat I Masculum et I femineum in decima. Et remanent xiij boviculi quorum vj Masculi. Idem respondet de xxxj vitulis de exitu.
ij s. iij d. ob. De quibus computat iij in Morina, pro coreis I d. ob. Et viij liberantur Instaurario. Et remanent xx vituli.

Summa averiorum restancium in dicta vaccaria xxxvj vacce I taurus v bovetti ix Juvence xiij boviculi quorum vj Masculi et xx vituli.

Johannes del Haregreves reddit compotum suum de xliij vaccis I tauro de rem̄. Et de vij de addicione. Summa Recepte L vacce I taurus. De quibus I liberatur S. le Geldhirde. Et v et I taurus liberantur Instaurario. Et remanent xliiij vacce I taurus. Idem respondet de vj bobus de addicione. Et liberantur Henrico Hare. Et respondet de xj boviculis de rem̄. Et remanent v bovetti et vj Juvence. Idem respondet

Compotus Terrarum Henrici de Lacy

v d.

de xiij vitulis de rem. De quibus computat ij in Morina pro coreo iiij d. Et I Masculum in decima. Et remanent x vituli quorum v Masculi. Idem respondet de xxvj vitulis de exitu. De quibus computat ij in Morina pro coreis I d. Et v liberantur Instaurario. Et remanent xix vituli.

Summa averiorum restancium in dicta vaccaria xliiij vacce I taurus v bovetti, vj Juvence, x boviculi quorum v Masculi et xix vituli. Item I bovettus taurellus receptus de Instaurario.

ij s. ij d. ob.

Adam pistor reddit compotum suum de xlj vaccis I tauro de rem. Et de iij de addicione. Et de ij receptis de Instaurario. Summa Recepte xlv vacce I taurus. De quibus computat ij liberatas S. le Geldhirde. Et remanent xliiij vacce I taurus. Idem respondet de v bobus de addicione. Et liberantur Henrico Hare. Idem respondet de x boviculis de rem. Et remanent ij bovetti et viij Juvence. Idem respondet de xiiij vitulis de rem. De quibus computat I in Morina pro coreo ij d. Et I femineum in decima. Et remanent xij boviculi quorum iiij Masculi. Idem debet ij s. pro emendacione boviculorum. Idem respondet de xiiij vitulis de exitu. Et de ij receptis de Instaurario. Summa Recepte xvj. De quibus computat I in Morina pro coreo ob. Et remanent xv vituli.

Summa averiorum restancium in dicta vaccaria xxxiiij vacce I taurus v bovetti viij Juvence xij boviculi quorum iij Masculi et xv vituli.

Roscindale.

Wills' de Dynlay loco Johannis Cleges reddit compotum suum de xxxix vaccis I tauro de rem. Et de v de addicione. Summa Recepte xliiij vacce I taurus. De quibus computat ij in Morina pro coreis iiij s. iiij d.

Et I liberatur S. le Geldhirde. Et ix vacce I taurus liberantur Instaurario. Et remanent xxxij vacce. Item ij vacce I taurus recepti de Instaurario. Idem respondet de iij bobus de addicione. Et liberantur Henrico Hare. Idem respondet de xiiij boviculis de rem. De quibus computat I strangulatum per Lupum pro coreo et carne xvjd. Et remanent v bovetti et viij Juvence. Idem respondet de xiij vitulis de rem. De quibus computat I strangulatum per lupum pro coreo iiijd. Et I femineum in decima. Et remanent xj boviculi quorum vj Masculi. Idem respondet de xxiiij vitulis de exitu. Et ij receptis de Instaurario. De quibus computat iiij in Morina pro coreis ijd. Et
vjs. viijd. ij liberantur Instaurario. Et I in vendicione pro vjd. Et remanent xv vituli.

Summa averiorum restancium in dicta vaccaria xxxiiij vacce I taurus v bovetti viij Juvence xj boviculi quorum vj Masculi et xv vituli.

Johannes de Cleges loco Will'i de Dynlay reddit compotum suum de xxxvij vaccis ij tauris de rem. Et de vj vaccis I tauro de addicione. Summa Recepte xliij vacce iij tauri. De quibus I strangulatam per lupum pro coreo et carne ijs. ijd. Et iiij In Morina pro coreis viijs. viijd. Et I vacca I taurus liberantur Instaurario. Et remanent xxxvij vacce ij tauri. Idem respondet de I bove de addicione. Et liberatur Henrico Hare. Idem respondet de xij boviculis de rem. De quibus computat I in Morina pro coreo xd. Et remanent vj bovetti et v Juvence. Idem respondet de xvj vitulis de rem. De quibus computat iiij in Morina pro coreis xijd. Et I Masculum in decima. Et remanent xj boviculi quorum v Masculi. Idem respondet de xxj vitulis de exitu. De quibus com-
xiijs. ixd. putat ij in Morina pro coreis Id. Et I in vendicione pro xijd. Et remanent xviij vituli.

Summa averiorum restancium in dicta vaccaria xxxvij vacce ij tauri vj bovetti v Juvence xj boviculi quorum v Masculi et xviij vituli.

Ricardus de Dunnockschaghe reddit compotum suum de xliiij vaccis ij tauris de rem̄. Et de iiij de addicione. Summa Recepte xlviij vacce ij tauri. De quibus computat I in Morina pro coreo ijs. ijd. Et I in vendicione pro vijs. Et ij liberantur S. le Geldhirde. Et ij liberantur Instaurario. Et remanent xlij vacce ij tauri. Idem respondet de vij bobus de addicione. Et liberantur Henrico Hare. Idem respondet de xij boviculis de rem̄. Et I invento super visum. Et remanent viij bovetti iiij Juvence. Idem respondet de xvij vitulis de rem̄. De quibus computat I in Morina pro coreo ijd. Et I femineum in decima. Et remanent xv boviculi quorum vj Masculi. Idem respondet de xx vitulis de exitu. De quibus computat vj in Morina pro coreis iijd. Et

xs. vijd. ij in vendicione pro xijd. Et ij liberantur Instaurario. Et I in decima. Et remanent ix vituli.

Summa averiorum restancium in dicta vaccaria xlij vacce ij tauri viij bovetti iiij Juvence xv boviculi quorum vj Masculi et ix vituli.

Henricus del Stockes reddit compotum suum de xxxj vaccis I tauro de rem̄. Et de ij vaccis I tauro de addicione. Et de ij vaccis receptis de Instaurario. Summa Recepte xliij vacce ij tauri. De quibus computat iij in Morina pro coreis vjs. vjd. Et ij liberantur S. le Geldhirde. Et ij liberantur Instaurario. Et remanent xxxii vacce ij tauri. Idem respondet de vj bobus de addicione. Et liberantur Henrico Hare. Idem respondet de xij boviculis de rem̄. Et remanent viij bovetti et iiij Juvence. Idem respondet de xviij

Comitis Lencolnie.

vitulis de rem. De quibus computat I in Morina pro coreo viijd. Et i Masculum in decima. Et remanent xvj boviculi quorum viij Masculi. Idem respondet de xiij vitulis de exitu. Et de ij receptis de Instaurario. Summa Recepte xvj. De quibus vijs. iiijd. ō. computat v in Morina pro coreis ijd. ob. Et remanent xj vituli.

Summa averiorum restancium in dicta vaccaria xxxvj vacce ij tauri viij bovetti iiij Juvence, xvj boviculi quorum viij Masculi et xj vituli.

Alanus Franceys loco Will'i de Cronschaghe reddit compotum suum de xl vaccis ij tauris de rem. Et de iiij vaccis de addicione. Et de iij receptis de Instaurario. Summa xlvij vacce ij tauri. De quibus computat iij in Morina pro coreis et carne vs. xd. Et ij liberantur S. le Geldhirde. Et lj liberantur Instaurario. Et remanent xl vacce ij tauri. Idem respondet de iiij bobus de addicione. Et liberantur Henrico Hare. Idem respondet de x boviculis de rem. Et iij strangulantur per lupum, pro corcis et carne ijs. Id. Et remanent iij bovetti et iiij Juvence. Idem respondet de xiij vitulis de rem. De quibus computat ij in Morina pro coreis iiijd. Et I Masculum in decima. Et remanent x boviculi quorum viij Masculi. Idem respondet de xvjI vitulis de exitu. Et de iij viijs. iiijd. ō. receptis de Instaurario. Summa Recepte xx vituli. De quibus computat iij in Morina pro coreis Id. ō. Et remanent xvjj vituli.

Summa averiorum restancium in dicta vaccaria, xl vacce ij tauri iij bovetti iiij Juvence x boviculi, quorum vij Masculi et xvij vituli.

Henricus de Berdeshul reddit compotum suum de xliiij vaccis I tauro de rem. Et de v de addicione. Et de ij receptis de Instaurario. Summa Recepte Lj vacce I taurus. De quibus computat I in Morina pro coreo xij d. Et ix liberantur S. le Geldhirde. Et remanent xlj vacce I taurus. Idem respondet de iiij bobus de addicione. Et liberantur Henrico Hare. Idem respondet de x boviculis de rem̄. De quibus computat I strangulatum per lupum pro coreo vj d. Et remanent iiij bovetti et v Juvence. Idem respondet de xviij vitulis de rem̄. De quibus computat I Masculum et I femineum in decima. Et remanent xvj boviculi quorum viij Masculi. Idem respondet de xviij vitulis de exitu. Et de ij receptis de Instaurario. Summa Recepte xx. De quibus computat ij in Morina pro coreis I d. Et ij liberantur S. le Geld-

xix d.   hirde. · Et remanent xvj vituli.

Summa averiorum restancium in dicta vaccaria xlj vacce I taurus iiij bovetti v Juvence xvj boviculi quorum viij Masculi et xvj vituli.

Thomas del Stockes reddit compotum suum de xxxix vaccis I tauro de rem̄. Et de ij de addicione. Summa Recepte xlj vacce I taurus. De quibus computat v liberantur S. le Geldhirde. Et remanent xxxvj vacce I taurus. Idem respondet de v bobus de addicione. Et liberatas Henrico Hare. Idem respondet de xj boviculis de rem. Et remanent v bovetti vj Juvence. Idem respondet de xiij vitulis de rem̄. De quibus computat I Masculum in decima. Et remanent xij

j d. ob.   boviculi quorum vj Masculi. Idem respondet de xix vitulis de exitu. De quibus computat iij in Morina pro coreis I d. ob. Et I liberatur S. le Geldhird. Et remanent xv vituli.

Summa averiorum restancium in dicta vaccaria xxxvj vacce I taurus v bovetti vj Juvence xij boviculi quorum vj Masculi et xv vituli.

Comitis Lencolnie.

Henricus de Dynlay reddit compotum suum de xxxiiij vaccis I tauro de rem̄. Et de vj de addicione. Et de I vacca recepta de Instaurario. Summa Recepte xlj vacce I taurus. De quibus computat I in Morina pro coreo ijs. ijd. Et iiij liberantur S. le Geldhirde. Et remanent xxxvj vacce I taurus. Idem respondet de v bobus de addicione. Et liberantur Henrico Hare. Idem respondet de xiiij boviculis de rem̄. De quibus computat I stangulatum pro coreo vjd. Et rem̄ vj bovetti et vij Juvence. Idem respondet de xvij vitulis de rem̄. De quibus computat ij in Morina pro coreis iiijd. Et ij femineos in decima. Et remanent xiij boviculi quorum vij Masculi. Idem respondet de xvj vitulis de exitu. Et de I recepto de Instaurario.

iijs. vd.   De quibus computat iij In Morina, pro coreis Id. Et I liberatur S. le Geldhirde. Et remanent xiij vituli.

Summa averiorum restancium in dicta vaccaria xxxvj vacce I taurus vj bovetti vij Juvence xiij boviculi quorum vij Masculi et xiij vituli.

Will's de Cronscaghe loco Roberti de Holme reddit compotum suum de xxxv vaccis ij tauris de rem̄. Et de xj de addicione. Et de iiij receptis de Instaurario. Summa Recepte L vacce ij tauri. De quibus computat I vaccam in Morina pro coreo ijs. ijd. Et vj liberantur S. le Geldhirde. Et I taurus liberatur Instaurario. Et remanent xliij vacce I taurus. Idem respondet de iij bobus de addicione. Et liberantur Henrico Hare. Idem respondet de xij boviculis de rem̄. De quibus computat I in vendicione pro xijd. Et remanent iij bovetti et viij Juvence. Idem respondet de xviij vitulis de rem̄. De quibus computat I Masculum et I femineum in decima. Et remanent xvj boviculi quorum vj Masculi. Idem respondet de

Compotus Terrarum Henrici de Lacy

xvij vitulis de exitu. Et de iiij receptis de Instaurario. Summa Recepte xxj. De quibus computat ij in Morina pro coreis I d. Et ij liberantur S. le
iij s. ix d. Geldhirde. Et j in vendicione pro vj d. Et remanent xvj vituli.

Summa averiorum restancium in dicta vaccaria xliij vacce I taurus iij bovetti et viij Juvence xvj boviculi quorum vj Masculi et xvj vituli.

Henricus de Reved loco Johanne de Werbertone reddit compotum suum de xlij vaccis I tauro de rem̄. Et de iij [vaccis] j tauro de addicione. Summa Recepte xlv vacce ij tauri. Item I tauro recepto de Instaurario De quibus computat ij in Morina pro coreis iiij s. iiij d. Et de·ij liber. S. le Geldhirde. Et ij I tauro liber. Instaurario. Et rem̄ xxxix vacce ij tauri. Idem respondet de vij bobus de addicione. Et liberantur Henrico Hare. Idem respondet de xiij boviculis de rem̄. De quibus computat I in Morina pro coreo x d. Et remanent v bovetti et vij Juvence. Idem respondet de xvj vitulis de rem̄. De quibus computat ij Masculos in decima. Et remanent xiiij boviculi quorum v Masculi. Idem respondet de xxij vitulis de exitu. De quibus computat iij in Morina
v s. iij d. ob. pro coreis I d. ō. Et iij liberantur S. le Geldhirde. Et ij liberantur Instaurario. Et remanent xv vituli.

Summa averiorum restancium in dicta vaccaria xxxij vacce I taurus v bovetti vij Juvence quorum vj Masculi et xv vituli.

Robertus de Couhope reddit compotum suum de xxxvij vaccis J tauro de rem̄. Et de v de addicione. Summa Recepte xlij vacce I taurus. De quibus computat ij in Morina pro coreis iiij s. iiij d. Et iij liberantur S. le

Comitis Lencolnie.

Geldhirde. Et v liberantur Instaurario. Et remanent xxxij vacce J taurus. Idem respondit de ij bobus de addicione. Et liberantur Henrico Hare. Idem respondit de xij boviculis de rem̄. Et remanent v bovetti et vjj Juvence. Idem respondet de xv vitulis de rem̄. De quibus computat I Masculum et I femineam in decima. Et remanent xiij boviculi quorum vj Masculi. Idem respondit de xxiij vitulis de exitu. De quibus computat iiij in Morina pro coreis ij d. Et J liberatur S. le Geldhirde. Et v liberantur Instaurario. Et J in vendicione pro viij d. Et remanent xij vituli.

vs. ij d.

Summa averiorum restancium in dicta vaccaria xxxij vacce J taurus v bovetti vij Juvence xiij boviculi quorum vj Masculi et xij vituli.

Akeringtone.

Rogerus de Catlou reddit compotum suum de īīīj.iiij vaccis de rem̄. Et de xvj vaccis ij tauris de addicione. Summa Recepte C vacce ij tauri. De quibus computat ij strangulatas per lupum pro coreis viij s. ix d. Et I vacca in vendicione pro vij s. vj d. Et iiij liberantur S. le Geldhirde. Et xxxj liberantur Instaurario. Et remanent Lxjj vacce ij tauri. Idem respondet de xj bobus de addicione. Et liberantur Will'o de Bagestondene. Idem respondet de xix boviculis de rem̄. Et rem. xj bovetti et eorum I taurellus et viij Juvence. Idem respondet de xxv vitulis de rem̄. Et de xviij receptis de S. le Geldhirde. Summa Recepte xliij. De quibus computat I in Morina pro coreo I d. Et v in decima. Et rem̄ xxxvj boviculi quorum xiij Masculi. Idem respondet de Lv vitulis de exitu. Et de ix receptis de Simone le Geldhird. Summa Recepte Lxiijj. De quibus computat I strangulatum per lupum pro coreo nichil. Et iiij in Morina pro

Item I vacca

coreis et carnibus vjd. ob. Et I in vendicione cum
xvjs. xd. o. vacca. Et ij in decima. Et xxx liberantur Instaurario.
Et remanent xxvj—vituli.

Summa averiorum restancium in dicta vaccaria Lxjj vacce ij tauri xj bovetti quorum I taurellus et viij Juvence xxxvj boviculi quorum xiij Masculi et xxvj vituli.

Mokot de Anteley reddit compotum suum de xlij vaccis I tauro de rem̄. Et de xj vaccis de addicione. Summa Recepte Liij vacce I taurus. De quibus computat iij in Morina pro coreis et carnibus xjs. ijd. Et iij
Item I liberantur S. le Geldhirde. Et I liberatur Instaurario.
vacce Et remanent xlvj vacce I taurus. Idem respondet de iij bobus de addicione. Et liberantur Henrico Hare. Idem respondet de xiij boviculis de rem̄. De quibus computat I in Morina pro coreo vjd. Et remanent v boviculi vij Juvence. Idem respondet de xix vitulis de rem̄. De quibus computat ij Masculos in decima. Et remanent xvij boviculi quorum iiij Masculi. Idem respondet de xx vitulis de exitu. De quibus computat ij in Morina pro coreis I d. ob. Et
xjs. ixd. ob. I liberatur S. le Geldhirde. Et I liberatur Instaurario.
Et remanent xvj vituli.

Summa averiorum restancium in dicta vaccaria xlvj vacce I taurus v bovetti vij Juvence xvij boviculi quorum iiij Masculi et xvj vituli.

Elias de Hayleghes reddit compotum suum de xxiiij vaccis I tauro de rem̄. Et de xiiij receptis de Instaurario. Summa Recepte xxxviij. De quibus computat ij liberatas S. le Geldhirde. Et remanent xxxvj vacce I taurus. Idem respondet de xxij vitulis de rem̄. De quibus computat I in decima. Et remanent xxj boviculi quorum xij Masculi. Idem respondet de v

vitulis de exitu. Et de xiiij receptis de Instaurario.
ob. Summa Recepte xix De quibus computat I in Morina pro coreo ob. Et remanent xviij vituli.

Summa averiorum restancium in dicta vaccaria xxxvj vacce I taurus xxj boviculi quorum xij Masculi et xviij vituli.

Will's de Antelay et Henricus Hare custodes boum reddunt compotum suum de Cv bobus I vacca de rem̄. Et de Cv bobus receptis de vaccariis ut supra. Summa Recepte CCx boves. Item v receptis de Instaurario, I vacca de quibus computat ij in Morina pro coreis xix d. Et Cxxvj liberantur S. le Geldhirde. Et
xix d. Lxxvij boves I vacca cum I vitulo liberantur Instaurario. Summa Mise CCv boves I vacca.

Et remanent in custodia Willi' de Antelay x boves.

Will's de Bakestonden custos averiorum sterilium de Akeringtone reddit compotum suum de xxxj bobus de rem̄. Et de xj receptis de vaccaria de Akeringtone ut supra. Et de xxxiij Receptis de S. le Geldhirde. Summa Recepte Lxxv. De quibus computat xxvj liberatos Gilberto de la Lieghe Instaurario. Et xliiij liberantur Johanni de Paldene Instaurario. Summa Mise Lxx boves.

Et remanent in custodia dicti Will'i v boues.

Simon le Geldhirde custos cromii reddit compotum suum de Lvj bobus de rem̄. Et de Cxxvj receptis de Henrico Hare ut supra. Summa Recepte C$_{iiij}^{xx}$ij. De quibus computat xxxiij liberatos Will'o de Bakestondene. Et Cxliiij liberantur Gilberto Instaurario. Et iij liberantur Johanni de Paldene Instaurario. Summa Mise CLxxix. Et ij furati. Et est quietus. Idem respondet de Lxix vaccis de rem̄. Et de Lxxix receptis de vaccariis ut supra. Summa Recepte Cxlviij. De quibus computat vj in Morina pro coreis vijs. ijd. Et Lxvij liberantur Gilberto Instaurario. Et Lxxiiij liberantur Johanni de Paldene Instaurario. Et de I furato per latrones. Et est quietus. Idem respondet de xviij vitulis de rem̄. Et liberantur vaccario de Akeringtone ut supra. Idem respondet de I vitulo de exitu. Et de xij receptis de vaccariis ut supra. De quibus computat ij in Morina pro coriis jd. Et ix liberantur vaccario de Akeringtone ut supra. Et ij liberantur Johanni de Paldene Instaurario. Et est quietus.

Gilbertus de la Lieghe et Johannes de Paldene Instauratores per testimonium aliorum Instauratorum reddunt compotum suum de xxiij bobus de rem̄. Et de Cxlvij receptis de Simone le Geldhirde ut supra. Et Lxx receptis de Will'o de Bakestandene ut supra. Et Lxxvij receptis de Will'o de Antelay ut supra. Summa Recepte CCCxvij. De quibus computat v liberatos Henrico Hare ut supra. Et CCxiij In vendicione ut Inferius. Et I furato per latrones. Et remanent iiij^{xx}.xviij boves. Idem respondet de CCxliij vaccis ix tauris receptis de vaccariis ut supra. Et I de empcione ut Inferius. Summa Recepte patet. De quibus computat Lxx vaccas v tauros liberatos vaccariis ut supra. Et CLxviij vaccas v taurum, In vendicione ut Inferius. Summa Mise CCxxxviij boves x tauri. Et remanent v vacce. Idem respondet de I bovetto taurello recepto de Roberto de Penhul ut supra. Et liberatur Johanni de Haregreves ut supra. Et est quietus. Idem respondet de Lxxiiij vitulis receptis de vaccariis ut supra. De quibus computat I in Morina coreum nullius valoris. Et Lxx liberantur vaccariis ut supra. Et ij in vendicione ut Inferius. Et remanet I vitulus.

Comitis Lencolnie. 87

Summa averiorum restancium in custodia Johannis de Paldene $\overset{xx}{iiij}$.xviij boves v vacce et ij vituli. Et I taurus inventus per recognicionem Johannes de Paldene.

Denarii.
Iidem Gilbertus et Johannes ut supra reddunt compotum suum de vijli. vjs. iijd. ob. receptis de coreis et carnibus supra venditis in compotis vaccariorum et custodum averiorum.
Et de Cvli. xiijs. ijd. receptis de CCxiij bobus venditis.
Et de Lxvijli. viijs. iiijd.—receptis de CLxviij vaccis v tauris et ij vitulis venditis.
Et de Lxs. receptis de Simone Noel Receptore de Cliderhou per I talliam.
Et de Lxs. receptis de Roberto filio Ade Receptore de Cliderhou per I talliam.
Summa Recepte C$\overset{xx}{iiij}$.vjli. vijs. ixd. ob.

De quibus computant xls. ob. In liberacione v pastorum custodiencium boves, vaccas bovettos, boviculos et vitulos apud Akeringtone, Hoddesdene et Penhul a festo Sancti Michaelis usque festum Sancte Elene.
Et xviijs. iiijd. ob. In liberacione iij pastorum a festo Sancte Elene usque festum Sancti Michaelis.
Et ixs. In stipendio eorundem per annum.
Et vs. vjd. In emendacione Hayarum apud Blackay et Haselingwurthe.
Et xs. xjd. In una loga estivali facta apud Okenheved.
Et viijs. vijd. In emendacione vaccariarum in tribus forestis.
Et xixd. In candelis emptis pro vaccaria de Akerigtone et Bakestondene et pro vitulis castrandis.
Et xiijd. In uno ferro empto pro vitulis signandis et averiis excoriandis.
Et viijs. vjd. In expensis Instauratoris pro averiis venditis in Nundinis de Boultone.

Et vjs. viijd. In uno tauro empto.
Et viijs. allocatos Instaurario pro expensis suis circa vitulos signandos.
Et xvjs. viijd. allocatos Instaurario hoc anno ex gracia pro laboribus suis.
Et Lxs. In feodo Instauratorum per annum.
Et vs. In stipendio clerici sui.
    Summa prima Mise ixli. xixs. xjd.
Idem computat xvjs. ijd. ob. allocatos Instauratori in quibus Comes ei tenebatur ultimo compoto suo.
Et CLxxiijli. xviijd. Liberatos Roberto filio Ade Receptori de Cliderhou presens recognovit.
    Summa Liberacionis CLxxiijli. xvijs. viijd. ob.
    Summa Summarum tocius Mise et Liberacionis C$^{xx}_{iiij}$.iijli. xvijs. vijd. ob.
Et sic debentur Comiti Ls. ijd.

Akeringtone.

Robertus de Rylay serviens de Akeringtone reddit compotum suum apud Ichtenhil xiiij die Maii Anno ut supra coram eodem et de eodem tempore.

De xvjs. vd. ob.	de arreragiis ultimi compoti.
De iijd.	de quodam curtilagio juxta Manerium.
De xviijd.	de herbagio vendito per loca.
De vjd.	de faldagio averiorum et I veteri plaustro vendito.
De ixs.	de uno bove vendito.
De xlviijs. vijd.	de xxv quarteriis iiij bussellis dimidio avene venditis.
De iiijli. xs.	de Simone Noel Receptori de Cliderhou per I talliam.
De ixli. xs.	de Roberto filio Ade Receptori de Cliderhou per I talliam.

    Summa Recepte xvijli. xvjs. iijd. ob.

Comitis Leucolnie.

De quibus computat viij d. in custu unius caruce tempore seminis.
Et vjs. viij d. In ij plaustris novis factis et aliis plaustris emendandis.
Et xvij s. xj d. In liberacione I carucarii tempore seminis qui est plaustrarius per residuum anni.
Et vij s. In stipendio ejusdem per annum.
Et iij s. iij d. In cibo et stipendio I fugantis carucam tempore seminis et herciatoris tempore eodem.
Et vj d. In pratis mundandis.
Et vj d. In bladis sarelandis.
Et xxvjs. ix d. In ͫ iiij acris I roda prati falcandis.
Et xxixs. vij d. In herba spargenda feno levando, cariando et tassando tam extra grangiam quam infra.
Et vj s. viij d. In xx plaustratis feni falcandis et levandis infra le Rodes.
Et viij s. ij d. In xij acris avene Metendis colligendis et ligandis.
Et vs. in domubus cooperiendis et emendandis.
In custu Molendini nichil.
Et ij s. xj d. In una via facienda per medium bosci de Akeringtone.
Et x d. in fimis coriandis et spargendis.
Et xxs. xd. ob. In haiis et fossatis faciendis et mundandis per loca.
Et xj s. In I bove empto.
Et iij s. ob. In xlj quarteriis dimidio avene triturandis et ventandis.
Et xlvj s. viij d. In vadiis servientis per annum.
Et vj s. ix d. In stipendo ejusdem.
  Summa prima Mise xli. iiij s. viij d.

Idem computat iiij d. In pratis Mundandis apud Bakestandene.
Et xxvij s. xj d. In xlvij acris et dimidio prati falcandis

ibidem herba spargenda feno levando et tassando et cariando.

Et xvd. In domubus cooperiendis et emendandis ibidem.

Et vs. ijd. I fossato Mundando et haiis faciendis ibidem.

Et vjd. In pratis Mundandis apud Hoddesdene.

Et xliiijs. In Lxxij acris prati falcandis ibidem herba spargenda feno levando cariando et tassando.

Et vs. in domubus cooperiendis et emendandis cum coopertura falcanda ibidem.

Et. iijs. vd. In fossatis mundandis et haiis faciendis ibidem.

Et xxxjs. ixd. ob. In domubus cooperiendis et emendandis apud Rilay, et fossatis Mundandis et haiis faciendis per loca, cum una loga estivali de novo facta ibidem pro boviculis.

Et xjs. iijd. In domubus cooperiendis et emendandis apud Antelay et fossatis Mundandis et haiis faciendis ibidem, cum una loga estivali de novo facta ibidem pro boviculis.

Summa Secunda Mise vjli. xs. vijd. ob.

Summa Summarum tocius Mise xvjli. xvs. iijd. ob.

Et debet serviens Comiti xxjs.

Grangia de Akeringtone.

Idem respondet de xliiijqr. iiijbus. di avene de exitu. Summa Recepte patet. De quibus computat xvqr. in Semine.

Avena. Et Iqr. In prebenda unius affri tempore seminis. Et iijqr. In prebenda boum per estimacionem. Et xxvqr. iiijbus. di. In vendicione ut supra. Summa Mise ut supra. Et est quietus.

Affri.

Idem respondet de I affro de rem. Summa Recepte patet. Et remanet I affrus Masculus.

Boves.

Idem respondet de xvj bobus de rem. Et de I de empcione. Summa Recepte xvij boves. De quibus computat I in vendicione ut supra. Et remanent xvj boves.

Standene.

Will's de Brunlay serviens de Standene, reddit compotum suum Loco ut supra et die coram eodem et de eodem tempore ut supra.

De Cxiij s. vij d.	de arreragiis ultimi compoti.
De vij s. iiij d.	de ix acris de dominicis positis ad firmam.
De xx s.	de prato de Grenlache vendito hoc anno.
De xxj s. viij d.	de xxvj acris terre in Hulcroftes hoc anno.
De xviij s.	de herbagio vendito per loca.
De xxj s. vij d.	de averiis agistatis in estate et yeme.
De Lxviij s.	de proficuis xxxj animalium emptorum et agistatorum in pastura.
De xxvij s. ij d. ob.	de faldagio hoc anno.
De xl s.	de faldagio animalium Abbatis de Whalleye.
De xl s.	de faldagio animalium Hugonis de Cliderhou.
De iij s.	de I pullo de vago vendito.
De viij s. vij d.	de subbosco vendito sub Manerio.
De iiij li. ij s.	de I affro et v bobus venditis.
De xiij s. viij d.	de xx coreo I affri et coreis et carnibus iiij boum Mortuum.
De xliij s. vj d. ob.	de iiij qr. v bus. frumenti I qr. vij bus. ordei et ij bus. fabarum.
De vij li. x s. iiij d. ob. qª.	de $\overset{xx}{\text{iiij}}$.iij qr. vij bus. avene venditis.

Summa tocius Recepte xxxiiij li. xviij s. vj d. ob. qª.

De quibus computat vj s. viij d. ob. In custu ij carucarum per annum cum stipendio fabri.

Et ijs. iiijd. In precaria xiiij carucarum.
Et xiijd. in ferratura affrorum per annum.
Et ijs. vijd. ob. In custu plaustrorum.
Et Lxxvjs. vjd. in liberacione iij carucariorum per annum.
Et xvijs. viijd. In stipendio eorundem.
Et vs. iiijd. In cibo et stipendio I herclantis per xiij septimanis.
Et xvjs. In cibo et stipendio ij custodiencium averia agistata.
Et viijs. ixd. ob. In cibo et stipendio unius custodientis averia de faldagio.
Et ijs. vjd. In bladis sarclandis.
Et xiiijs. In xlviij acris prati falcandis.
Et viijs. iijd. In herba spargenda feno levando et tassando.
Et xxxixs. iiijd. ob. In cibo et stipendio Metentium colligencium et ligancium blada in autumpno.
Et vs. iijd. In domubus cooperiendis et emendandis.
Et xiijd. In ij tribulis uno picosio et aliis Minutis emptis.
Et vs. vjd. In fossatis et haiis faciendis.
Et xls. In ij affris et ij bobus emptis.
Et xiijs. iiijd. ob. qᵃ. In vij qr. frumenti iij qr. v bus. ordei et CLxvij qr. di. avene triturandis et ventandis.
Et xlvs. vjd. In vadiis servientis per annum.
Et vjs. viijd. In stipendio ejusdem.
Et xls. liberatos Simoni Noel Receptori de Cliderhou, ut in compoto.
Et xijli. liberatas Roberto filio Ade Receptori de Cliderhou per I talliam.
Et xijs. vijd. In bobus et vaccis Hugonis de Cliderhou custodiendis captis pro diversis districcionibus.

    Summa tocius Mise et liberacionis xxxli. xijs. Id. ob. qᵃ. Et sic debit serviens Comiti iiijli. vjs. vd. De quibus dicit se liberasse Roberto de Hephale Senescallo xxijs. in xj qr. avene quos petit sibi allocari. Postea allocantur ei vs. vjd. In iiij bus. frumenti et iiij bus. ordei emptis.

Comitis Lencolnie.

Grangia de Standene.
Idem respondet de viij qr. v bus. frumenti de exitu. Et iiij bus. de empcione ut supra. Summa Recepte ix qr. I bus. De quibus computat iiij qr. di in semine. Et iiij qr. v bus. vendicione ut supra. Et est quietus.

Ordium.
Idem respondet de iij qr. iij bus. ordei de exitu. Et iiij bus. de empcione. Summa Recepte iij qr. vij bus. De quibus computat ij qr. in semine. Et I qr. vij bus. in vendicione ut supra. Et est quietus.

Fabe.
Idem respondet de ij bus. fabarum de exitu. Summa Recepte patet. Et totum in vendicione ut supra.
Et est quietus.

Avena.
Idem respondet de I qr. ij bus. di avene de rem̅. Et de C$_{\overline{iiij}}^{xx}$.viij qr. iij bus. di. Summa Recepte C$_{\overline{iiij}}^{xx}$.ix qr. vj bus. De quibus computat $_{\overline{iiij}}^{xx}$.xiiij qr. in semine. Et v qr. di In prebenda boum. Et vj qr. iiij bus. in prebenda affrorum. Et $_{\overline{iiij}}^{xx}$.iij qr. vij bus. In vendicione ut supra. Summa Mise ut supra. Et est quietus.

Affri.
Idem respondet de ij affris de rem̅. Et de ij de empcione. Summa Recepte iiij affri. De quibus computat I in Morina coreum venditur. Et I in vendicione ut supra. Et remanent ij affri Masculi.

Boves.
Idem respondet de xxvij bobus de rem̅. Et de ij de empcione. Summa Recepte xxix boum. De quibus computat iiij in Morina de coreis responsum est. Et v in vendicione ut supra. Et remanent xx boves.

Ichtenhil.
Johannes parcarius de Ichtenhil reddit compotum suum ibidem xvj die Maij Anno regni regis Edwardi xxxiiij coram domino Will'o de Nunny videlicet ab incrastino

sancti Michaelis Anno regni regis Edwardi xxxij usque incrastinum Sancti Michaelis Anno regni regis Edwardi xxxiij.

De x s.	de I bove vendito.
De v s. viij d.	de coreis I bovis ij Jumentorum et iiij pullorum.
De iiij li. x s.	de Simone Noel Receptore de Cliderhou.
De vij li.	de Roberto filio Ade Receptore de Cliderhou.

Summa Recepte xij li. v s. viij d.

De quibus computat x d. In custu caruce tempore seminis.
Et iiij s. iiij d. In ij novis plaustris factis et aliis custubus pro eisdem.
Et xxxvij s. In liberacione ij carucariorum per annum.
Et vj s. vj d. In stipendio ij hominum pro caruca et pro plaustris per annum.
Et xxiij s. xj d. In Lxxj acris et iij rodis prati falcandis.
Et xxij d. In herba falcanda in Foresta.
Et xv s. ix d. In dicta herba spargenda feno levando et tassando.
Et xviij d. In bladis vigilandis.
Et iiij s. xj d. ob. In vij acris avene Metendis colligendis et ligandis.
Et x s. I d. q^n. In domubus cooperiendis et emendandis.
Et xvij s. iij d. In fossatis Mundandis et haiis faciendis per loca.
Et ij s. q^n. In emendacione palicii.
Et xx d. In busca prosternenda pro Manerio.
Et vij s. vj d. In Jumentis et pullanis capiendis et faldandis per tres vices et pullis signandis et capistris emptis pro eisdem.
Et viij s. ij d. In stipendio et cibo custodiencium pullanos per xix septimanas.

Comitis Lencolnie.

Et vs. vjd. In Jumentis venientibus de Cridelinges custodientibus et prebenda eorundem per unum Mensem, videlicet a tempore quo venerunt de Cridelinges usque ponerentur in parco.
Et xlvs. vjd. In vadiis parcarii per annum.
Et xiijs. iiijd. In roba ejusdem.
Et xixd. In liberacione garcionis parcarii per annum.
Et v. In stipendio ejusdem.
Et xixs. ijd. In vadiis Henrici le Hallehyne a festo Sancti Marci usque festum Sancti Michaelis per litteram Comitis et sic de anno in annum quousque Comes aliud inde preceperit capiendo per septimanam quinque denarios.
Et iiijs. iiijd. allocantur parcario in quibus Comes ei tenebatur super ultimo compoto suo.
    Summa tocius Mise xijli. xvjs. ijd. Et sic debentur parcario xs. vjd.

Grangia de Ichtenhil.
Idem ut supra reddit compotum suum de xxvij quarteriis avene de exitu. Summa Recepte patet. De quibus computat xj quarterias in semine. Et xvj quarterias In sustentacione Jumentorum pullorum et ferarum.
    Et est quietus.

Boves.
Idem respondet de xxj bobus de rem̅. Summa Recepte patet. De quibus computat I in Morina de coreo responsum est. Et I in vendicione ut supra.
    Et remanent xix boves.

Equicium.
Idem respondet de xxxv Jumentis de rem̅. Et de xj de addicione. Et de iiij receptis de proposito de Cridelinges. Summa Recepte Liiij. De quibus computat ij in Morina corea venduntur et vj in vendicione ut in Compoto Roberti filii Ade Receptoris de Cliderhou. Summa Mise viij. Et remanent xlvj Jumenta.

Runcini.
Idem respondet de I stalone ferranto recepto de stabulo Comitis. Et de x Runcinis de addicione. Et de viij Receptis de equiciario parci de Dynebeghe. Summa Recepte xix Runcini. De quibus computat xvij In vendicione ut in compoto Receptoris ut supra. Summa Mise xvij. Et remanent ij stalones.

Pullani.
Idem respondet de xv pullanis de rem. Summa Recepte patet. De quibus computat I in Morina coreum venditur.
Et remanent vj pulli et viij pultrices in tercio anno.

Pullani.
Idem respondet de xxi pullanis de rem. Summa Recepte patet. De quibus computat iiij in Morina corea venduntur et ij in decima.
Et remanent xv pullani super annum quorum x Masculi.

Pullani.
Idem respondet de xxvj pullanis de exitu. Summa Recepte patet. De quibus computat ij in vendicione ut in compoto Receptoris. Et remanent xxiiij pullani.

Simon Noel Receptor de Cliderhou, reddit compotum suum apud Ichtenhil xxx die Marcii regni regis Edwardi xxxiij coram eodem ut supra, videlicet ab incrastino Sancti Michaelis Anno regni regis Edwardi xxxij usque diem supradictum.

De $\overset{C}{\text{iiij.}}\overset{xx}{\text{iiij.}}$v li. x s. ob. q^a. de arreragiis ultimi compoti.
De xiiij li. vij s. iij d. de redditu de Rachedal* termino Marcij.
De xxv s. de redditu Will'i de Mara termino eodem.
De iiij s. de redditu Ade de Prestwyche in Totingtone termino predicto.

Comitis Lencolnie.

De ijs.   de redditu Johannis Banaster in Penwortham termino eodem.
De iijs.   de redditu de Adelingtone et Okesbure termino eodem.
De ijs.   de redditu de Standisse et Langtre termino eodem.
De ixd.   de redditu de Queltone termino predicto.
De xxs. iijd.   de redditu de Baldwynhil termino eodem et Purificacione.
De xs.   de Thaynagio de Twyseltone termino Marcii.
De Lxxjs. vjd.   de vj bobus emptis ut Inferio venditis.
De xls.   de Serviente de Standene per I talliam.

Summa Recepte D^{c}viijli. xvs. ixd. ob. q^a.

De quibus computat xxjd. In domubus de Colne cooperiendis et emendandis et alnetis scapulandis pro Mensis et formulis.

Et vs. In ij rotis de novo factis pro Molendino de Brunley.

Et ijs. datis Carpentario in parte solucionis dimidie Marce pro emendacione Molendini de Clevachre.

Et iijs. ixd. In domubus infra Castrum cooperiendis et emendandis.

Et xixd. In una olla enea et unum pocinet emendandis.

Et xs. In feno empto pro Castro.

Et xli. In feodo Senescalli pro tribus quarteriis anni.

Et Lxxvs. In feodo et roba Constabularii pro dimidio anno.

Et xxijs. ixd. In vadiis Janitoris Castri pro dimidio anno.

Et vjs. viijd. solutis Abbati de Sallay pro una lampade invenienda ibidem pro anima Comitis Johannis.

Et xiijs. In vadiis Warennarii custodientis boscum de Salthul Dounum et Wurchestone pro dimidio anno.

Et ijs. xd. ob. qᵃ. In expensis Instauratoris pro averiis vendendis apud Ichtenhil.
Et iiijli. xvijd. ob. In expensis audiencium compotum ante hunc compotum.
Et xxvjs. In vadiis duorum custodiencium Marchias foreste de Penhul et Roscindale per dimidium annum.
Et xviijd. In litteris portandis per loca.
Et xxjs. vd. ob. In $\substack{C\\iiij}$ Marcis salvo ducendis usque Pontemfractem per vices.
Et ijs. ixd. In una bissa carianda usque Burtone juxta Lincolniam precepto Comitis.
Et xviijd. In panno elemosinario cariando de Pontefracto usque Cliderhou.
Et vjd. In faldis emendandis apud Brunlay et Rachedale.
Et iiijli. viijs. ob. qᵃ. In expensis Senescalli pro Curiis tenendis per tempus compoti.
Et xls. In expensis Senescalli usque Dynebeghe, Londinium et Eboracum ad mandatum Comitis.
  Summa prima expense xxxli. viijs. vijd. ob.

Idem computat Lxxiiijs. In vj bobus emptis pro cariagio meremii Warderobe et petre pro calce, et carbonibus Marinis pro calce comburendo.
Et Lvjs. ō. qᵃ. In meremio prosternendo et scapulando pro Wardroba, et libera petra frangenda pro eadem, et petra frangenda pro calce, et I toridulari pro calce comburendo.
Et xxijli. xs. solutos carpentariis in parte stipendiorum suorum pro meremio prosturnendo et palicio faciendo pro parte pro parco de Alvedene et Musdene residuum fit per Robertum filium Ade Receptori de Cliderhou ut Inferius.
Et xiili. liberatos Roberto Receptori de Cliderhou per J talliam.
Et iiiili. xs. liberatis Roberto de Rylay proposito de Akerington per J talliam.

Et iiiili. xs. liberatos Johanni parcario de Ichtenhul per J talliam.
Et Lxs. liberatos Gilberto de la Lyeghe Instauratori per J talliam.
Et CCLxvjli. xiijs. iiijd. Liberatos Olivero de Stanesfend Receptori Pontifracti per J talliam.
Et Cxxviijli. xiijs. viijd. Liberatos Roberto filio Ade Receptori de Cliderhou per iij tallias ut patet Inferius.
Summa Secunda expense et liberacionis ͞iiijxlviijli. vijs. ob. q^a.
Summa Summarum omnium expense et Liberacionis ͞iiijLxxvijli. xiijs. viijd. ob. q^a. Et sic debet Receptor Comiti xxxli. xiijd. ob.

Robertus filius Ade Receptor de Cliderhou reddit compotum suum Loco et die et coram eodem ut supra videlicet a xxx die Marcii anno regni regis Edwardi xxxiij usque festum Sancti Michaelis proximo sequens.

Colne.

De xxijli. xiijs. vijd. o.	de redditu de Colne cum Membris et operibus arent. termino Egidii.
De iijs. vjd.	de x acris et dimidia terre appropriatis ibidem hoc anno primo.
De xjli. ijs.	de firma Molendini de Colne et Walfredene deducta decima.
De xxiiijs.	de firma Molendini fulleretici ibidem.
De iiijli. vjs. xd.	de finibus pro ingressu terrarum ibidem.
De xlis. viijd.	de perquisitis Curie ibidem.
De iiiis. vjd.	de Merchetto v Mulierum.
	De Leyrwico nihil.
De xijd.	de Thisteltakes hoc anno.
De xxxjs.	de Inparcamentis averiorum in Troudene.

De xvj s.   de carbonibus Marinis ibidem.
De xixs. ij d.   de herbagio yemali ibidem.
De xvs. ij d.   de herbagio estivali ibidem.
De iij s. xj d.   de feno vendito ibidem.
De vij s. viij d.   de ij boviculis et I porco de vago.

Summa prima Recepte xlvj li. x s. ob.

Haselingdene.
De iiij li. vj s. viij d. ob.   de redditis ibidem termino Egidii cum incremento anni precedentis.

De xij d.   de iij acris apruviatis hoc anno primo.

De xiij s. iiij d.   de firma Molendini ibidem.
De Lxvij s. viij d.   de herbagio yemali in Roscindale.
De Cvs. x d.   de herbagio estivali ibidem.
De xx s.   de herbagio de Derplaghe.
De xx d.   de herbagio de primerolsykes.
De xxvj s. v d.   de feno vendito ibidem. De Minera nihil.

Summa Secunda Recepte xvj li. vij d. ob.

Totington.
De xiiii li. viii s. xj d.   de redditu ibidem termino Pentecostes, residuum per S. Noel.

De xx s. iij d.   de Lx acris iij rodis terre apruviatis hoc anno primo.

De iij s.   de redditu Ricardi de Radecleve pro xx acris terre per cartam Comitis.

De x d.   de firma ejusdem pro ij acris et dimidio terre ad voluntatem Comitis.

De xij d.   de firma Henrici de Bury pro terra de Schuttleswurthe.

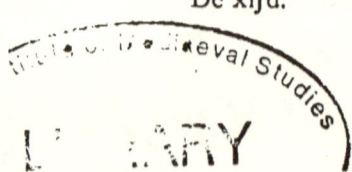

Comitis Lencolnie.

De I d. ob.	de I li. Cymini de Galfrido de Chadertone pro Shillingbotham.
De Lxvj s. viij d.	de firma Molendinorum de Totingtone, deducta decima.
De vj s. viij d.	de stallagio ibidem.
De xiiij s.	de herbagio de Couhope hoc anno.
De Lxvj s. x d.	de herbagio de Aldene, Musdene, et Ugdene, et non plus propter parcum ibidem de novo constructum.
De xvij s. viij d.	de herbagio foreste de Totingtone.
De xvj s. iij d.	de pannagio ibidem.
De xij d.	de veteri busca vendita ibidem.
De xxxvj s. viij d.	de busca vendita pro J forgio per xvj septimanas.
De iiij li. vij s. x d.	de finibus pro ingressu terrarum de Totingtone.
De vj li. vs. iiij d.	de perquisitis Curie ibidem.
De vj s. vj d.	de Imparcamentis averioram ibidem.
De ij s.	de uno boviculo de vago ibidem.
De iiij li. x s.	de Scutagio ij feodorum et quarte partis I Militis in Totingtone pro exercitu Scocie de anno regni regis Edwardi xxviij

Summa tercia Recepte xlij li. xj s. vj d. ob.

Rachedale.

De v s.	de viij^{va} parte Molendini de Rachedale.
De xiij d.	de iij acris I roda terre apruviate hoc anno primo.

De xxvj s. viij d.   de firma heredis Ade de Balschaghe pro Bedeleria.
De Liij s. iiij d.   de tcoloneo fori et Nundini et stallagio ibidem.
De xxvij s. x d.   de finibus pro ingressu terrarum ibidem.
De iiij li. xij s.   de perquisitis Curie ibidem.

Summa Quarta Recepte xli. vs. xjd.

Rommesgreve.
De xxxiij s. iiij d.   de herbagio yemali et estivali ibidem.
De vij s. vj d.   de veteri busca vendita ibidem.
De iiij li. vj s. J d. ob.   de firma de Wurchestone termino Egidii.

Hoddesdene.
D viij d.   de dimidia acra terre apruviate hoc anno primo.
De ij d.   de redditu Ade filii Wyot pro ij colariis.
De xlvj s. ix d. ob.   de dominico ibidem posito ad firmam.

Wurchestone.
De xxj s. vij d. ob.   de firma Molendini ibidem deducta decima.
De Lviij s. ij d.   de finibus pro ingressu terrarum ibidem.
De xx s.   de perquisitis Curie ibidem.

Penhiltone.
De iij s.   de imparcamentis averiorum ibidem.
De vj li. iiij s. iij d.   de firma de penhiltone cum incremento anni precedentis.
De ij d.   de J placca vasti apruviati hoc anno primo.

Comitis Lencolnie.

Ichtenhil.

De I d.	de herede Henrici de Blakeburne pro $\overset{xx}{iiij}$ acris terre.
De xvij s. xj d.	de finibus pro ingressu terrarum ibidem.
De xviii s. viij d.	de perquisitis Halmoti ibidem.
De xviij d.	de Merchettis ij Mulierum.
De xij d.	de Leyrwito unius Mulieris.
De vs. vj d.	de Inparcamentis averiorum ibidem.
De Liij s. iiij d.	de firma de Ichtenhil termino Egidii.
De xiiij li. vj s. x d.	de finibus pro ingressu terrarum ibidem.
De Lxxvj s.	de perquisitis halmoti ibidem.
De iij s. vj d.	de Merchetto duarum Mulierum De Leyrwyto nihil.
De ii s. vj d.	de Thisteltackes ibidem.
De Cvj s. x d.	de Imparcamentis averiorum ibidem.
De Cxiij s. ij d.	de herbagio yemali in Penhil.
De vj li. ii s. x d.	de herbagio estivali ibidem.
De xvi s. viij d.	de feno vendito ibidem.
De xx s. ij d.	de veteri busca vendita ibidem pro Meremio et focali.
De vij s. iiij d.	de veteri busca vendita ibidem pro cineribus.
De xviij d.	de petra vendita ibidem pro coopertura domorum.
De v s. vj d.	de ix fraxinis venditis.
De viij s.	de iij pultricis I pullano et I jumenta de vago.

Summa Quinta Recepte Lxiij li. x s. vij d. ob.

Habringham.
De iiij li. xiiij s. x d.   de firma de Habringham termino Egidii.
De xij d.   de iij acris terre apruviatis hoc anno primo.
Padingham.
De xj li. xij d.   de firma de Padyham termino predicto.
De iiij li. xiij s.   de firma Molendini ibidem deducta decima.
De vj s. viij d.   de operibus remissis ibidem.
Brunlay.
De xiij li. x s. I d. ob.   de firma de Brunlay termino predicto.
De iij s. iiij d.   de operibus remissis ibidem.
De ix li. viij s. v d.   de firma Molendini ibidem deducta decima.
De xxiiij s.   de firma Molendini Fulleretici ibidem.
Brerecleve.
De x d.   de Mensura conducta ibidem.
De Cix s. x d. ob.   de firma de Brerecleve termino predicto.
De iij d.   de iij rodis terre apruviate hoc anno primo.
Parva Merclesdene.
De iiij li. iiij s. iiij d. ob. de firma de parva Merkelesdene termino predicto.
De xiiij d.   de operibus remissis ibidem.
De vj s.   de firma de Chirche termino predicto.
Chirche.
De xvij d. ob.   de firma Ade de Simondstone.
De xiiij s. iij d.   de Johanne de Blakeburne pro xxviij acris et dimidia in Berdeswurthgrave.

De ijs. vjd.	de firma ejusdem pro v acris terre invente ibidem et preceptum est quod terra quam idem Johannes tenet Mensuretur.
De vs. vjd.	de firma de Burdeswurthe et vllesbothe.
De xiijs. iiijd.	de redditu Hugonis de Cliderhou pro terra quondam Thome de Hiltone in Salesbyry quam idem Hugo tenet in Thaynagio. Et sciendum quod heres dicti Hugonis tenetur pro supradicto tenemento in xls. de Relevio. Et pro tenemento quondam Johannis de Salebyry in aliis xls. Et eciam pro tenemento quondam Johannis filii Gilberti in eadem, in aliis xls. cum tempus relevii acciderit. De undecim solidis de firma Ade le Tasker pro tenemento quondam Magistri Henrici de Claytone in Salebyry nichil quia reddebatur eidem Henrico per Comitem.
De Id.	de redditu Ricardi de Tyndyhevede quam solebat reddere Thome de Hiltone in Salebyry.

Summa Sexta Recepte Lvijli. iis.

Penwurtham.
De xliiijs. viijd.	de firma assartorum et coteriorum ibidem termino predicto.

Compotus Terrarum Henrici de Lacy

De xx s.	de firma Ade Ploket pro xl acris terre ibidem termino Michaelis.
De iij s.	de firma ejusdem pro uno tofto et dimidia acra terre ad voluntatem Comitis.
De viij li. xiij s. iiij d.	de pratis dominicis et piscaria positis ad firmam in anno sequenti reddet quatuordecim Marcas.
De I d.	de I placea inter prioratum et le Motehalle ad voluntatem.
De xv s.	de herbagio de Middleford. De panagio nichil.
De vj s. viij d.	de firma de Blacshaghe.
De xix s. ix d.	de Incremento ejusdem per cartas Comitis hoc anno primo.
De viij s. v d. q^a	de Warda Castri Lancastrie.
De xxvj s. viij d.	de piscaria de Northmeles.
De viij s. I d. ob.	de Roberto de Northmeles.
De xij d.	de firma de Galeweylandes.
De vj d.	de redditu Henrici de Whalley pro dimidia libra piperis.
De I d.	de redditu Roberti de Eukestone pro tenemento in eadem.
De ij s.	de redditu de Northmeles.
De xviij s. I d. ob.	de firma que vocatur sakepe.
De xxv s.	de redditu Willielmi de Mara termino Pentecostes.
De xvj s.	de firma tenementi quondam Johannis David atte Halghe.
De xxx s.	de Thoma de Leyland pro bedeleria de Penwortham.
De iiij s.	de turbis venditis ibidem.
De xv s. iiij d.	de finibus pro ingressu terrarum.

Comitis Lencolnie.

De vijli. xiiijs. iiijd.   de perquisitis Curie ibidem.
De vijs. viijd.   de custodia terre et heredis Ricardi de Stokeport pro Birkedale.
De Cs.   de Scutagio ij feodorum et dimidii Militum in Penwortham de exercitu Scocie de anno regni regis xxviij.

Summa Septima Recepte xxxvjli. iiijs. ixd. q^a.

Dounum.

De viijli. xiijs. ob.   de firma de Dounum termino Egidii. Et non plus quia sex denarii de redditu Magistri Henrici de Dounum relaxantur eidem precepto Comitis.
De iiijs.   de firma cujusdam assarti ibidem termino eodem.
De Lxxiijs. iiijd.   de dominico ibidem posito ad firma.
De xd.   de pastura de Grenhou et I curtilagio ibidem hoc anno primo.
De Liiijs.   de firma Molendini ibidem deducta decima.
De xs.   de redditu Alexandri de Keuerdale.
De Id.   de redditu magistri Henrici de Claytone.
De xijd.   de redditu Walteri de Wadingtone.
De Id. ob.   de I pari cirotecarum de redditu Ricardi clerici.
De Lxvijs.   de finibus pro ingressu terrarum ibidem.
De xxxjs. vjd.   de perquisitis Halmoti ibidem.

Compotus Terrarum Henrici de Lacy

De vjd.   de Imparcamentis averiorum.
De vs.   de turbis ibidem venditis.
    Summa octava Recepte xxjli. vd.

Akerigtone.

De xxxiiijs. xjd.	de firma Lx acrarum et I rode terre ibidem.
De vijs.	de una placea que vocatur Pesecroftes.
De xiijs. iiijd. ob.	de Incremento terre invente ibidem.
De iiijs.	de firma Aule Grangie et Coquine positis ad firmam.
De xviijd.	de ij acris terre positis ad firmam apud Akeringtone.
De xxiijs. iijd. ob. q.	de terra arabili apud Antelay posita ad firmam.
De xxxvjs.	de firma Molendini ibidem deducta decima.
De iijs. Id. ob.	de firma vj acrarum et I rode terre in Dunschopfal.
De xxiiijs. ijd.	de herbagio yemali et estivali apud Akerington.
De vjs. viijd.	de herbagio de Brocholhirstes.
De xiijs. vjd.	de finibus pro ingressu terrarum ibidem.
De xvjs. iiijd.	de perquisitis Halmoti ibidem.
De xjs. vjd.	de Imparcamentis averiorum ibidem.
De xvs.	de xij fraxinis ibidem.

Hoddesdene.

De vjs. xjd.	de averiis agistatis in Hoddesdene.

Huncotes.

De Cs. xjd.	de firma de Huncotes termino predicto.

Comitis Lencolnie.   109

Clivachre.
- De vjli. xvijs. ixd. — de firma tenencium per cartas in Clivachre.
- De iiijli. viijs. vijd. — de firma assartorum et coteriorum ibidem.
- De vjd. — de redditu Oliveri de Stanesfeud pro viij acris terre ibidem et pro xij acris terre in Brunley.
- De vjd. — de dimidia libra piperis de redditu Ade filii Mathei de Ormerode.
- De vd. — de ij paribus cirotecarum I pari calcarium de redditu Mathei de Berecroftes, Johannis filii Mathei et Ade Fabri.
- De Liiijs. — de firma Molendini ibidem deducta decima.
- De vjs. ijd. — de averiis agistatis in communi pastura ibidem.
- De vjs. viijd. — de Minera ferri per x septimanas vendita.

Summa Nona Recepte xxxjli. ijs. ixd. ob. qa.

Cliderhou.
- De viijli. xs. vjd. — de firma Thaynorum termino eodem.
- De iijs. iiijd. — de Galfrido de Simonstone pro relaxacione Secte Curie.
- De iiijd. — de firma Dyote le Arousmythe et Dinarie sororis sue pro uno cotagio ad terminum vite.
- De iijs. viijd. — de firma unius cotagii que fuit Roberti le Arousmythe.
- De ijs. vjd. — de Will. fil. Henrici pro ij acris et dim. subtus Baldwynhul.

De vjd.	de I placea subtus Aulam placitorum.
De ijs.	de herbagio fossatorum Castri.
De xijd.	de I placea pro forgeo sub Castro hoc anno primo.
De vjs.	de herbagio gardini.
De iijs. iiijd.	de fructu gardini hoc anno.
De xxd.	de ingressu v prisonum ad portam Castri.
De vjli. xiijs. iiijd.	de firma Burgencium de Cliderhou termino predicto.
De vijli. vjs. viijd.	de teoloneo fori et Nundini, et stallagio.
De xijli.	de firma Molendini deducta decima.
De ijs.	de firma Johannis le Arblaster.
De vs.	de firma de Sandwele et Salewele.
De vjs.	de firma de David Scoles.
De iiijs.	de firma Thome Le Sureys pro attachiamento stagni.
De xxvs. viijd. ob.	de firma dominicarum terrarum sub Salthul.
De vjli. xs.	de finibus pro ingressu terrarum.
De xxli.	de fine Roberti de Holdene pro pluribus transgressionibus quibus convictus fuit coram Comitem.
De Lxvjs. viijd.	de fine Nicholai de Holdene filii sui pro transgressione facta in foresta de venacione Comitis.
De xls.	de fine Henrici Banastre pro eadem.

Comitis Lencolnie.

De iijs. iiijd.	de fine Radulfi de Levesay pro eadem.
De xxvijli. vijs. ixd.	de perquisitis Curie de Cliderhou.
De Ljs. ijd.	de catallis Willielmi Hoome fugitivi.
De xxs.	de Relevio heredis Alicie de Simondstane pro tenemento in eadem.
De iijs. iijd. ob.	de Relevio heredis Henrici de Couhope pro tenemento in Clivachre.
De iiijd.	de Relevio heredis Petri de Dounum.
De xxxviijs.	de inparcamentis averiorum liberorum pro evasionibus in foresta.
De Lxs.	de Ade de Cloghe pro serjantia libere Curie.
De xxxjs. vd.	de Warda Castri Lancastrie.
De xxjli. vjs. viijd.	de firma Wapentagie de Stayncleve.
De xiiijs. vjd.	de duabus partibus cujusdam tenementi in Snelleshou.
De Ciiijs. vijd.	de exitu duarum parcium terre quondam Ade de Ristone.
De vjs. viijd.	de firma Molendini de Schypen.
De $\overset{xx}{iiii}$.vijli.	de albo xxix vaccariarum posito ad firmam.
De CLxxiijli. xviijd.	de Gilberto de La Leigh et Johanne de Paldene Instauratoribus ut in compoto.
De xlvijli. iijs. iiijd.	de ix Runcinis venditis de Ichtenhil.
De vjli. xjs.	de vj Jumentis venditis.

De xxxli. iiijs. de viij Runcinis de Wallia venditis.
De xviijli. xviijs. de vij carratis et xxxvj petris plumbi venditis.

Summa decima Recepte $\overset{C}{_{iiij}}\overset{xx}{_{iiij}}$.xvijli. xixs. ixd.

De Cxxviijli. xiijs. viijd. de Simone de Noel Receptore de Cliderhou ut in compoto suo.

De vijli. xiijs. Id. de Scutagio de Blakeburneschyre pro parte de exercitu Scocie de Anno regni regis Edwardi xxviij, de residuo respondeatur in compoto sequenti.

De xxxixs. vjd. de Scutagio de Boulaund pro parte de eodem exercitu de residuo respondeatur in compoto sequenti particule patent in cedula huic appensa.

De xijli. de serviente de Standene ut in compoto.

De Lxvjli. xiijs. iiijd. de Thome Receptori de Dynbeghe per I talliam.

De $\overset{xx}{_{iiij}}$.vli. de Abbate et Conventu de Whalleye pro debito in quo tenebantur Comiti ex Mutuo eis facto per dominum W. de Nony per scriptum obligatorium.

De xiijli. vjs. viijd. de Edmundo Talbot quos habuit de Comite ex prestito per manus domini Nicholai de Redinges Receptori Hospicii Comitis ut patet in compoto suo.

Comitis Lencolnie.

De viijli. ixs. iijd. de xviij bobus venditis.
Summa undecima CCCxxiijli. xvs. vjd.
Summa Summarum tocius Recepte M᷉Cxlvjli. vjs.
Item xijli. Recepte de Simone Noel ut in Compoto.

Mise.

De quibus computat vs. xjd. In vj acris prati falcandis herba spargenda feno levando et cariando et tassando.

Et xiijs. ob. In emendacione capitis Stagni de Colne.

Et xijs. xjd. In Molendinis per patriam emendandis residuum emendaciones fit per firmarios Molendinarum.

Et xxvjs. iiijd. In domibus Infra Castram Cooperiendis et emendandis.

Et ijs. In emendacione Aule de Penwortham.

Et Lxvjs. viijd. In feodo Senescalli pro parte residuum recepit per Simonem Noel ut in compoto supra.

Er Lxxvs. In feodo et roba Constabularii per tempus Compoti.

Et xxjs. xjd. ob. In vadiis Janitoris Castri per dictum tempus.

Et xvijs. viijd. In faldis faciendis per Magistrum Forestarium, et ramis prosternendis pro feris et Mensis secandis.

Et vjli. ijs. ijd. ob. qa. In expensis Senescalli et aliorum tenencium Curiam pro parte.

Et xxjs. vd. ob. In expensis Senescalli et aliorum faciendum visum Instauri et pro vaccariis ponendis.

Et xxijs. vjd. qa. In expensis Senescalli Instauratoris et aliorum pro pullis vendendis.

Et Lxxs. xd. ob. In expensis domini W. de Nony, Henrici de Scrope apud Ichtenhil per iiij dies pro diversis negociis Comitis.

Et xijs. iijd. in vadiis Warennarii custodientis boscum de Salthil per tempus compoti.

Et vjs. xjd. In expensis Instauratoris per diversas Nundinas pro Instauro vendendo.

Et vjd. solutis Waltero de Wadingtone pro annua firma ei debita.

Et L s. solutis pro Warda Castri Lancastrie termino Johannis Baptiste.
Et C s. solutis Willielmo de Cathertone pro annua firma ei debita ad terminum Vite de Manerio de Dounum pro scripto Comitis.
Et vs. xj d. In decasu firme Roberti de Ormerode pro J bovata terre in Clivachre ei concessa per cartam Comitis ad terminum vite.
Et xj s. iiij d. In decasu firme Willielmi de Penhiltone quos reddere consuevit per annum pro xxxiiij acris terre in Habringham quos Comes ei remisit ad terminum vite.
Et vs. ix d. ob. In decasu firme de Totingtone pro I placea terre quę redditur Priori de Brettone ut jus suum de cetero deleantur a compoto.
Et x d. In decasu firme vij acrarum terre quas Isabella de Gouildforde tenuit ☛ de cetero deleantur de compoto firmarum de Ichtenhil.
Et xxvj s. v d. In decasu firmarum hoc anno particule patent in compoto huic rotulo appensa.
Et iiij s. cavenacio et percameno empto pro compoto et pro Curia.
Et x li. ij s. ix d. ob. q^a. In expensis iiij stalonum et I equi venientium de Hospicio Comitis comorancium apud Standene et Ichtenhil per annum, cum prebenda furfure ferratura Marchancia et aliis emptis pro eisdem cum vadiis garcionum custodencium eosdem per dictum tempus et stipendiis eorundem.
Et xxj s. allocatis vaccariis de Roscindale Penhul et Troudene pro vaccis teneribus deficientibus in vaccariis.
Summa prima expense xlvj li. iiij s. I d. q^a.

Idem computat ij s. iiij d. In litteris portandis per loca.
Et xliij s. ij d. In expensis Receptoris et aliorum ducentium denarios per quinque vices usque Pontefractam.

Et vs. In vadiis custodiencium Marchetas Foreste de Penhul et Roscindale per quinque septimanas residuum per Simonem Noel.
Et vijs. ixd. In sale empta pro venacione salianda et venacionem capiendam.
Et vijs. viijd. In iij cervis et dimidio et xij damis cariandis usque Pontefractam.
Et xijs. ijd. In vij carratis plumbi carriantis de Bakestandene usque Bradeforde.
Et iiijs. vijd. In uno rete cariando usque Merlande pannum pauperum querendum apud Pontemfractam et barellis cariandis usque Altoftes.
Et xxs. vd. ob. In expensis xvj esparvariorum apud Cliderhou, et garcionum portancium eosdem Londinio cum gallis emptis pro eisdem.
Et xxd. In lecto Comitis cariando usque Dynebeghe.
Et Lli. xs. vd. q^a. In $^{C\,xx}_{ix.\,v.}$vj perticatis palicii faciendis et plantandis circa parcum de Musbyre cum cariagio dicti palicii de bosco de Totingtone pro parte. Residuum fit per Simonem Noel ut patet in compoto suo.
Et viijli. xvijs. ixd. In xviij bobus emptis pro cariagio palicii.
Et xxs. datis per Comitem Will'o le Waynwright et Ricardo de Helay factoribus palicii parci de Musbyry, et specialiter eis quam aliis factoribus quia Melius operabantur et plus quam alii.
  Summa Secunda Lxxvli. xijs. xjd. ob. q^a.

Idem computat vijli. liberatas Johanni parcario de Ichtenhil ut in compoto.
Et ixli. xs. liberatos preposito de Akeringtone ut in compoto.
Et Lxs. liberatos Johanni de Paldene Instauratori ut in compoto.
Et xxxvli. vjs. liberatos domino Nicholao de Redinges Receptori Hospicii Comitis ut in compoto.

Et DCC.xxxij li. vs. ij d. liberatos Olivero Receptori Pontisfracti ut in compoto.
Et xviij li. xviij s. liberatos eidem Olivero in plumbo ut in compoto suo.
Summa Liberacionis DCCCv li. xix s. ij d.

Minera.
Idem computat viij li. viij s. I d. ob. in $\overset{xx}{\underset{iiii}{}}$.xj cariagiis vj discis et dimidio Minere emptis de operantibus in Minera, unde ix disce faciunt cariagium prece cariagii xxij d.
Et xiij li. xiij s. iij d. In ix carratis et dimidio, septe ped, et I petra plumbi emptis de eisdem, unde vj petre faciunt ped, et xxv ped, faciunt carratum.
Et vij s. v d. In busca prostruenda et amputanda pro Minera predicta comburenda.
Et viij s. viij d. ob. In dicta busca et Minera carianda usque le Boole.
Et xxxvj s. vj d. In expensis comburendi supradictam Mineram.
Et vij s. viij d. In I pari follium de novo faciendo pro dicta Minera comburenda.
Et ij s. v j d. In bilantibus faciendis et ligandis cum ferre pro dicto plumbo ponderando et aliis utensilibus necessariis faciendis.
Et v s. viij d. In una parva domo facienda facta pro plumbo imponendo et I fâlda facienda pro Minera imponenda.
Et xiij s. iiij d. datos operantibus in Minera per Comitem pro quadam fovea facienda sub terra pro aqua extrahenda de aliis foveis.
Et x s. dat operantibus in Minera per Comitem.
Et xxx s. In vadiis Hugonis le Welmaker existentibus per xxiiij septimanas ultra Mineram.
Et xlij s. in vadiis Elye de Assenhirste existentibus ultra operatores Minere per xlij septimanas.
Summa expense circa Mineram xxx li. vij s. ij d.

Comitis Lencolnie.

Summa Summarum tocius expense et Liberacionis $^{C}_{ix.}$Lviijli. iijs. vd. Et sic debet Receptor Comiti CCli. iis. vijd. de quibus vigniti quinque Marce sunt de fine Roberti de Holedene de quo fine Receptor oneratur supra, et attermantur per Comitem solvendo per annum quinque Marcas quousque plenarie persolvantur.

Caune.
    De xijd.   de Decasu firme Roberti filii Gamele de una bovata terre in magna merclesdene.
    De iijd.   de decasu firme unius placie in eadem quam Ricardus Sharl tenuit.

Bronelay.
    De xiijs.   de decasu firme Ade Caboun.
    De ijs.   de decasu firme vj acrarum terre quas J. de Leicroft tenuit.

Brereclive.
    De xviijs.   de decasu firme Ricardi de Wyndhil in Brereclive.

Parva Merclesdene.
    De ixd.   de decasu firme J tofti et di acre terre quas Galfridus filius Thome tenuit.
    De vjd.   de decasu firme J tofti quod Will. Swetemilke tenuit.
    De xvjd.   de de casu firme iiij acrarum terre in eadem que monstratur in solucioni.

Rachdale.
    De xijd.   de de casu firme unius Burgagie quas Wil. Galle tenuit.
    De vjd.   de decasu firme Ade marchaunt.

COMPOTUS OF THE LANDS OF HENRY DE LACY, EARL OF LINCOLN.

AKERINGTONE.

Robert de Heppehale, Seneschall, and Robert de Reyleye, Sergeant, rendered their compotus at Ichtenhille, 30 Jan. 1297, before Sir William de Nony and Thomas de Fisheburne, from 30 Sep. 1295 to 30 Sep. 1296.

	£	s.	d.
Arrears of the last compotus	2	13	7¾
A curtilage near the vaccary this year 3d., Herbage sold in various places 4s. A plot for flax 1d. Old wagon sold 4d. Old cottage near Hoddesden sold 6d.		5	0
A plot called Reylayker let		6	8
Cheese 82½ stone, butter 27¼ stone	2	10	2
Received from Simon Noel by one tally	2	15	0
Total receipts	13	2	11¾

Payments and remittances.

	£	s.	d.
Ploughing and harrowing 21d. 2 wagons, etc., and 2 axes bought 3s. 9½d.		5	6½
Food and wages of a man leading the wagons and cart during the year, and carrying hay and fencing 25s. 5½d. A helper 7s.	1	12	5½
Repair of the mill, a millstone and iron bought		1	1
Making hedges and bridges	1	2	1½
A tripud, salt, etc., for the dairy		3	9
Reaping corn 6d., collecting and trimming branches in the park 9d.		1	3
Mowing meadows, making and stacking hay	2	10	5
Oats, mowing 11¼ acres 5s. 9d.; threshing and winnowing 53 quarters 3s. 10½d.		9	7½
Hoddesdene, cleaning the house 3s. 6d.; repairing hedges 2s. 1d.; haymaking 29s.; rebuilding and roofing a house 19s. ¾d.	2	14	1¾
Paid to Mary widow of William de Bradeschac for her dower from her husbands freehold in Le Bradehevyd		3	0
To the Sergeant for his service	1	6	8
Total payments and remittances	11	2	4½
Due to the Earl	2	0	7¼

Comitis Lencolnie.

AKERINGTON GRANGE.
Robert de Ryleye rendered his compotus of the produce of the grange of the fruits of autumn 1295.

> Oats. Produce 53 quarter 3 bushels, from which he counts 16 qrs. for seed, 1 qr. provender of workhorses and oxen and 37 qr. 3 bus. sold as above.
> Workhorses one Mare and one foal of last year and a foal born.
> Oxen. 12 oxen of last year.
> Dairy, 156 cheeses with 16 made after Michaelmas, From which he counts 16 for tithe and 140 weighing 82 stone sold as above.
> Butter. 27¼ stone, clear of tithe, all sold as above.

COLNE.
Robert de Heppehale, Seneschal, and Simoni Noel, Receiver, rendered their compotus at Ichtenhille, 30 Jan. 1297, before Sir William de Nony and Thomas de Fisscheburne, from 29 Sept. 1295 to 29 Sept. 1296.

	£	s.	d.
Arrears of the last compotus	481	11	8
Rent of Kaune with its members and arrears of marks, 1 Sept.	22	11	8
Rent of the mill of Kaune and Walfred, deducting tithe	12	16	0
Rent of the fulling mill of Kaune, 1 Sept.	1	13	4¼
Fine of the lands of Robert Molendarius, Adam son of Richard Benedict, and of William son of Adam de Alcancotes		11	0
Small fines of Kaune lands	1	9	10
Fees of the Hallmote there	1	0	8
Merchats of Elena daughter of Will. de Rediker and of Christiana daughter of Adam de Wodehouses		13	4

TROCHDENE.

Attachments of Cattle 22s. 6., Sea Coal 10s., cattle agisted 12s. 2d., hay sold 3s. 7.	2	8	3
First total of Receipts with arrears	526	4	2¼

HASLENDENE.

Rent of Haselingdene 1 Sept. 3l. 6s. 5¼., of the mill 29 Sept. 13s. 4d.	3	19	9¼

Compotus Terrarum Henrici de Lacy

	£	s.	d.
Winter herbage in Roseyndale 33s. 10; 80 cattle of the Abbot of Whalley agisted there 13s. 4d. Cattle agisted there in summer 49s. 10d.	4	15	0
Herbage of Derplaghe 20s.; of primerolsyke 20d. Hay sold there to the Abbot of Whalley 13s. 4d.; to others of the country 4s. 2d.	1	19	2
A forge for iron farmed out in Roscyndale	3	0	0
Second total of Receipts	14	15	11¼

TOTINGTONE.

	£	s.	d.
Rent of Totington at Easter and 29 Sept.	13	12	6¼
Rent of Richard de Radeclive for 20 acres by the Earl's charter 3s.; for 2¼ acres, enclosed by ditches with the 20 acres, and held at the Earl's will 10d.; of the lord of Bury for the land of Shuttelesworthe 12d.; Geoffrey de Chadertone for Shillingbothim for 1 lb. of cummin 1½d. Totingtone mill deducting tithe 26s.	1	10	11½
Stallage there		6	8
Herbage of Couhoppe 14s.; of Alvedene, Musedene and Uggedene 106s. 8d.; of the Wythns 10s.	6	10	8
Cattle agisted in Totingtone forest 6s. 4d.; nothing for Oaks, *Hucetum* and ore this year; pannage 15s. 5d.; fines of lands 38s. 2d.; court fees 43. 10d.; impounding cattle 12s.	3	16	9
Third total of Receipts	27	17	8

RACHEDALE.

	£	s.	d.
Rent, on 11 Nov.—Burghers 6s.; divers tenants 52s. 2d. Hugh de Elaunde, 159s. 9½d.	10	17	11½
One eighth part of the Mill		5	0
Rent of the Abbot of Whalley for 6 bovates 6s.; of the tenency formerly John de Byrun's 42s. 9½d. of the same for a tenement in Butterworth 2s.	2	10	9½
Tolls of fairs and market there, and stallage	2	13	8
Adam de Balghschaes heir for the bedelry	1	16	8
Fines of lands 43s. 2d; court fees 84s. 4d.	6	7	6
Reliefs of Henry son of Richard son of Henry for his fathers land			8
Revenue of the lands formerly Henry son of Patrick's, now in the Earls hand by felony of Ranulph son and heir of the same Henry		2	0
Fourth total of Receipts	24	0	11

Comitis Lencolnie.

		£	s.	d.

ROMESGREVE.
Summer herbage there sold this year — 1 0 4
For Ashes, Hucetum and oak trees nothing this year

HODDESDENE.
Herbage of Hoddesdene sold — 4 6
Old brushwood for a forge for 13 weeks — 13 0

WORSTONE.
Rent of Worstone 1 Sept. — 4 6 1½
Rent of Adam de Wyot for 2 collars, 1 Sept. — 2
Demesne lands let — 2 0 0
Rent of the mill there, deducting tithe — 1 4 0
Fines of lands 18s. 4d, fees of Hallemote 9s. 6d. — 1 17 10

PENNYLTONE.
Rent of Penniltone and Wymondeshouses, 1 Sept. — 6 4 2
Rent of Henry de Blakburne for 80 acres — 1
Fees of the Hallemote — 4 6
Nothing this year for fine of land and impounding cattle.

ICHTENHILLE.
Rent of Ichtenhille, 1 Sept. — 2 13 4
Fines of lands there this year — 3 15 6
Fees of the Hallmote — 1 19 2
Letherwyte of 5 women, Nothing for Marchet — 9 4
Escapes of cattle in the forest of Pennehille — 3 11 10
Thisteltack of Natives — 2 6
Winter herbage in Pennehille — 2 13 0
Summer herbage there — 2 5 0
Hay sold there — 18 10
Fine of Adam de Heley for the goods of his children coming to the Earl — 6 8
Sold — 17 ash trees 10s.; old brushwood 6s.; a stray mare 3s. — 19 0
80 wild boars — 3 6 1

Fifth total of Receipts — 41 4 11½

HABRINGEHAM.
Rent of Habringgeham, 1 Sept. — 4 14 4

PADINGHAM.
Rent of Padingham, 1 Sept. — 11 1 0
Rent of Padingham Mill, deducting tithe — 4 12 0
Works remitted in Padingham — 6 8

Compotus Terrarum Henrici de Lacy

BRUNLEY.

Rent of Brunley with the increase, 12s., of last year	13	8	5¼
Increase of the toft held by Robert Smith in Brunly		1	0
Works remitted there		3	4
Rent of Brunley Mill deducting tithe	10	0	0
Rent of the fulling mill there, this year the first		6	8
Rent of Brereclive, 1 Sept.	5	7	9¼

MERCLESDENE.

Rent of Little Merclesden, 1 Sept.	3	19	0¼
Works remitted there		1	2
Rent of Chirche 6s.; of Adam de Simondestone, 1 Sept., 1s. 5¼d.; of Tho. de Hiltone 13s. 4d.; of Berdeworthe and Ulvesbothe 5s. 6d.	1	6	3¼
A Mesuage and 7 acres in the Earl's hand by the felony of Wil. de Berdeworthe in Berdeworth		3	9
Increase of the same tenement		1	6
Rent of John de Blackburne for 28½ acres of land at Berdworthgrene		14	3
Sixth total of Receipts	56	7	3

PENNEWORTHAM.

Rent of Cottiers and assarts, 29 Sept.	2	4	4
Rent of Hugh (Hagonis) Ploket 1s. 8d.; of the same for 1 toft and ¼ acre of land held at will 3s.; for the demesne meadows and fisheries there, 29 Sept. 153s. 4d.	7	18	0
Rent of the Prior of Pennewortham for one plot next the priory			1
Ward of Lancaster Castle, 24 June		8	5¼
Herbage of Middelforde		15	0
Pannage there, deducting tithe	1	4	0
Fishery of Northmeles, 29 Sept.	1	6	8
Rent of Robert de Meles 8s. 1d.; of Galwaylandes 1s.		9	1
Rent of Roger de Walley for ¼ lb. pepper, 1 Sept.			6
Rent of Robert de Holande for a tenement in Eakestone			1
Rent of Adelingtone and Dokesbyry, 11 Nov.		3	0
Rent of Stanedisse and Langetre 2s.; of Northmeles, 11 Nov., 2s.; of Weltone, Nov. 11, 9d.		4	9
Sackefe, 29 Sept.		18	1¼
Rent of Sir William de la Mere, 11 Nov. and Whitsuntide	2	10	0

Comitis Lencolnie.

Rent of the tenement formerly of John de Deyethalghe, 29 Sept.		16	0
Henry Motoun for the beadelry	1	10	0
Fines for entering upon lands there	1	5	0
Fees of the Court there	4	9	2
Wood of Wreck sold			6
Peats sold at Pennewortham		1	4
Custody of the land and heir of Richard de Stockport until his majority		7	8
Ward of the land and heir of John de Neutone given to the Earl by the grant of Adam de Frekiltone	2	13	4
Seventh sum of Receipt £27 10s. ¾d., also 53s. 4d.	30	3	4¾

DOUNUM.

Rent of an assart there held by the Parson of Walley		4	0
Rent of Dounam with the increase of last year, 1 Sept.	8	11	5½
Desmesnes there let, 1 Sept.	3	13	4
Rent of the Mill there, deducting tithe	2	14	0
Peats sold there		2	0½
Rent of Alexander de Keuerdale, 1 Sept.		10	0
Rent of Master Henry de Claytone			1
Rent of Will. de Wadingtone, 1 Sept.		1	0
Rent of Richard clerk of Dounam for one pair of gloves			1½
Fines and fees of the Hallmote there		10	6
Impounding cattle		2	0
Eighth total of Receipts	16	8	6½

AKERINGTON.

Rent of 52 acres 1 rood of land let	1	11	9
A plot called Pesecroft		7	0
The Hall, Kitchen and Grange let		4	0
3 vaccaries there let, 1 Sept.	5	3	1¾
Rent of Mill, deducting tithe	1	16	8
5 acres of waste lately let		2	6
Fines for entering upon lands 17s. 4d.; fees 1s.; impounding cattle 6s. 6d.	1	4	10
Brushwood and Ore sold to a forge there for 27 weeks	1	14	0
Herbage of Brockolehurst		6	8

HUNCOTES.

Rent of Huncotes, 1 Sept.	5	0	11

Compotus Terrarum Henrici de Lacy

CLIVACHER.

Rent of divers holding by charter in Clivacher, 1 Sept.	6	13	8
Rent of Cottiers and Assarts there, 1 Sept.	4	6	3
Rent of Oliver de Stanesfend for 8 acres in Clivacher and 6 in Brunley held by the Earl's charter			6
¼ lb. pepper, rent of Adam son of Matthew			10
2 pairs of gloves, 1 pair of spurs, rent of Matthew de Bercroft, John son of Mathew and Adam the smith, 1 Sept.			5
Rent of Mill, tithe deducted	3	12	0
Relief of the son and heir of Ivo de Clivacher		1	7½
Fees of the Hallmote 1s. 6d.; impounding cattle 1s.		2	6
Sea coals sold there			3
Cattle agisted in the common pasture of Clivacher		5	4
Ninth total of Receipts	32	15	10¾

CLIDERHOWE.

Rent of Baldwynhille, 11 Nov. and Whitsuntide	1	0	3
Rent of the Thayns there, 1 Sept.	9	0	6
Galfrid de Simondestone for relaxation of suit of court		3	4
Rent of Dyote le Arrousmythe for his life and that of Dinaria his sister for one Cottage			4
William son of Henry for 2 acres of land under Baldwynhille		2	6
Rent of messuage formerly of Robert li Arrousmythe		3	4
Herbage of the castle ditches		1	6
Herbage of the Garden and a toft adjacent		3	0
Fruit of the Garden		8	0
Rent of the burgesses there, 29 Sept.	6	13	4
Toll of the Fair and Markets there	8	0	0
Rent of the Mill there, deducting tithe	12	0	0
Rent of Walter le Alblaster, 29 Sept.		2	0
Rent of Sandwelle and Salewelle		4	0
Rent of John de Danyscales 6s.; two years rent not charged to the Receiver 12s.		18	0
Rent of Ranulph de Mittone for attachment of the Mill there		2	0
Rent of land under Salthille this year	2	2	8½
Fines for entering upon lands there this year	4	1	6
Fees of the Court there this year	12	16	10
Relief of the heiresses of Richard de Tounley for tenements in Touneley, Coldecotes and Snodd-			

Comitis Lencolnie. 125

worth 10s.; for tenements in Brunschaghe 18s. 5d.	1	8	5
Impounding freemen for evasions in the forest	1	2	6
Fine of Adam de Dynley for a transgression in the forest	2	0	0
Fine of Richard del Tyndeheved because he is not prosecuted		13	4
Rent of Henry de Boltone for the Beadelry	3	0	0
Warde of Lancaster Castle	1	11	5
Rent of the Wapentak of Stainiclif	23	6	0
Received from Gilbert Instaurator as in compotus	77	18	4
Produce of 27 vaccaries let out	81	0	0
Thomas, Serjeant of Standen as in compotus	15	10	0
Arrears of William son of Margery		9	11
Goods of Elias Thayn felon beheaded, particulars in a certain cedule appended to this roll	6	10	0
Relief of the heirs of Adam de Tockholes for a tenement there		2	0
Profits of a tenement called Snelleshowe in the Earl's hand after the death of Peter de Cestria, viz., for this year and last year	2	2	6
Tenth total of Receipts	253	14	6¼
Sum total of the whole Receipts	1043	13	4

Expenses.

Repairing the Hall and Grange at Kaune	2	1½
Haymaking, 3 acres of meadow	2	4½
Cost of Kaune water mill with repair of outer wheel	13	1
Repairing the Fulling mill of Kaune	12	8
Repairing Worchestone Mill and its outer wheel	2	11
Repairing Dounam Mill	1	4
Repairing Totingtone Mill	1	6
Repairing Brunley Mill with 2 millstones lately bought	3	7
Repairing Clivacher Mill	3	6
Repairing Padyngham Mill	12	10
Repairing houses below the castle		3½

Repairing Pennewortham Hall and Roscyndale Hall		2	0
Fee and Robe of the Seneschal per annum	13	6	8
Fee and Robe of the Constable per annum	7	10	0
Wages of the parker of Ichtenhille per annum	2	5	6
A yearly rent due to Walter de Wadingtone			6
To the Abbot of Salley for finding a lamp for the soul of Earl John		6	8

Compotus Terrarum Henrici de Lacy

	£	s.	d.
Ward of Lancaster Castle	2	10	0
Expenses of the Constable and Gilbert Instaurator selling the Earl's stock in the Markets of Boltone and St. Egidius		14	8
Expenses of the Seneschal, Constable and Instaurator for views made and colts marked		4	0½
Wages of one Warrener keeping Salthille, Dounum Wood and Worstone	1	6	0
Expenses of hearing the compotus before this	3	11	3½
Diminution of Rents shown by a cedule appended to this roll		18	5
Expenses of taking wild boars		6	8
Wages of the Porter per annum	2	5	6
Canvass and parchment bought for this year and the 3 last years		8	0
First total of Expences	43	10	11½

Foreign Expences.

	£	s.	d.
Wages to the keeper of the Marches of the Forest of Rachedam and Bernolswyke this year	1	6	0
Bringing 190li. safely from Cliderhowe to Buckeby and carrying money 5 times to Pontefract	1	12	4
Taking 5 Colts from Cliderhou to Buckeby by order of the Earl for hay, oats, litter, with the expenses of takers in returning		12	0
Given de Huddelestone by the Earl's letter	3	8	0
Allowed to Mabota, Maid of Alesya de Lascy, for herbage, with which the Receiver is charged in the last compotus		10	0
Allowed to John del Barouforde of the rent of the vaccary which he holds		10	0
Fulling Mill at Brunley built anew	2	12	6½
Second total of Expences	10	11	11½

Delivered.

	£	s.	d.
Delivered to Peter, Provost of Ichtenhille by one tally	6	7	0
Delivered to the Provost of Akerintone as in compotus	2	15	0
Delivered to Thomas de Raynevelle by one tally written by the hand of Robert de Sulkestone, clerk	183	6	8
Delivered to Oliver de Stanesfend as in compotus	354	0	0
Sum of the whole delivery £546 13 8			

Comitis Lencolnie.

Sum total of the whole expences & delivery 600 16 7
So the Receiver owes the Earl £442 16s. 9d.
Of which 14s. are arrears of Hen. de Kyghley.
Afterwards he was allowed 6s. 8d. for tithe of
the wild boars. And 13s. 4d. for the Merchat
of 2 women with which he was unjustly charged
above in Kaune, because the women are of free
condition.

ICHTENHILLE.

Robert de Heppehale, Seneschall, and Peter de Ruddeby rendered the compotus from 4 March 1296 to 30 Sept. 1296, before Sir William de Nony and Thomas de Fissheburne at Ictenhille.

One work horse and 17 oxen agisted in Rohille	7	9
3 oxen sold	1 16	0
Hides of 9 mares, 2 foals of the third year and 7 foals of the second year	4	9
4 quarters of Oat sold	9	0
Received from Simon Noel as in compotus	6 12	0
Arrears of William son of Margeria on the last compotus	9	11¼
Total	9 19	7¼

Expences.

Cost of Carts 2d.; of wagons, with one made anew, and grease bought for them 1s. 10d.; 2 servants for the carts and wagons 20s. 5d.	1 2	5
Food and wages of one harrower		2½
Two men keeping foals in the stable for 10 weeks	7	6
Their wages during the time of the compotus	3	6
Repairing houses	7	11¼
4½ quarters of oats sold	7	1
1 tripod, 1 iron for marking colts		10
Cutting and carrying fuel	1	8
Repairs of Paling	4	6
Repairing ditches and hedges about Hegham and in the park	18	10½
Mowing 60½ acres of meadow	17	7¾
Making and stacking the hay	12	7

Compotus Terrarum Henrici de Lacy

Reaping, gathering and binding 16 acres of oats	6	10½
Selling foals, halters bought for them and expences of those who helped to fold and take them	5	2½
Provender of 2 stallions, iron for them and expences of grooms keeping them and taking them from Ichtenhill to Pontefract	11	3
Turning the course of Kelder water at Whytacre to save the paling	8	6
Expences of the Seneschal and others taking 16 Stags in the forest, and 5 Does in the park, with the carriage of 6 Stags and 4 Does from Ichtenhille to Pontefract	11	3
Repairing the pailing about the fishpond, and the fence about Rohille	1	7½
Delivered to Simon Noel Receiver as in compotus	9	11¼
Total of Expences and Delivery	8 13	2¼

So the Serjeant owes the Earl 26s. 4¼d.
•Afterwards 6s. 8d. were allowed him for his Robe for this year. And 9s. 1d. for making anew and erecting a Cross in the Market of Brunley.

ICHTENHILLE GRANGE.

The same renders his compotus of the produce of the grange of the fruits of autumn 1295 before the same, as above.

Oats. 27 quarters produce received from William son of Margeria; 4½ qr. bought as above; total 31½ qr. From which he counts 15 qr. 2 bushels for seed, 16 qr. 6 bus. provender of foals from 4 March to the feast of St. Elena, and 4 qr. sold as above.

Oxen. 17 received from William son of Margeria as in compotus, of which 3 are sold and 14 oxen remain.

Horses. Remainder 52 mares, of which 9 died of murrain their hides accounted for above, 1 delivered to William de Stopham by the Earl's letter. And 42 mares remain.

Runcini. Remainder 2, of which one delivered to the provost of Tanschelf as in compotus. And 1 remains.

Two-year-olds. Remainder 29 foals in the same year, of which 2 in murrain, hides accounted for above. And 27 foals in the third year remain, of which 14 are males.

Foals. Remainder 22 foals, of which 7 in murrain, hides accounted for above, and 1 in tithe. And 14 foals in the second year remain, of which 6 are male.
Foals of the year. 22, of which 1 in murrain, hide of no value. And 21 remain.

TROCHDENE.

The Instaurator of Blakeburnschyre, Robert de Heppehale, and the Instaurators and cowkeepers render their compotus at Ictenhille, 26 Jan. 1297, from 30 Sept. 1295 to 29 Sept. 1296.

3s. 2½d.

Adam, son of John, renders his compotus of 36 cows and 2 bulls of the remainder, and 6 cows of addition, and 1 received from the Instaurator; total 43 cows and 2 bulls. Of which he counts one in murrain, flesh and hide 14d.; 2 delivered to Simon le Geldhirde, and 5 with 1 bull to the Instaurator; 35 cows and one bull remain. Also 4 oxen of addition, delivered to Geoffrey le Parker. Also 9 yearlings of the remainder. Of which 1 strangled by the wolf, flesh and hide 6d. 5 steers and 3 heifers remain. Also 15 calves of the remainder, of which 2 in tithe, and 13 yearlings remain, of which 6 are males. Also 25 calves of the year, and 1 received from the Instaurator; total 26. Of which 2 in murrain, flesh and hide ½d.; 1 sold, 6d.; 5 delivered to the Instaurator, and 1 to Simon le Geldehirde: and 13 calves remain.

Total cattle remaining in this vaccary: 35 cows, 1 bull, 5 steers, 3 heifers, 13 yearlings (6 males), and 17 calves.

2s. 11d.

Matilda, wife of Jordan del Bothe, renders a compotus of 44 cows and 1 bull of the remainder and 7 of addition; total 50 cows, 1 bull. Of which she counts 1 in murrain, hide and flesh 20d.; 3 delivered to Simon le Geldehirde, and 2 cows to the Instaurator: 43 cows and 1 bull remain. Also 5 oxen of addition, delivered to Geoffrey le Parker. Also 9 yearlings of the remainder; of which one in murrain, hide 2d. And 3 steers and 5 heifers remain. Also 17 calves of the remainder; of which 1 strangled by the wolf, flesh and hide 12d.; one in tithe. 15 yearlings (9 males) remain. Also 23 calves of the year; of which 2 delivered to Simon le Geldehirde, and 2 to the Instaurator; and 3 in murrain, hides 1d.: and 16 calves of the year remain.

Total of the cattle remaining in this vaccary: 44 cows, 1 bull, 3 steers, 5 heifers, 15 yearlings (9 males), and 16 calves.

S

Emma del Munkerode renders her compotus of 41 cows and 1 bull of the remainder and 4 of addition; total 45 cows, 1 bull. Of which she counts 3 delivered to Simon le Geldehirde, and 3 delivered to the Instaurator with 1 bull: 39 cows remain. Also 5 oxen of addition, delivered to Geoffrey le Parker. Also 12 yearlings of the remainder; 5 steers and 7 heifers remain. Also 15 calves of the remainder; of which 1 in tithe: 14 yearlings (6 males) remain. Also 1 young bull received from the Instaurator. Also 22 calves of the year: of which 1 in murrain, hide of no value; 1 delivered to Simon le Geldehirde, and 3 to the Instaurator: 17 calves remain.

Total of the cattle remaining in this vaccary: 39 cows, 5 steers, 7 heifers, also 1 steer bull received from the Instaurator, 13 yearlings (6 males), and 17 calves.

Henry de Emot in the place of Adam son of Maulke renders his compotus of 40 cows and 1 bull of the remainder, and 6 of addition; total 46 cows, 1 bull. Of which he counts 1 in murrain, hide and flesh 2s.; 2 delivered to Simon le Geldehirde, and 4 to the Instaurator. 39 cows, 1 bull remain. Also 4 oxen of addition, delivered to G. the parker. Also 14 yearlings of the remainder: 5 steers and 9 heifers remain. Also 26 calves of the year: of which 6 in murrain, hides and

2s. 6¼d. flesh 6¼d.; 1 delivered to Simon le Geldehirde, and 4 to the Instaurator: 15 calves remain.

Total of the cattle remaining in this vaccary: 39 cows, 1 bull, 5 steers, 9 heifers, 8 yearlings, 4 young heifers, and 15 calves.

Peter del Fernyside renders his compotus of 38 cows and 1 bull of the remainder, and 7 of addition, and 3 received from the Instaurator: total 49 cows, 1 bull. Of which he counts 1 strangled by the wolf, hide and flesh 4d.; 1 in murrain, hide and flesh 22d.; 7 delivered to S. le Geldehirde: 40 cows,

2s. 11¼d. 1 bull remain, Also 6 oxen of addition, delivered to G. the parker. Also 15 yearlings of the remainder; of which 1 strangled by the wolf, hide and flesh 6d.; 1 in murrain, hide 3d.; 8 steers, 5 heifers remain. Also 17 yearlings of the remainder: of which 2 in tithe: 15 yearlings (9 males) remain. Also 16 calves of the year, and 4 received from the Instaurator: total 20: of which 2 in murrain, hide ¼d.; 1 delivered to Simon le Geldehirde; 17 calves remain.

Total of the cattle remaining in this vaccary: 40 cows, 1 bull, 8 steers, 5 heifers, 15 yearlings (9 males), and 17 calves.

Total of the money in the forest of Trochden 10s. 7¼d.

PENNEHILLE.

Richard de Birchenleye renders his compotus of 44 cows and 1 bull of the remainder, and 3 of addition; total 47 cows, 1 bull. Of which he counts 3 delivered to Simon le Geldehirde, and 8 to the Instaurator: 36 cows, 1 bull remain. Also 1 ox of the remainder, and 4 of addition, delivered to G. the parker. Also 13 yearlings of the remainder; 6 steers, 7 heifers remain. Also 15 calves of the remainder: of which 2 in tithe, and 1 delivered to the Instaurator: 12 yearlings remain (9 males). Also 24 calves of the year: of which 4 in murrain, flesh and hides 2d.; 7 delivered to the Instaurator: 13 calves remain.

2d.

Total of the cattle remaining in this vaccary: 32 cows, 1 bull, 6 steers, 6 heifers, 12 yearlings (9 males), and 13 calves.

Richard son of Benedict renders his compotus of 43 calves and 1 bull of the remainder, and 5 of addition, and 4 received from the Instaurator; total 51 cows, 1 bull. Of which 2 in murrain, hides and flesh 4s. 5d.; 3 delivered to S. le Geldehirde, and 1 to the Instaurator: 45 cows and bull remain. Also 4 oxen of addition, delivered to G. the parker. Also 13 yearlings of the remainder; of which 1 in murrain, hide and flesh 12d.: 6 steers and 6 heifers remain. Also 16 calves of the remainder: of which 1 in tithe: 15 yearlings remain (6 males). Also 15 calves of the year, and 4 received from the Instaurator: total 19: of which 1 in murrain, hide of no value; 1 delivered to S. le Geldehirde; and 2 sold 5d.; 16 calves remain.

5s. 10d.

Total of the cattle remaining in this vaccary; 45 cows, 1 bull, 6 steers, 6 heifers, 15 yearlings (6 males), and 16 calves.

Henry son of Kitte renders his compotus of 42 cows and 1 bull of the remainder, and 6 of addition, and 1 received from the Instaurator: total 49 cows and 1 bull, also 1 bull of addition. Of which he counts 3 delivered to S. le Geldehirde, and 2 to the Instaurator: 44 cows and 2 bulls remain. Also 1 ox of addition delivered to G. the parker. Also 10 yearlings of the remainder: 3 steers and 7 heifers remain. Also 13 calves of the remainder: of which 1 in tithe: 13 yearlings remain (5 males). Also 19 calves of the year, and 1 received from the Instaurator: total 20: of which 3 in murrain, hides 1d.; 2 delivered to the Instaurator: and 10 calves remain.

1d.

Total of the cattle remaining in this vaccary: 44 cows, 2 bulls, 3 steers, 7 heifers, 12 yearlings (5 males) and 15 calves. Afterwards one cow is allowed to him because it was taken away by robbers; it is forgiven by the Earl.

William de Penniltone renders his account of 36 cows and 2 bulls of the remainder, and 7 of addition : total 43 cows and 2 bulls. Of which 1 in murrain, hide and flesh 22d.; 2 delivered to S. le Geldehirde, and 1 to the Instaurator : 39 cows and 2 bulls remain. Also 2 oxen of addition, delivered to G. the parker. Also 14 yearlings of the remainder : 9 steers and 5 heifers remain. Also 14 calves of the remainder : of which 2 in murrain, hide and flesh 4d.; 1 in tithe : 11 yearlings remain (5 males), Also 23 calves of the year : of which 2 in murrain, hides 1d.; 1 delivered to S. le Geldehirde, and 2 to the Instaurator : 18 calves remain.

Total of the cattle remaining in this vaccary : 39 cows, 2 bulls, 9 steers, 5 heifers, 11 yearlings (5 males), and 18 calves.

Benne de Holcoumbe renders his compotus of 46 cows and 1 bull of the remainder, and 4 of addition, and 1 received from the Instaurator; total 51 cows and 1 bull. Of which he counts 3 in murrain, hides and flesh 3s. 8d.; 1 delivered to S. le Geldehirde, and 5 to the Instaurator : 42 cows and 1 bull remain. Also 5 oxen of addition, delivered to G. the parker. Also 10 yearlings of the remainder ; 8 steers and 2 heifers remain. Also 13 calves of the remainder : of which 1 in tithe : 12 yearlings remain (5 males). Also 22 calves of the year, and 2 received from the Instaurator : total 24; of which 4 in murrain, hides 3d.; 5 delivered to the Instaurator : 14 calves remain.

3s. 11d.

Total of the cattle remaining in this vaccary : 42 cows, 1 bull, 8 steers, 2 heifers, 12 yearlings (5 males), and 13 calves.

John del Haregreves in the place of William son of Hawysia renders his account of 41 cows and 1 bull of the remainder, and 6 of addition, and 6 received from the Instaurator : total 53 cows and 1 bull. Of which he counts 1 delivered to S. le Geldhirde : 52 cows, 1 bull remain. Also 2 oxen of addition delivered to G. the parker. Also 9 yearlings of the remainder : of which 1 sold, 16d.: 3 male steers and 5 heifers remain. Also 15 calves of the remainder : of which 1 in murrain, hide 3d.; 1 in tithe : 13 yearlings remain (7 males). Also 12 calves of the year, and 6 received from the Instaurator : total 18 : of which 3 in murrain, hides 1d., 15 calves remain.

Total of the cattle remaining in this vaccary : 52 cows, 1 bull, 3 steers, 5 heifers, 13 yearlings (7 males), and 15 calves.

William son of Gryffry renders his compotus of 41 cows and 1 bull of the remainder, and 6 of addition, and 3 received from the Instaurator : total 50 cows and 1 bull. Of which he counts 1 sold, 3s. 6d.; 2 delivered to S. le Geldehirde : 47

Comitis Lencolnie.

3s. 6d.

cows, 1 bull remain. Also 3 oxen and 1 bull of addition: of which 3 are delivered to G. the parker; 1 bull remains. Also 10 yearlings of the remainder: 7 steers, 3 heifers remain. Also 16 calves of the remainder, and 3 received from the Instaurator; total 18: of which 2 in murrain, hides ½d.: 16 calves remain (5 males).

Total of the cattle remaining in this vaccary: 47 cows, 2 bulls, 7 steers, 3 heifers, 13 yearlings (5 male), 16 calves.

John del Barouford in place of whom Thomas son of Alan renders his compotus of 36 cows and 1 bull of the remainder, and 9 of addition, and 1 received from the Instaurator: total 46 cows and 1 bull. Of which he counts 2 delivered to S. le Geldhirde, and 4 to the Instaurator: 40 cows and 1 bull remain. Also 9 oxen of addition delivered to G. the parker. Also 13 yearlings of the remainder: 5 steers and 8 heifers remain. Also 8 calves of the remainder, and 1 received from the Instaurator; of which he counts 1 in tithe: 13 yearlings remain (7 males). Also 23 calves of the year: of which 1 in murrain, hide of no value; 2 delivered to S. le Geldhirde, and 4 to the Instaurator; 16 calves remain.

Total of the cattle remaining in the vaccary: 40 cows, 1 bull, 5 steers, 8 heifers, 13 yearlings (7 males), and 16 calves.

Adam son of Nicholas renders his compotus of 40 cows and 1 bull of the remainder, and 2 of addition, and 3 received from the Instaurator: total 45 cows, 1 bull. Of which 2 delivered to S. le Geldhirde; 2 in murrain, hides and flesh 3s. 6d.; 41 cows, 1 bull remain. Also 5 oxen of addition, delivered to G. the parker. Also 12 yearlings of the remainder; 8 steers and 4 heifers remain. Also 14 calves of the remainder: of which 1 in murrain, hide 4d.; 1 in tithe: 12 yearlings remain (4 males). Also 16 calves of the year, and 3 received

4s. 11d.

from the Instaurator, total 19: of which 2 in murrain, hides 1d.: 17 calves remain. Also he owes 12d. for calves badly kept.

Total of the cattle remaining in this vaccary: 41 cows, 1 bull, 8 steers, 4 heifers, 12 yearlings (4 males), and 17 calves.

William Gougge in place of Richard de Bercroft renders his compotus of 41 cows and 1 bull of the remainder, and 4 of addition, and 2 from the Instaurator; total 47 cows, 1 bull. Of which 1 in murrain, flesh and hide 2s. 4½d., 4 delivered to Simon le Geldehirde, 2 to the Instaurator: 40 cows and 1 bull remain. Also 3 oxen of addition, delivered to G. the parker. Also 12 yearlings of the remainder: of which 1 strangled by the wolf, hide and flesh 12d.: 7 steers and 4

3s. 5½d.

heifers remain. Also 14 calves of the remainder: of which

2 in tithe: 14 yearlings remain (6 males). Also 19 calves of the year, and 2 received from the Instaurator: total 21: of which 3 in murrain, hide 1d.; 2 delivered to the Instaurator: 16 calves remain.

Total of the cattle remaining in this vaccary: 40 cows, 1 bull, 7 steers, 4 heifers, 12 yearlings (6 males) and 16 calves.

1s. 10½d.

Robert Attebrigge renders his compotus of 39 cows and 1 bull of the remainder, and 5 of addition, total 43 cows and 1 bull. Of which 1 in murrain, hide and flesh 18d.; 2 delivered to Simon le Geldhirde: 41 cows and 1 bull remain. Also 3 oxen of addition, delivered to G. the parker. Also 10 yearlings of the remainder: of which 1 in murrain, hide and flesh 1½d.: 4 steers and 5 heifers remain. Also 14 calves of the remainder: of which 2 in murrain, hides and flesh 2d.: 12 yearlings remain (4 males). Also 17 calves of the year, and 2 of cows which were in doubt, total 19: of which 2 in murrain, hide 1d., 1 delivered to Simon le Geldhirde: 16 calves remain.

. Total of the cattle remaining in this vaccary: 41 cows, 1 bull, 4 steers, 5 heifers, 12 yearlings (4 males), and 16 calves.

Total of the money on the forest of Pennehille 27s. 8¼d.

ROSCYNDALE.

1d.

Henry del Estock renders his compotus of 35 cows and 1 bull of the remainder, and 3 of addition, and 2 from the Instaurator; total 41 cows and 1 bull. Of which he counts 2 delivered to Simon le Geldhirde and 5 to the Instaurator: 39 cows and 1 bull remain. Also 5 oxen of addition, delivered to G. the parker. Also 15 yearlings of the remainder: 10 steers and 5 heifers remain. Also 12 calves of the remainder and 1 from the Instaurator; total 13: of which 1 in tithe: 12 yearlings remain (7 males). Also 24 calves of the year, and 1 received from the Instaurator; total 25: of which 2 in murrain, hide 1d.; 4 delivered to the Instaurator: 19 calves remain.

Total of the cattle remaining in this vaccary: 39 cows, 1 bull, 10 steers, 5 heifers, 12 yearlings (7 males), and 19 calves. Afterwards 1 cow was allowed to the said Henry of which it was testified on the compotus that she had been taken away by robbers.

Henry de Houghton in whose place John de Pycoppe renders his compotus of 28 cows and 1 bull of the remainder, and 5 of addition, and 3 from the Instaurator: total 46 cows and 1 bull. Of which he counts 1 strangled by the wolf, hide and

Comitis Lencolnie.

flesh 3s.; 2 delivered to the Instaurator: 43 cows and 1 bull remain. Also 6 oxen of addition, delivered to G. the parker. Also 12 yearlings of the remainder: 8 steers remain (of which 1 is a young bull) and 4 heifers. Also 18 calves of the remainder: of which 2 in tithe; 1 in murrain, hide 1d.: 15 yearlings remain (10 males). Also 16 calves of the year, and 3 received from the Instaurator, total 19: of which 4 in murrain, hide and flesh 8½d.: 15 calves remain.

3s. 9½d.

Total of the cattle remaining in this vaccary: 43 cows, 1 bull, 8 steers (1 a young bull), 4 heifers, 15 yearlings (10 males), and 15 calves.

John son of Odousa in place of Adam de Wordhille renders his compotus of 37 cows and 1 bull of the remainder, and 6 of addition, and 6 received from the Instaurator: total 49 cows and 1 bull. Of which 2 in murrain, bides and flesh 2s. 10d.; 2 delivered to the Instaurator: 43 cows and 1 bull remain. Also 6 oxen of addition, delivered to G. the parker. Also 9 yearlings of the remainder: of which 1 strangled by the wolf, hide and flesh 16d.: 4 steers and 4 heifers remain. Also 15 calves of the remainder: of which 3 in murrain, hides and flesh 9d.; and 1 in tithe: 9 yearlings remain (6 males). Also 15 calves of the year and 5 from the Instaurator: total 20: of which 3 in murrain, hides 1d.: 17 calves remain.

5s.

Total of the cattle remaining in this vaccary: 43 cows, 1 bull, 4 steers, 4 heifers, 11 yearlings (6 males) and 17 calves.

Robert de Couhoppe in place of Cecilia de Heleye renders his compotus of 37 cows and 1 bull of the remainder, and 4 of addition, and 5 received from the Instaurator, total 46 cows and 1 bull. Of which 1 in murrain, hide and flesh 12d.; 3 delivered to S. le Geldhirde, and 1 to the Instaurator: 41 cows and 1 bull remain. Also 5 oxen of addition, delivered to G. the parker. Also 9 yearlings of the remainder: of which 1 sold 10d.: 7 steers and 1 heifer remain. Also 13 calves of the remainder: of which 1 in tithe: 12 yearlings remain (7 males). Also 12 calves of the year, and 6 received from the Instaurator: total 18: of which 4 in murrain, hides ½d.; 14 calves remain. Richard son of Cecilia de Heley made a fine of 10s. for 4 calves lost by defect of custody of the same Cecilia.

22½d.
also 10s.

Total of the cattle remaining in this vaccary: 41 cows, 1 bull, 7 steers, 1 heifer, 12 yearlings (7 males), and 14 calves. Pledges of the said 10s. Henry del Estocke and Richard de Heley.

Richard de Dunnockschae renders his compotus of 35 cows and

1 bull of the remainder, and 1 of addition, and 1 received from the Instaurator: total 37 cows and 1 bull. Of which 1 strangled by the wolf, hide and flesh 6s.; 1 delivered to S. le Geldhirde, and 3 cows and 1 bull to the Instaurator: 32 cows remain. Also 8 oxen of addition, delivered to G. the parker. Also 12 yearlings of the remainder; 6 steers (of which 1 a young bull), and 6 heifers remain. Also 12 calves of the remainder: of which 1 strangled by the wolf, hide and flesh 9d.; and 1 in tithe; 10 yearlings remain (5 males). Also 21 calves of the year, and 1 received from the Instaurator: total 22: of which 2 in murrain, hides 1d.; 1 delivered to G. le Geldhirde and 3 to the Instaurator: 16 calves remain.

6s. 10d.

Total of the cattle remaining in this vaccary: 32 cows, 6 steers (1 a young bull), 6 heifers, 10 yearlings (5 males), 16 calves.

Richard de Bercroft in place of Robert de Couhoppe renders his compotus of 35 cows and 2 bulls of the remainder, and 3 of addition: total 38 cows and 2 bulls. Of which 4 delivered to the Instaurator: 34 cows and 2 bulls remain. Also 5 oxen of addition, delivered to G. the parker. Also 11 yearlings of the remainder; 3 steers and 8 heifers remain. Also 14 calves of the remainder: of which 2 in murrain, hides 18d.: 12 yearlings remain (6 males). Also 20 calves of the year: of which 5 in murrain, hides 2½d.; 2 delivered to the Instaurator: 13 calves remain.

12½d.
also 5s. 8d.

Total of the cattle remaining in this vaccary: 33 cows, 2 bulls, 3 steers, 8 heifers, 12 yearlings (6 males), 13 calves. Afterwards 1 cow was sold in addition to the compotus for 5s.

Thomas del Estocke renders his compotus of 32 cows and 1 bull of the remainder, and 9 of addition, and 4 received from the Instaurator: total 45 cows and 1 bull. Of which 2 delivered to the Instaurator, and 4 to S. le Geldhirde, and 1 strangled by the wolf, hide and flesh 4s. 10d.: 39 cows and 1 bull remain. Also 2 oxen of addition, delivered to G. the parker. Also 11 yearlings of the remainder: 6 steers and 5 heifers remain. Also 12 calves of the remainder: of which 1 strangled by the wolf, hide and flesh 9d.; and 1 in tithe: 9 yearlings remain (6 males). Also 14 calves of the year, and 4 received from the Instaurator: total 18: of which 3 in murrain, hide and flesh 3d.: 15 calves remain.

5s. 10d.

Total of the cattle remaining in this vaccary: 39 cows, 1 bull, 6 steers, 5 heifers, 10 yearlings (6 males), and 15 calves.

Henry de Hoghtone in the place of Henry de Berdeshille renders his compotus of 34 cows and 1 bull of the remainder, and

Comitis Lencolnie.

9 of addition, and 3 received from the Instaurator: total 46 cows and 1 bull. Of which 1 in murrain, hide and flesh 3s. 4d.; 1 delivered to Simon le Geldhirde: 44 cows and 1 bull. Also 2 oxen of addition, delivered to G. the parker. Also 10 yearlings of the remainder, and 1 received from the Instaurator, and one found by the Seneschal's inspection: total 12: 8 steers remain (1 a young bull), and 4 heifers. Also 16 calves of the remainder: of which 2 in murrain, hide 6d.; and 1 in tithe: 13 yearlings remain (5 males). Also 20 calves of the year, and two received from the Instaurator: total 22: of which 2 in murrain, hides 1d.; and one delivered to the Instaurator, and 1 to S. le Geldhirde: 18 calves remain.

4s. 11d.

Total of the cattle remaining in this vaccary: 44 cows, 1 bull, 8 steers (1 a young bull), 4 heifers, 13 yearlings (5 males), 17 calves.

William de Dynley in the place of Christiana de Dynley renders his compotus of 41 cows and 1 bull of the remainder, and 4 of addition, total 45 cows and 1 bull. Of which he counts 1 in murrain, hide and flesh 4s.; and 2 delivered to the Instaurator, and 2 to S. le Geldhirde: 40 cows and 1 bull remain. Also 4 oxen of addition, delivered to G. the parker. Also 10 yearlings of the remainder: 5 steers and 5 heifers remain. Also 18 calves of the remainder: of which 2 in tithe, 1 delivered to the Instaurator; 15 yearlings remain (5 males). Also 21 calves of the year: of which 2 in murrain, flesh and hides 1d.; 1 delivered to S. le Geldhyrde, and 1 to the Instaurator: 16 calves remain.

4s. 1d.
also 4s.

Total of the cattle remaining in 'this vaccary: 40 cows, 1 bull, 5 steers, 5 heifers, 15 yearlings (5 males), and 15 calves. Afterwards 1 cow and 1 calf were sold in addition to the compotus for 4s.

Alan de Roclif renders his compotus of 29 cows of the remainder, and 1 of addition, and 6 received from the Instaurator, total 36 cows. Of which 1 strangled by the wolf, flesh and hide 5s.: 35 cows remain. Also 9 oxen of addition, delivered to G. the parker. Also 13 yearlings of the remainder: of which 1 in murrain, hide and flesh 12d.: 7 steers remain (of which 1 a young bull), and 6 heifers. Also 18 calves of the remainder: of which 1 in tithe; and 1 in murrain, hide 10½d.; 18 yearlings remain (7 males). Also 12 calves of the year, and 6 received from the Instaurator, total 18: of which 3 in murrain, hide 1d.: 15 calves remain.

6s. 11½d.

Total of the cattle remaining in this vaccary: 35 cows, 7

T

steers (1 young bull), 6 heifers, 16 yearlings (7 males), and 15 calves.

William son of Andrew in the place of Robert de Anteley renders his compotus of 39 cows and 1 bull of the remainder, and 7 of addition, and 4 cows from the Instaurator, total 50 cows and 1 bull. Of which 1 in murrain, hide and flesh 2s. 6d.: 1 delivered to S. le Geldhird and 2 to the Instaurator: 46 cows and 1 bull remain. Also 6 oxen of addition, delivered to G. the parker. Also 9 yearlings of the remainder: of which 1 in murrain, hide 16d.: 5 steers and 3 heifers remain. Also 17 calves of the remainder: of which 1 in murrain, hide 1d.; and 1 in tithe: 15 yearlings remain (7 males). Also 15 calves of the year, and 4 received from the Instaurator: total 19: of which 5 in murrain, hides 2d.: 14 calves remain.

4s. 1d.

Total of the cattle remaining in this vaccary: 46 cows, 1 bull, 5 steers, 3 heifers, 15 yearlings (7 males), and 14 calves. Afterwards 1 cow was sold in addition to the compotus for 4s.

Total of the money of the Forest of Trochdene 66s. 2d.

Vaccary of Akeringtone.

Makocke de Anteley renders his compotus of 100 cows and 1 bull of the remainder, and 13 of addition with 3 bulls, total 114 cows and 4 bulls. Of which 3 delivered to S. le Geldhirde, and 3 to the Instaurator; 2 in murrain, flesh and hide 4s. 9d.; and 1 bull delivered to the Instaurator: 106 cows and 3 bulls remain. Also 18 oxen of addition and 6 oxen of the remainder, total 24: of which 6 delivered to William de Anteley, and 18 to G. the parker. Also 56 yearlings of the remainder: of which 2 in murrain, hides and flesh 2s.; 1 sold for 15d.; 1 delivered to the Instaurator: 52 steers remain of which 28 males and 24 females. Also 36 calves of the remainder: of which 2 in tithe; 3 strangled by the wolf, hides and flesh 20d.: 31 yearlings remain (19 males). Also 48 calves of the year, and 2 received from the Instaurator, total 50: of which 4 in murrain, hides 4d., 46 calves remain.

10s.

Total of the cattle remaining in this vaccary: 106 cows, 3 bulls, 24 steers, 24 heifers, 31 yearlings (19 males), and 46 calves.

Geoffrey the parker renders his compotus of 3 oxen of the remainder, and 137 oxen received from the cowkeepers as above, total 140 oxen: of which 2 strangled by the wolf,

hides and flesh 4s.; 3 delivered to Gilbert the Instaurator
4s. and 135 delivered to Simon le Geldhirde: total as above.
Simon le Geldhirde renders his compotus of 135 oxen received from Geoffrey the parker as above, 135 remain. Also 60 cows received from the cowkeepers: of which 3 in murrain;
3s. 4½d. hides and flesh 3s. 4d., and 31 delivered to G. the Instaurator: 26 cows remain. Also 12 calves received from the cowkeepers as above, and 2 issue of the cows of Croin' in custody of the same, total 14: of which 1 in murrain, hide ½d., and 13 delivered to the Instaurator.

Total of the cattle remaining in the custody of the said Simon: 135 oxen, 26 cows.

William de Anteley renders his compotus of 122 oxen of the remainder, and 6 received from the cowkeeper of Akeryngtone, total 128: of which 2 in murrain, hides and flesh 13d.; and 126 delivered to G. the Instaurator.

Total of the money of Akeryngtone and of the keepers of the oxen and cattle of Crom. 18s. 5d.

Gilbert son of Michael, Chief Instaurator, Peter de Bradleye, Richard, clerk, Instaurator of Pennehille, Henry del Estocke, Instaurator of Roscyndale, William de Rocheleye, Instaurator of Trochdene render their compotus of 42 cows of the remainder, and 94 cows and 4 bulls received from the cowkeepers as in the compotus: total 136 cows and 4 bulls. Of which 60 delivered to the cowkeepers as in the compotus; and 72 cows and 4 bulls sold as below: 4 cows remain. Also 54 oxen of the remainder, and 129 oxen received from the keeper of the cattle of Crom'; total 183 oxen: of which 137 oxen sold as below: 46 oxen remain. Also 1 yearling of the remainder, and 1 steer received from the cowkeeper of Akeringtone: of which 1 steer delivered to the cowkeeper of Roscyndale as in the compotus: and 1 steer, a young bull, remains. Also 2 yearlings received from the cowkeeper of Roscindale and delivered to other cowkeepers of these forests. Also 60 calves received from the cowkeepers and 9 calves received from the heifers of Hoddesdene; total 59 calves: of which 59 delivered to cowkeepers as in the compotus, and 11 sold as below.

Total of the cattle remaining in the custody of the said G., 4 cows, 46 oxen, 1 bull steer. Afterwards 4 oxen were sold as below.

Money received. Gilbert son of Michael answers for £6 3s. 11d. received from the hides and flesh of dead animals in the forest of Trochdene, Pennehille and Roscyndale and others

Compotus Terrarum Henrici de Lacy

as in the compotus of the said cowkeepers. £57 13s. 6d. for 137 oxen sold: 10s. for 3 oxen sold as above: 24s. for 4 bulls sold as above: £24 9s. 10d. for 72 cows and 11 calves sold as above.

Total received £90 2s. 3d.

Expenses.

	£	s.	d.
Allowance to 2 keeping oxen and 1 keeping cows at Hoddesdene and Akeringtone 48s. 1½d. Their yearly wages 8s.	2	16	1½
Food and wages of 1 helping them at times		5	6
Food and wages of 1 keeping the cows of Croym. in Hegham for 21 weeks in summer and of 1 keeping the yearlings at Standene for 12 weeks in winter		9	3
Removing, and rebuilding there, 1 house for yearlings in Sapedene		5	10
Removing, and rebuilding there, 1 oxhouse at Rughley		19	9½
Building anew one barn at Wynewelle in Trochdene Forest	1	2	1½
Repairing 1 house thrown down by 1 oak there		3	6
Repairing vaccaries in Roscyndale Forest		1	8
Making hedges round meadows at the new hall in Rosendale and Blakay		5	4
Cutting *houcetum* and branches for barren cattle		5	9
Driving away cattle in different places			9
An iron bought for marking cattle			2
Wages of 1 man guarding calves from the Wolf		1	2
Forgiven Matilda del Bothe for one cow taken away by robbers		3	0
Fee of Gilbert the Instaurator yearly	2	0	0
Allowed to the Instaurator of the forrests for marking cattle and for the wages of his clerks		8	0
Due to Gilbert from the last compotus	1	0	8½
Delivered to Simon Noel, who being present acknowledged it	77	18	4
Total of Expences and Delivery	88	6	11½

So Gilbert owes the Lord Earl 35s. 3½d. Afterwards 8s. were allowed to Gilbert paid to Adam de Shippewelbothym which he paid for cutting down and shaping timber taken from the same for the Earls use for building 1 barn at Blakay. So he owes 27s. 3½d. clear.

Comitis Lencolnie.

STANDENE.

Robert de Heppehale, Seneschall, and Thomas, Sergeant there, render their compotus at Ichtenhille, 30 Jan. 1295, before the same and for the same year as above.

	£	s.	d.
Arrears of the last Compotus	14	18	7½
Grenelache meadow sold this year	1	0	0
Meadow sold in various places this year	1	0	0
66 cattle agisted there by the head this year	1	11	6
Wheat sold, 5 bushels		5	5
Oats sold, 70 qr. 6½ bus.	10	17	7½
Foldage there this year	1	13	10
Total of the whole receipt	31	7	0

Expenses.

	£	s.	d.
Cost of one cart for the year with the smith's wages		3	3½
Making 3 hedges for oxen			3
Making anew 2 waggons		2	8
Allowances of 2 carters by the year 40s. 4d., their wages 8s.	2	8	4
Food and wages of one keeping oxen and agisted cattle in summer		10	6
Food and wages of one harrower in seedtime		3	4
Food and wages of one helping the keeper of oxen and agisted cattle in summer		2	6
Roofing houses		1	10
Reaping corn		1	0
Mowing 35½ acres of meadow at Standene and at the new meadow of Cliderhowe		16	0¾
Wages of 109 men reaping corn as if for one day		17	7½
Seed wheat sold 1 qr. 5 bus.		13	9
Thrashing and winnowing 101 qr. 6 bus. of oats		6	3½
Yearly wages of the Sergeant at 1½d. a day	2	5	6
His Robe		6	8
Delivered to Simon Noel, who being present acknowledged it	15	10	0
Total of the whole expences and delivery	24	9	7½

And so he owes the Earl 6l. 17s. 4¾d., of which 70s. 7¾d. are arrears of Ralph son of Lucke for-

142   *Compotus Terrarum Henrici de Lacy*

> merly provost ; and 37s. 1¼d. are arrears of Jordan formerly provost. So Thomas owes 24s. 7¾d. clear.

Grange of Standen.

The same render their accounts of the grange for the harvest of 1295, before the same, as above.

> Wheat : 5 bushels produce and 1 qr. 5 bus. produce of the grange ; total 2 qr. 1 bus. Of which 1 qr. 5 bus. for seed and 5 bus. sold.
> Oats : produce of the grange 121 qr. 6½ bus. ; of which 51 qr. for seed and 70 qr. 6½ bus. sold.
> Oxen : 17 oxen of the remainder. 17 oxen remain.

Halton.

William de Wambwelle, Receiver, renders his Compotus at Haltone 15 Nov. before William de Nony and Thomas de Fisseburne from 30 Sep. 1295 to 30 Sep. 1296.

	£	s.	d.
Arrears of the last compotus	80	9	6
Rent of Haltone, 11 Nov.	5	8	5
Rent of John Boydel for one plot at the kiln			1
Rent of Runcouer upper and lower with 6d. rent of Thomas the parker as in the last compotus Nov. 11 and June 24	7	2	9½
Increase of the rent of Robert dolle for 1 acre of land found by measurement of the 5 acres of land which he bought from Richard the clerk		1	1
Rent of Robert the parker for a plot of waste in Haltone		2	0
Rent of Gilbert the smith for a plot of waste at the forge, this year being the first		1	6
The Earl's oxhouse let, this year being the first		3	0
115 acres 3½ roods and 1 plot in Bondeth and Chyrchefeld, 29 Sept.	5	15	3½
35 acres 3½ roods and 3 plots of land in Haltone wood, let 29 Sept.	1	15	9
Rent of a horse mill, this year, being the first, and next year it shall pay 10s.		5	0
Fishery of Runcouer, 2 Feb. and 29 Sep.	1	0	0
Fishery by a weir, 29 Sep.		1	0

Comitis Lencolnie. 143

	£	s.	d.
Another fishery there this year		1	6
Fishery of Bodeworht		1	0
Rent of Whyteley with *breda*, 11 Nov. and 27 June	5	6	11½
Rent of Thomas de Bartone for the demesnes of Anderbuske, 11 Nov.	1	2	0
Rent of Anderbuske, 11 Nov. and 24 June	1	13	10
10 acres of land which John Segersteyn holds there at the same terms		10	0
Rent of Cronleycroft at the same terms		3	3
3 acres 1 rood of waste let at the same terms		10	0
Rents, 11 Nov., of Northcotes 11s. 11½d.; of Penre 6s. 8d.; of Aldredley 5s.; of Lysenker 13s. 4d.; of Byrcheles 12s.; of Thomas de Makelesfelde in the same 1s.; of Toft 7s.; of Hulle and Walmefelde 3s. 1d.; of Coten 7s. 11d.; of Endesbyre and Pexhille 40s.	5	7	11½
Rent of Gropenhalle, 24 June			4
Rent of divers tenents in Chester, 11 Nov. and 24 June		12	6
1lb. of cummin of the rent of Ranulph de Deresbyre for 1 burgage in Chester, 24 June			¾
Rent of 1 saltwork in Northwic, at the same terms	1	0	0
Rent of the Moor, at the same terms	4	9	0½
1lb. of pepper of the rent of Simon le Buter, 24 June		1	8
1 pair of Gloves of the rent of Felewelle		1	0
Stallage of Felewelle and a fourth part of the fishery of the same, 29 Sep.	5	6	8
Fishery of Lower Waletone, 24 June		2	0
Tenents of Langdendale for keeping the roads toward Chester Markets		3	4
54½ acres of demesne land of Halton, let 29 Sep., deducting tithe and *redecima*	1	13	2
First Total of Receipt with arrears	134	11	8½
1 plot of pasture in the Marsh let to the bonders, this year the first		6	8
Herbage sold in various places		5	0
14 oxen, 15 steers and yearliugs agisted in the park	1	0	2
Pannage of the park nothing			
Produce of 10 cows let, rent deducted	1	10	0
Cattle agisted in Northewode	3	13	2
Old brushwood sold there		19	8
Pannage of Whytteley, deducting tithe and *redecima*		10	3½

Compotus Terrarum Henrici de Lacy

	£	s.	d.
Pannage of the foreign wood before Hultone		9	0
Pannage of Halton and Runcouer, deducting tithe and *redecima*		11	6¼
32 hogs of the pannage of Haltone, Runcouer, Whitteley sold, deducting tithe and *redecima*	3	12	0
Autumnal works, ploughing and streteward	5	0	0
Fines of divers vills for Marketgalt this year		17	5½
Fines and fees of the free Court of Haltone	14	16	0
Reliefs nothing			
Merchat of Margareta daughter of Alan de Haltone and of Margeria daughter of Adam de Cliftone		12	0
Fees of the Halimote of Haltone and fines for entering land	3	8	2
Goods of dead serfs nothing this year.			
Merchat of Margeria daughter of Adam Lenke, of Amabilia daughter of Richard de Whitteley and of Alicia daughter of Richard de la Grene of the same	1	6	8
Fees of the halimote of Whitteley and fines for entering land	1	18	4
Goods of dead serfs nothing this year.			
Tallage of the bondsmen of Haltone		10	0
Tallage of the bondsmen of Runcouer, Upper and Lower	2	13	8
Tallage of the bondsmen of Whitteley who should give tallage every third year	2	13	4
Toll of Haltone Market this year	16	11	6
Toll of beer there		6	9
Rent of Whitteley Mill 11 Nov. and 24 June	1	4	0
Ward of cattle in the fold of Halton Castle		16	0
Sergeantcy of the free Hundred of Haltone this year	21	0	0
Advowsons this year	5	0	0
3 foresters of Norhtwode for the bailiwick of the forestry	2	5	0
Wild honey, nothing this year.			
One foal and 1 filly sold as estrays		8	0
Old hay sold		14	0
Ward of Endesbyre and Pexhille until the heir was of age		17	5½
Fine of Robert son and heir of Robert de Mascy, under age, who was abducted and married by Richard de Mustone, the marriage of which heir belonged to the Earl because he held his tenements in Wale-			

Comitis Lencolnie. 145

	£	s.	d.
ton and Sale by military service of the heir of Ranulph Starky, who was under age and in the Earls ward, and the said Robert de Mascy is of full age. Therefore nothing from the proceeds of the wardship of his lands	8	0	0
Wardship of the land and heir of Ralph Starky in Nettone	3	13	8
Wardship of the land and heir of Thomas de Waletone in Hattone	1	5	0
Wardship of the land and heir of Geoffrey Chedel in Cliftone	6	1	8½
Wardship of the land and heir of Richard de Whittely, and not more because 5 shillings are assigned to the mother for wardship of the heir	1	0	0
Wardship of the land and heir of Hugh de Duttone in Bekewycke 24 June	1	2	1½
Pepper and other things sold in addition to the compotus as below		16	0
Fees of the Halimote of the tenants at the ward of Feltone		5	6
Second total of Receipt	117	13	9½

WYDENESSE.

Rent of Wydenesse Apeltone with *breda* 25 Dec. and 24 June	8	19	1½
Rent of Uptone, 29 Sept.	2	9	0¾
Demesnes there let, 25 Dec. and 24 June	3	10	0
Rent of 2 mills there, at the same terms	1	10	1
Rent of Henry le Waleys for 1 rood of land and one horse mill where before was a hand mill		7	0
From the men of Runcouer for having peats		2	0
The Rent called Sacfe, at the same terms	1	6	1
Repe silver, 29 Sep.		6	8
Rent of Richard de Doningtone, 8 Sep.		2	8
Oxsegalte nothing this year, for it is only every third year, which will be next year.			
Mediety of the goods of Richard de Dentone, serf of the Earl deceased	1	6	8
Fine of Richard son of Richard de Dentone for his fathers land held in Dentone	5	6	8
Fine of Phillip de la Leghe, who married the daughter			

U

Compotus Terrarum Henrici de Lacy

	£	s.	d.
of Roger de Wydnesse, serf of the Earl, for Rogers lands held in Wydenesse	2	13	4
Fine of William son of Dobbe de Uptone for the tenement which John Magge, serf of the Earl, held	2	13	4
Merchat of Amabilla daughter of William de Upton, Margeria daughter of Richard de Dentone, Alicia daughter of William son of Edde, and Margeria daughter of W. de Assebroke		18	0
Fees of the Halimote and small fines	2	12	9
Relief of Richard son of Henry for the mediety of the Mill of Dentone		9	0
Small fines of free men for entering land	1	15	0
Fees of the free Court of Wydeness,	3	5	8
Chevage of 15 men		1	3
Chevage of Ranulph de Wydeness		6	8
Pannage of Wydenesse deducting tithe and redecima		9	0¾
Fine of the forester of Wydenesse for the bailwick of the forest	1	0	0
From Robert Le Noreys for the serjeancy of the free court of Wydeness	3	0	0
Tallage of the bondmen of Wydeness, this year, who give tallage only every third year	13	6	8
Third Total of Receipt	57	16	4½
Nicholas Frodesham for his arrears by 2 tallies which remain with the Receiver	13	7	0
The Provost of Congleton, by 2 tallies	22	3	4
Fourth Total of Receipt	35	10	4
Sum Total of the whole Receipts	345	13	2½

Expenses of the Manor.

	£	s.	d.
Roofing and repairing houses within the Castle and stalls in the market		15	10
2 millstones bought for the horsemill		7	7
Food and wages of 1 carter, and shoeing horses yearly		19	0
Mowing meadows and carrying hay		7	7
Wages and robe of the parker yearly	1	12	8
Expenses of the keepers of the market this year		12	10
6 cows with 6 calves bought	1	19	3
Fee of the Seneschall yearly	6	13	4

Comitis Lencolnie.

	£	s.	d.
Fee and robe of the Constable yearly	7	10	0
Carrying letters to various places		5	4
Expenses of those conducting Tuder ab carwar and his 4 fellows hostages from Haltone to Pontefract	1	6	6
Expenses of Thomas de Fisseburne for his visits and of John de Blakeburne for 1 visit	1	11	0
Given to pleaders and clerks in Cheshire for the Earls business	1	2	0
Paid to the executors of Sir Walthivus Darderne in part payment of £60 in which the Earl is bound to him by his written security for quit claim of the dower of Congleton Manor for which Margeria mother of the said Walthivus sued the Earl as her dower whereof letters of acquittance remain with the receiver	15	0	0
Falling off of the rent of the tenants of the heir of Ranulph de Starky in Stretton this year		8	6
Removing 141½ roods of old paling and planting there 13 roods of new paling and 27 roods of hedge made round the park		12	10
Carrying £163 twice to Pontefract		6	6
Delivered to Oliver de Stanefeld constable of Pontefract as in the compotus	186	10	0
Total of the whole expense and delivery	228	14	0

And so the receiver owes the Earl 117l. 12s. ½d.

Workhorses. The same answers for 2 workhorses of the remainder. 2 male workhorses remain.

Oxen. 1 ox of the remainder, and 1 of addition. 2 oxen remain.

Cows. 8 cows and 1 bull and 2 of addition and 6 bought as above. 16 cows and 1 bull remain.

Steers. 2 yearlings of the remainder. 2 steers (1 male) remain.

Yearlings. 6 calves of the remainder. 6 yearlings remain (5 males.)

Calves. 7 calves born, 6 bought as above, total 13. Of which 1 in tithe. 12 calves remain (7 males.)

Pepper, cummin, gloves, arrows, knives, lances.

The same answers for 2 lances and 12 barbed arrows of the remainder, 1 lb. of pepper, 1 lb. of cummin of the rent of the Prior of Norton in Aston, 1 lb. of pepper of the rent of Chester, 1 lb. of pepper for the rent of Simon le Rotes for a tenement in More.

1 pair of furred gloves of the rent of Thellewelle.

Compotus Terrarum Henrici de Lacy

6 barbed arrows of the rent of Sproscroft.
1 pair of spurs of the rent of Penre.
1 knife of the rent of Aydrop Mylingtone.
1 lance of the rent of the heir of Nicholas de Leycestria.
9 lbs of pepper, 3 lbs of cummin of the aforesaid rent for the three years last past with which the receiver was not charged.
3 pairs of furred gloves, 18 arrows, 3 pairs of spurs, 3 knives, 3 lances of aforesaid rent for the three years last past with which the receiver was not charged. From which he counts 4 pair of gloves, 4 lbs of pepper sold as in this compotus and the three last compoti, and all the rest sold in addition to the compotus.

CONGLETONE.

William de Wambwelle constable of the Castle of Haltone and Alexander Mercer provost render their compotus at Haltone 16 Nov. 1297 before Sir W. de Nony and T. de Fisseburne, namely from 12 Dec. 1294 to 30 Sept. 1295.

	£	s.	d.
Rents there 24 June.	14	5	8¼
Demesnes there let at the same term	1	5	8¼
Rent of the millstone rock let at the same term		10	0
The common oven let		8 6	8
Rent of the mill this year		8 6	8
Toll of the fair and market		6	8
Herbage of the garden 2s; of the flaskes 2s; of various places 2s. 6d.		6	6
Apples sold			11
Fines and fees of the Court		2 8	0
Total of the whole Receipt	26	18	2

Expenses of the Manor and delivery.

	£	s.	d.
Repairing houses			8
Mowing 4 acres of mead, making and carrying the hay		6	2
Delivered to William de Wambewelle as in the Compotus	21	12	0
Allowed the provost for his service		5	0
Falling off of rents this year		6	6
Total of the whole expense and delivery	22	10	5

So the provost owes the Earl, 4l. 7s. 9d.

CONGLETONE.

William de Hesketh Seneschal and Alexander Mercer provost renders his compotus at the place and day and before the same as above namely from 30 Sept. 1295 to 30 Sept. 1296.

	£	s.	d.
Arrears of the compotus as above	4	7	9
Rents of freemen and burgesses there, 11 Nov. and 24 June	28	11	5
Demesnes let, 27¼ acres	2	11	5
Rent of the Rock of Millstones let this year	1	0	0
The Common Oven let this year		8	0
Rent of the Mill this year	8	0	0
Toll of the fair and market		10	0
Herbage and fruit of the garden		3	3
Herbage of flaskes		2	0
Herbage sold from waste lands		1	4
The Dovecot sold		3	4
Fines and fees of the Court	1	5	3
4 acres of meadow of the demesnes let		10	6
Hay of the same meadow from last year sold		17	0
Total of the whole Receipt	48	11	4

Expenses of the Manor and delivery.

	£	s.	d.
Making hedges round the garden			4
Allowed the provost for his service yearly		6	8
Paid Sir Nicholas de Leyburne 24 June which the Earl granted to him for his life by charter and besides the same Sir Nicholas shall have for his life ten pounds from the Manor of Congleton by the same charter to be paid him 11 Nov. and 24 June	5	0	0
Paid Sir Robert brother of the same Sir Nicholas 24 June by the Earls charter in the form aforesaid by the hands of William de Wambewelle	5	0	0
Delivered to William de Wambewelle, who being present acknowledged it	22	3	4
Falling off of rents this year		13	0
Total of the whole expense and delivery	33	3	4

So the provost owes the Earl 15l. 8s.

COMPOTUS OF THE LANDS OF HENRY DE LACY, EARL OF LINCOLN. 33 EDW. I.

HALTONE.

William de Heskeyth, Seneschal, and William de Wambewell, Receiver of Haltone, render their compotus at Haltone 21 Feb. 1307 before Sir William de Nony and Robert de Silkestone namely from 30 Sept. 1304 to 30 Sept. 1305.

	£	s.	d.
Arrears of the last compotus	132	3	8¾
Total of the arrears	132	3	8¾
Rent of Haltone, 11 Nov.	5	13	9
The Earls Oxhouse let		3	0
Rent of Runcoure lower and upper, 11 Nov. and 24 June	7	3	10¼
A plot of waste approved there, this year the first			1
115 acres 3 roods in Bondheth and Chirchfelde	5	15	9
35 acres 3 roods of land in Haltone wood	1	15	9
Thomas the parker for one cottage in Runcoure			6
Rent of 4 Mills, 2 Feb. and 29 Sep.	4	0	0
Fishery of Runcoure	1	0	0
Fishery by nets there. Fishery by Weir, nothing	1		8
A certain fishery between Haltone and Runcoure, this year the first		6	8
Fishery of Budwurthe	1		0
Rent of Whitlay with *breda*, 11 Nov. and 24 June	5	16	11¼
John le Segerstayn for 10 acres of land there, at the said terms		10	0
22 acres 1 rood of land there, at the said terms	1	2	3
5 acres of land there let		5	0
4 plots there approved, this year the first		16	0
Rent of Thomas de Bartone for the demesnes of Andrebusk	1	2	0
Rent of Andrebuske, at the said terms	1	13	0
Increase of the Rent of Roger the smith in the same, this year the first		4	0

Comitis Lencolnie. 151

	£	s.	d.
Rent of Cornleycroft, at the said terms		10	0
Rent of Norhcote, 11 Nov.		11	11½
Rent of Penre, 11 Nov.		6	8
Rent of Aldredelay, at the said terms		5	0
Rent of Lesynker, 11 Nov.		13	4
Rent of Byrchels, at the same terms		12	0
Rent of Thomas de Macklesfelde 12d.; of Endesbyre and Peschille 40s.; of Toftes 7s.; of Hulm 3s. 1d.; of Cottem 7s. 11d.; with said term	2	19	0
Rent of Gropenhale, 24 June			4
Rent of divers tenants in Chester, at the said terms		13	6
1 lb. of cummin of the rent of Ranulph de Deresbyre in the same			1
1 lb. of pepper of the rent of Ranulph le Roler in the same		1	0
A pair of gloves of the rent of Thellewelle, 29 Sep.		1	0
Rent of a certain saltwork in Northwyc, at the said terms	1	0	0
Rent of More, at the said terms	3	13	3½
A plot approved there, this year the first			1
17 head of cattle agisted in the common pasture there		1	5
Stallage and a fourth part of the fishery of Thellewelle	5	6	8
Fishery of Nether Waltone, 24 June		2	0
Tenents of Langdendale for ward of the roads, which they are accustomed to make towards the markets of Chester		3	4
Passage of the boat nothing.			
53¼ acres of the demesnes of Haltone, deducting *redecima*	3	1	3¾
One plot of pasture let to the bondsmen of Halton		6	8
Rent of the water Mill in Whytlay deducting tithe	1	4	0
Second Total of Receipt	60	4	8¾
10 oxen, 6 cows before calving sold	7	10	0
Milk of cows, herbage at the park, herbage in various places, nothing.			
Fines of the townships of Strettone, Comberbache, Coggishil and Aldewyke with the fine of William de Wyrisbanke for cattle agisted in Northwode	2	17	2
155 cattle agisted there by the head		12	11
Old brushwood sold there by cartloads	1	0	6
Balliwick of the forestry there	2	5	0

	£	s.	d.
Thisteltacke of Northwode this year	1	9	10
Thisteltacke of Runcoure, Helton and More		14	9
Haltone and Runcoure for estrays in Astmore		9	0
Autumn works, ploughing [?] and stretewarde	5	13	4
Markethgalt of Haltone		16	9½
Fees of the free Court of Haltone	9	19	0
Merchat of Alice Lille		3	0
Small fines and fees of the Halmote	2	14	8
Fine of Henry de Troforde for entering the land of W. his brother	1	4	0
Chattels of Richard le Mercer, a Fugitive		9	2
Fees of the halmote of Whytlay	1	13	3
Fine of John de Bartone for entering the tenement which the vicar of Budworthe held	2	0	0
Fine of Thomas del Strete for entering 2 acres of land approved from the waste	1	6	8
Ward of cattle in the fold		5	2
A stray ox sold		6	0
Tallage of the bondmen of Haltone		19	2
Tallage of the bondmen of Runcoure	4	8	9
Tallage of the bondmen of Whitlay	4	13	4
Tallage of the bondmen of More		9	6
Wild honey and wax sold		8	9
Toll of Halton Markets	17	0	10
Toll of beer in the said Markets		9	2
Toll of the Markets of St. Katherine		4	9
William Danyel for the serjeantcy of the Hundred of Haltone	23	0	0
Richard Starky for pleadings	7	6	8
Wardship of the land and heir of the lord of Hul super Daneno [?]		10	0
2 workhorses sold and 1 colt		16	6
Third Total of Receipt	103	17	7½

WEDENES.

	£	s.	d.
Rent of Wedenes, Apeltone and Dentone with the *breda* of Apultone 11 Nov. and 24 June	9	3	9¼
Rent of Uptone, 29 Sept.	2	10	0¾
1 cottage and 3 acres of land there		2	0
Demesnes of Wydenes, 25 Dec. and 24 June	3	10	0
Rent of 3 Mills there, at the said terms	1	16	9

Comitis Lencolnie. 153

	£	s.	d.
Alan de More for 1 rood of land and 1 Horse mill		7	0
Serfs of Runcoure for having peat		2	0
Rent called Sakefe, Oxgalt nothing	1	6	1
Repe silure, 29 Sep.		6	8
Rent of Richard de Doningtone, 8 Sept.		2	8
Rent of Richard de Molyneus for 14 acres of land in Baynele		1	2
Alan Wulnet and William de Holforde for ½ acre of land			2
Fine of William de Uptone and his fellows for entering 1 acre of waste approved, this year being the first	1	1	8
Fine of John son of Andrew de Dentone for entering the land which John de Dentone his grandfather held	2	0	0
Merchat of Matilda daughter of William de Uptone		4	0
Fees of the Halmote of Wedenes		6	0	0
Fees of the Free Court of Wedenes		4	9	2
Chevage of Ranulph de Wedenes, 6s. 8d.; of 26 bondmen 2s. 2d.		8	10
Thisteltake of Wedenes		12	0
Sergeantcy of the Free Court of Wedenes		3	0	0
Fine of the Forester of Wedenes for the bailiwick		1	0	0
Tallage of the bondsmen of Wedenes, who give every third year	20	0	0
Alexander provost of Dongletone by one tally	5	10	0
John provost of Congletone by 2 tallies	22	5	0
Nicholas de Frodesham in part payment of his arrears	26	13	4
Three Knight's fees and the 8th part and 40th part of 1 fee in Wydenes for the army of Scotland for 28 Edw. I., 1300		6	6	0
Fourth Total of Receipt	118	18	4
Sum Total of the whole Receipt	415	4	5

Expences.

	£	s.	d.
Repairing and covering houses within the Castle		3	7
Covering the hall of pleas with boards made and nails bought		15	0
Removing a house and rebuilding it next the grange, for steers		4	0
Mowing 16 acres of meadow, spreading the grass, gathering, carrying and stacking the hay		14	10
Forage bought for the Earl's cattle		7	6

X

	£	s.	d.
Pay of one keeping them in winter and cutting down firewood for the Castle and branches for the wild animals		10	8
Mending the park paling in places		6	0
Expences of keeping the Markets		12	3
Redecima of Haltone Mill		4	0
Fee of William de Heskeythe, Seneschall, yearly	6	13	4
Robes of the same	2	10	0
Fee and robes of the Receiver yearly	7	10	0
Fee of the Porter yearly		13	4
Wages and stipends of the parker yearly	1	12	8
Fee of William de Midgelay, counsel, yearly		13	4
First total of Receipt	23	10	6
Carrying letter to various places			8
Bringing money safely three times to Pontefract		5	0
Given to the Friars Preachers of Chester by the Earls letter	1	0	0
Remitted to Richard son of Richard de Dentone for the Earl, for a fine made for entering his fathers land, with which the Receiver was charged in the last compotus		16	0
Paid to the Earl of Lancaster by the hands of Simon de Baldrestene his Receiver of Lancaster for 3 Knights fees in Wedenes for the army of Scotland 24 Edw. I. 1296.	6	0	0
Delivered to Oliver, Receiver of Pontefract, as in the compotus	187	0	0
Delivered to Sir Nicholas de Readinge, Receiver of the household of the Earl, as in the compotus	44	17	2
Second Total of Expence and Delivery	239	17	10
Sum Total of the whole Expence and Delivery	263	9	4

And the Receiver owes the Earl £152 15s. 1d.

Pepper, Cummin, Gloves, Arrows, Lances, Knives, Spurs. The same answers for 2 lbs. of pepper, 2 lbs. of Cummin, 12 arrows, 2 pairs of spurs, 2 knives, 2 lances. 1 lb. of pepper, 1 lb. of cummin, rent of the Prior of Nortone. 1 lb. of pepper, 1 lb. of cummin, rent in Chester. 1 lb. of pepper, rent of Simon le Roter for 24 acres of land in More. 1 pair of furred gloves, rent of Thellewelle. 6 barbed arrows, rent of Spronthescrofte. 1 pair of white spurs, rent of

Comitis Lencolnie. 155

Penre. 1 knife, rent of Endropa de Milington. 1 lance, rent of Roger de Leycestria. From which he counts 1 lb. of pepper, 1 lb. of cummin, 1 pair of furred gloves sold as above. And 4 lbs. of pepper, 3 lbs. of cummin, 18 barbed arrows, 3 pair of white spurs, 3 knives and 3 lances remain.

Workhorses. The same answers for 4 workhorses of the remainder and 1 of addition. Total of Receipt 5 workhorses, of which he counts 2 sold as above. 3 workhorses remain, of which 1 mare with 1 foal of the year.

Foals. Also 1 foal of the remainder in the second year. One male foal in the third year remains.

Foals. Also 1 foal of the remainder, sold as above.

Oxen. Also 12 oxen of the remainder and 5 of addition, total 17 oxen. Of which he counts 10 sold as above, and 7 oxen remain.

Cows. Also 46 cows, 2 bulls of the remainder, and 10 cows 1 bull of addition, total 56 cows 3 bulls. Of which 6 sold as above, and 50 cows, 3 bulls remain.

Steers. Also 20 yearlings of the remainder. 7 steers and 13 heifers remain.

Yearlings. Also 35 calves of the remainder. 35 yearlings remain.

Calves. 12 calves of the year, of which 2 in tithe and redecima. 10 calves remain.

CONGLETON.

William de Heskeythe, Seneschal, and Alexander le Mercer and John de Bradake, provosts of Congletone, render their compotus, at the place and day, before the same and for the same time as above.

	£	s.	d.
Arrears of the last compotus	10	11	0
Rent of free bonders and cottiers at 2 terms	30	9	3¾
26 acres 3 roods of demesne land	1	15	8
The Rock of Millstones let	1	6	8
The Common Oven let		10	0
Rent of the Mill, deducting tithe	8	0	0
Toll of the fair and Markets	1	10	0
The grass and fruit of the garden, and the dove cote, both let		6	8
Vesture of 4 acres of meadow, sold		10	6

	£	s.	d.
The Pasture called Flaskes, sold		2	0
Fees of the Court	1	17	3
Total of the whole Receipt	56	19	0¾

Of which he counts

	£	s.	d.
Allowed the provost for his services		6	8
Paid Sir Nicholas de Leyburne, 11 Nov. and 25 June, for a yearly rent due to him for life by the Earls writ	10	0	0
Paid Sir Robert his brother in the aforesaid form	10	0	0
Expences of six men of Haltoneschyre for making the Bounds of the waste of Congletone		4	9
Delivered to William, Receiver of Haltone, as in the compotus	37	15	0
Total of the whole Expence and delivery	48	6	5

And so they owe the Earl £8s 12. 7¾d.

INSTAURUM OF BLAKEBURNESCHYRE.

Edmund Talbot, Seneschal, and John de Paledene, Instaurator, with the other Instaurators and cowkeepers render their compotus at Ichtenhil 9 May 1306 before Sir Wiliiam de Nony, that is, from 30 Sept. 1304 to 30 Sep. 1305.

TROUDENE.

3s. 11¼d.

John del Bothe renders his compotus of 39 cows and 1 bull of the remainder, and 5 cows of addition; total 44 cows, and 1 bull. Of which he counts 1 bull in murrain, hide and flesh 3s. 11d.; 2 delivered to S. le Geldhirde, and 4 to the Instaurator : 38 cows and 1 bull remain. Also 1 ox of addition, delivered to Henry Hare keeper of the oxen. Also 12 yearlings of the remainder : 6 steers and 6 heifers remain. Also 15 calves of the remainder, of which 1 male in tithe : 14 yearlings (8 males) remain. Also 20 calves of the year : of which 1 in murrain, hide ¼d; 1 delivered to Simon le Geldhirde, and 3 to the Instaurator : 15 calves remain.

Total of the cattle remaining in this vaccary ; 38 cows, 6 steers (of which 1 a young bull), 6 heifers, 14 yearlings (8 males) and 15 calves.

Adam son of Jurdan renders his compotus of 40 cows and 1 bull of the remainder, and 8 cows of addition, and 1 received from

Comitis Lencolnie.   157

the Instaurator; total 49 cows and 1 bull. Of which he counts 2 in murrain, hides 3s. 2d.; 1 delivered to S. le Geldhlrde and 4 to the Instaurator: 42 cows and 1 bull remain. Also 4 oxen of addition, delivered to Henry Hare. Also 13 yearlings of the remainder: 6 steers and 7 heifers remain. Also 14 calves of the remainder; of which 2 males in tithe; 12 yearlings (6 males) remain. Also 15 calves of the year, and 1 received from the Instaurator; total 16: of which 3 in murrain, hides 1d.: 14 calves remain.

3s. 3d.

Total of the cattle remaining in this vaccary: 42 cows, 1 bull, 6 steers, 7 heifers, 12 yearlings (6 males) and 14 calves.

Robert son of John renders his compotus of 33 cows and 1 bull of the remainder, and 1 cow of addition, and 5 received from the Instaurator; total 39 cows and 1 bull, of which he counts 2 cows and 1 bull delivered to the Instaurator; 37 cows remain. Also 10 yearlings of the remainder, of which 1 sold for 2s.; 6 steers, and of them 1 young bull, and 3 heifers remain; of which one in murrain, hide 2d.; and one female in tithe; 11 yearlings (4 males) remain. Also 11 calves of the year, and 5 received from the Instaurator;

2s. 2½d.

total 16, of which 1 in murrain, hide ½d., 15 calves remain.

Total of the cattle remaining in this vaccary: 37 cows 6 steers (and of them one young bull), 3 heifers, 11 yearlings (4 males), and 15 calves.

Juliana de Bothe renders her compotus of 38 cows and 1 bull of the remainder, and 4 of addition, and 2 bulls received from the Instaurator; total 42 cows and 3 bulls. Of which he counts 1 bull and 1 cow in murrain, hides and flesh 8s. 10d.; 5 cows and 1 bull delivered to the Instaurator and 2 to S. le Geldhirde: 34 cows and 1 bull remain. Also 5 oxen of addition, delivered to Henry Hare. Also 9 yearlings of the

8s. 10½d.

remainder; 4 steers and 5 heifers remain. Also 16 calves of the remainder; of which 1 male and 1 female in tithe; 14 yearlings (8 males) remain. Also 21 calves of the year, of which 1 in murrain, hide ½d.; 5 delivered to the Instaurator; 15 calves remain.

Total of the cattle remaining in this vaccary: 34 cows, 1 bull, 4 steers, 5 heifers, 14 yearlings (8 males) and 15 calves.

Ranulphus de Fernyside in place of Godfrey de Lothresdene renders his compotus of 40 cows and 1 bull of the remainder, and 2 of addition, and 3 received from the Instaurator; total 45 cows and 1 bull. Of which he counts 1 in murrain, hide and flesh 2s. 6d.; 2 delivered to S. le Geldhirde, and 4 to the Instaurator: 38 cows and 1 bull remain. Also 4 oxen of addition, delivered to Henry Hare. Also 14 yearlings of the remainder; 6 steers and 8 heifers remain. Also 14 calves of the remainder; of which one male in tithe; 14 yearlings (8 males) remain. Also the same owes 18d. for calves badly kept. Also he answers for 14 calves of the year, and 3 received from the Instaurator; total 17; of which 2 in murrain, hides 1d.: 15 calves remain.

4s.

Total of the cattle remaining in this vaccary; 38 cows, 1 bull, 6 steers, 8 heifers, 13 yearlings (8 males), and 15 calves.

PENHUL.

Richard son of Benedict renders his compotus of 38 cows of the remainder, and 3 of addition, and 7 cows and 1 bull received from the Instaurator; total 48 cows and 1 bull. Of which he counts 5 delivered to S. le Geldhirde; 43 cows and 1 bull remain. Also 2 oxen of addition. delivered to Henry Hare. Also 11 yearlings of the remainder; 5 steers and 6 heifers remain. Also 17 calves of the remainder: of which 2 in murrain, hides 7d.; 1 male and 1 female in tithe: 13 yearlings (9 males) remain. Also 12 calves of the year, and 7 received from the Instaurator; total 19; of which 1 in murrain, hide ½d.: 18 calves remain.

7½d.

Total of the cattle remaining in this vaccary: 43 cows, 1 bull, 5 steers, 6 heifers, 13 yearlings (9 males), and 18 calves.

Robert de Holcombe renders his compotus of 41 cows and 1 bull of the remainder, and 7 of addition, and 7 received from the Instaurator: total 55 cows and 1 bull. Of which he counts 1 in murrain, hide 2s. 2d.; and 4 delivered to S. le Geldhirde, and 2 to the Instaurator; 48 cows and 1 bull remain. Also 6 oxen of addition, delivered to Henry Hare. Also 9 yearlings of the remainder; 4 steers and 5 heifers remain. Also 16 calves of the remainder: of which 1 female in tithe: 15 yearlings (6 males) remain. Also 11 calves of the year, and 7 from the Instaurator; total 18: of which 2 in murrain, hides 1d.: 16 calves remain.

2s. 3d.

Total of the cattle remaining in this vaccary: 48 cows, 1 bull, 4 steers, 5 heifers, 15 yearlings (6 males) and 16 calves.

William son of Hauwysia renders his compotus of 38 cows and 1 bull, and 5 of addition, and 7 received from the Instaurator: total 50 cows and 1 bull. Of which he counts 2 delivered to S. le Geldhird, and 3 to the Instaurator: 45 cows and 1 bull remain. Also 6 oxen of addition, delivered to Henry Hare.

Comitis Lencolnie.

	Also 13 yearlings of the remainder: 7 steers and 6 heifers remain. Also 17 calves of the remainder: of which 2 in murrain, hides 4d.; and 1 male and 1 female in tithe: 13 yearlings (9 males) remain. And the same owes 2s. 6d. for the improvement of the yearlings. Also 14 calves of the year,
2s. 10d.	and 7 received from the Instaurator; total 21 : of which 3 delivered to the Instaurator: 18 calves remain.

Total of the cattle remaining in this vaccary; 45 cows, 1 bull, 7 steers, 6 heifers, 13 yearlings (9 males), and 18 calves.

Adam son of Nicholas in place of Adam de Grangia renders his compotus of 34 cows and 1 bull of the remainder, and 8 of addition, and 3 received from the Instaurator; total 45 cows and 1 bull. Of which he counts 1 in murrain, hide 2s. 2d.; and 2 delivered to the Instaurator: 42 cows and 1 bull remain. Also 3 oxen of addition, delivered to Henry Hare. Also 12 yearlings of the remainder: of which 1 in murrain, hide 11d; 6 steers remain, and of them 1 young bull and 5 heifers. Also 15 calves of the remainder; of which 1 male in tithe: 13 yearlings (6 males) remain. Also 12 calves of the year, and 3 received from the Instaurator; total 15 : of which 3 in murrain, hides ½d.: 12 calves remain.

Total of the cattle remaining in this vaccary: 42 cows, 1 bull, 6 steers (1 young bull), 5 heifers, 14 yearlings (6 males), and 12 calves.

	Robert de Merkelesdene renders his compotus of 46 cows, 1 bull of the remainder, and 2 of addition; total 48 cows and 1 bull. Of which he counts 1 in murrain, hide 2s. 2d.: 2 delivered to S. le Geldhirde, and 3 to the Instaurator; 41 cows and 1 bull. Also 3 oxen of addition, delivered to Henry Hare. Also 13 yearlings of the remainder: of which 1 steer, a young bull, delivered to the Instaurator: 8 steers remain, of them 1 young bull, and 4 heifers. Also 15 calves of the remainder; of which 1 male and 1 female in tithe;
2s. 3d.	13 yearlings (5 males) remain. Also 20 calves of the year; of which 2 in murrain, hides 1d.; and 1 delivered to the Instaurator: 17 calves remain.

Total of the cattle remaining in this vaccary: 41 cows, 1 bull, 8 steers (1 young bull), 4 heifers, 13 yearlings (5 males), and 17 calves.

Henry son of Christiana renders his compotus of 46 cows and 1 bull of the remainder, and 5 of addition, and 3 received from the Instaurator: total 53 cows and 1 bull. Of which he counts 1 in murrain, hide and flesh 2s. 10d. ; and two delivered to S. le Geldhirde: 50 cows and 1 bull remain.

Compotus Terrarum Henrici de Lacy

3s. 4½d.

Also 2 oxen of addition, delivered to Henry Hare. Also 13 yearlings of the remainder : of which 1 in murrain, hide 6d.: 12 yearlings (7 males) remain. Also 13 calves of the remainder: of which 1 male in tithe: 12 yearlings (7 males) remain. Also 13 calves of the year, and 3 received from the Instaurator : total 15 : of which 1 in murrain, hide ½d. : 14 calves remain.

Total of the cattle remaining in this vaccary : 50 cows, 1 bull, 7 steers, 5 heifers, 12 yearlings (4 males), and 14 calves.

Richard de Bradelay in place of Adam son of Peter renders his compotus of 46 cows and 2 bulls of the remainder, and 5 of addition, and 4 received from the Instaurator ; total 55 cows and 2 bulls. Of which he counts 8 delivered to S. le Geldhirde, and 4 cows and 1 bull to the Instaurator : 43 cows and 1 bull remain. Also 1 ox of addition, delivered to Henry Hare. Also 13 yearlings of the remainder : of which 1 in murrain, hide 6d : 7 steers and 5 heifers remain. Also 16 calves of the remainder. Of which one in murrain, hide 4d :

12d.

1 male in tithe : 14 yearlings (7 males) remain. Also 15 calves of the year, and 4 received from the Instaurator ; total 19 : of which 4 in murrain, hide 2d. : 15 calves remain.

Total of the cattle remaining in this vaccary : 43 cows, 1 bull, 7 steers, 5 heifers, 14 yearlings (7 males), and 15 calves. Of which the said Adam answers for 1 calf.

William del Wode in place of William de Penhiltone renders his compotus of 42 cows and 2 bulls of the remainder, and 3 of addition : total 45 cows and 2 bulls. Of which he counts 1 cow in murrain, hide 2s. 2d.; and 8 cows and 1 bull delivered to the Instaurator : 36 cows and 1 bull remain. Also 6 oxen of addition, delivered to Henry Hare. Also 13 yearlings of the remainder, and 1 found on view : 5 steers and 9 heifers remain. Also 15 calves of the remainder : of which 1 male

2s. 3½d.

and 1 female in tithe : 13 yearlings (6 males) remain. Also 31 calves of the year : of which 3 in murrain, hides 1½d.; and 8 delivered to the Instaurator : 20 calves remain.

Total of the cattle remaining in this vaccary : 36 cows, 1 bull, 5 steers, 9 heifers, 13 yearlings (6 males), and 20 calves.

John del Haregreves renders his compotus of 43 cows and 1 bull of the remainder, 7 of addition : total 50 cows and 1 bull. Of which 1 is delivered to S. le Geldhirde, and 5 and 1 bull to the Instaurator : 44 cows and 1 bull remain. Also 6 oxen of addition, delivered to Henry Hare. Also 11 yearlings of the remainder : 5 steers and 6 heifers remain. Also 13 calves of the remainder : of which 2 in murrain, hide 4d.; and 1

Comitis Lencolnie.

5d. male in tithe : 10 calves (5 males) remain. Also 26 calves of the year : of which 2 in murrain, hides 1d.; and 5 delivered to the Instaurator : 19 calves remain.
Total of the cattle remaining in this vaccary: 44 cows, 1 bull, 5 steers, 6 heifers, 10 yearlings (5 males), and 19 calves. Also 1 steer, a young bull, received from the Instaurator.
Adam the baker renders his compotus of 41 cows and 1 bull of the remainder, and 3 of addition, and 2 received from the Instaurator : total 45 cows and 1 bull. Of which he counts 2 delivered to S. le Geldhirde : 44 cows and 1 bull remain. Also 5 oxen of addition, delivered to Henry Hare. Also 10 yearlings of the remainder : 2 steers and 7 heifers remain. Also 14 calves of the remainder: of which 1 in murrain, hide 2d.; and 1 female in tithe : 12 yearlings (5 males) remain.

2s. 2½d. The same owes 2s. for the improvement of the yearlings. Also 14 calves of the year, and 2 received from the Instaurator : total 16 : of which 1 in murrain, hide ½d : 15 calves remain.
Total of the cattle remaining in this vaccary : 34 cows, 1 bull, 5 steers, 8 heifers, 12 yearlings (3 males), and 15 calves.

ROSCINDALE.

William de Dynlay in place of John Cleges renders his compotus of 39 cows and 1 bull of the remainder, and 5 of addition ; total 44 cows and 1 bull. Of which 2 in murrain, hides 4s. 4d.; 1 delivered to S. le Geldhirde, and 9 cows and 1 bull to the Instaurator ; 32 cows remain. Also 2 cows and 1 bull received from the Instaurator. Also 3 oxen of addition, delivered to Henry Hare. Also 14 yearlings of the remainder ; of which 1 strangled by the wolf, hide and flesh 16d.; 5 steers and 8 heifers remain. Also 13 calves of the remainder ; of which 1 strangled by the wolf, hide 4d ; and 1 female in tithe ; 11 yearlings (6 males) remain. Also

6s. 8d. 24 calves of the year, and 2 received from the Instaurator ; of which 4 in murrain, hides 2d ; 2 delivered to the Instaurator ; and 1 sold for 6d.: 15 calves remain.
Total of the cattle remaining in this vaccary : 34 cows, 1 bull, 5 steers, 8 heifers, 11 yearlings (6 males), and 15 calves.
John de Cleges in place of William de Dynlay renders his compotus of 37 cows and 2 bulls of the remainder, and 6 cows and 1 bull of addition. Total 43 cows and 3 bulls. Of which 1 strangled by wolf, hide and flesh, 2s. 2d.; and 4 in

murrain, hides 8s. 8d.; and 1 cow and 1 bull delivered to the Instaurator: 37 cows and 1 bull remain. Also 1 ox of addition, delivered to Henry Hare. Also 12 yearlings of the remainder: of which 1 in murrain, hide 10d.; 6 steers and 5 heifers remain. Also 16 calves of the remainder; of which 4 in murrain, hides 12d.; and 1 male in tithe: 11 yearlings (5 males) remain. Also 21 calves of the year: of which 2 in murrain, hides 1d.; and 1 sold for 12d.: 18 calves remain.

13s. 9d.

Total of the cattle remaining in this vaccary: 37 cows, 2 bulls, 6 steers, 5 heifers, 11 yearlings (5 males), and 18 calves.

Richard de Dunnockschaghe renders his compotus of 44 cows and 2 bulls of the remainder, and 4 of addition: total 48 cows and 2 bulls. Of which he counts 1 in murrain, hide 2s. 2d.; 1 sold for 7s.; 2 delivered to S. le Geldhirde, and 2 to the Instaurator: 42 cows 2 bulls remain. Also 7 oxen of addition, delivered to Henry Hare. Also 12 yearlings of the remainder; and 1 found on view: 8 steers, 4 heifers remain. Also 17 calves of the remainder: of which 1 in murrain, hide 2d.; and 1 female in tithe; 15 yearlings (6 males) remain.

10s. 7d.

Also 20 calves of the year: of which 6 in murrain, hides 3d.; 2 sold for 12d.; 2 delivered to the Instaurator; and 1 in tithe: 9 calves remain.

Total of the cattle remaining in this vaccary; 42 cows, 2 bulls, 8 steers, 4 heifers, 15 yearlings (6 males), and 9 calves.

Henry del Stockes renders his compotus of 31 cows and 1 bull of the remainder, 2 cows and 1 bull of addition, and 2 cows received from the Instaurator: total 43 cows and 2 bulls. Of which he counts 3 in murrain, hides 6s. 6d.; 2 delivered to S. le Geldhirde, and 2 to the Instaurator: 32 cows and 2 bulls remain. Also 6 oxen of addition, delivered to Henry Hare. Also 12 yearlings of the remainder: 8 steers and 4 heifers remain. Also 18 calves of the remainder: of which 1 in murrain, hide 8d.; and 1 male in tithe: 16 yearlings (8 males)

7s. 4½d.

remain. Also 13 calves of the year; and 2 received from the Instaurator: total 16: of which 5 in murrain, hides 2½d.: 11 calves remain.

Total of the cattle remaining in this vaccary: 36 cows, 2 bulls, 8 steers, 4 heifers, 16 yearlings (8 males), and 9 calves.

Alan Franceys in place of William de Cronschaghe renders his compotus of 40 cows and 2 bulls of the remainder, and 4 cows of addition, and 3 received from the Instaurator: total 47 cows and 2 bulls. Of which he counts 3 in murrain, hides and flesh 5s. 10d.; 2 delivered to S. le Geldhirde, and 2 to the Instaurator: 40 cows and 2 bulls remain. Also 4 oxen of

Comitis Lencolnie.

addition, delivered to Henry Hare. Also 10 yearlings of the remainder: of which 3 strangled by the wolf, hides and flesh 2s. 1d.: 3 steers and 4 heifers remain. Also 13 calves of the remainder: of which 2 in murrain, hides 4d.; and 1 male in tithe: 10 yearling (8 males) remain. Also 17 calves of the year; and 3 received from the Instaurator: total 20 calves: of which 3 in murrain, hides 1½d.: 17 calves remain.

8s. 4½d.

Total of the cattle remaining in this vaccary: 40 cows, 2 bulls, 3 steers, 4 heifers, 10 yearlings (7 males), and 17 calves.

Henry de Berdeshul renders his compotus of 44 cows and 1 bull of the remainder, and 5 of addition, and 2 received from the Instaurator: total 51 cows and 1 bull: of which he counts 1 in murrain, hide 12d.; and 9 delivered to S. le Geldbirde: 41 cows and 1 bull remain. Also 4 oxen of addition, delivered to Henry Hare. Also 10 yearlings of the remainder: of which 1 strangled by the wolf, hide 6d.: 4 steers and 5 heifers remain. Also 18 calves of the remainder; of which 1 male and 1 female in tithe; 16 yearlings (8 males) remain. Also 18 calves of the year, and 2 received from the Instaurator: total 20: of which 2 in murrain, hides 1d.; and 2 delivered to S. le Geldhirde: 16 calves remain.

1s. 7d.

Total of the cattle remaining in this vaccary: 41 cows, 1 bull, 4 steers, 5 heifers, 16 yearlings (8 males), and 16 calves.

Thomas del Stockes renders his compotus of 39 cows and 1 bull of the remainder, and 2 of addition: total 41 cows and 1 bull: of which he counts 5 delivered to S. le Geldhirde: 36 cows and 1 bull remain. Also 5 oxen of addition, delivered to Henry Hare. Also 11 yearlings of the remainder; 5 steers and 6 heifers remain. Also 13 calves of the remainder: of which 1 male in tithe: 12 yearlings (6 males) remain. Also 19 calves of the year: of which 3 in murrain, hides 1½d.; and 1 delivered to S. le Geldbird: 15 calves remain.

1½d.

Total of the cattle remaining in this vaccary: 36 cows, 1 bull, 5 steers, 6 heifers, 12 yearlings (6 males), and 15 calves.

Henry de Dynlay renders his compotus of 34 cows and 1 bull of the remainder, and 6 of addition, and 1 cow received from the Instaurator: total 41 cows and 1 bull: of which he counts 1 in murrain, hide 2s. 2d.; and 4 delivered to S. le Geldhirde: 36 cows and 1 bull remain. Also 5 oxen of addition, delivered to Henry Hare. Also 14 yearlings of the remainder: of which 1 strangled, hide 6d.; 6 steers and 7 heifers remain. Also 17 calves of the remainder: of which 2 in murrain, hides 4d.; and 2 females in tithe: 13 yearlings (7 males) remain. Also 16 calves of the year; and 1 received from the Instaurator; of which 3 in murrain, hides 1d.; and 1 delivered to S. le Geldhirde: 13 calves remain.

3s. 5d.

Total of the cattle remaining in this vaccary: 36 cows, 1 bull, 6 steers, 7 heifers, 13 yearlings (7 males), and 13 calves.

William de Cronscaghe in place of Robert de Holme renders his compotus of 35 cows and 2 bulls of the remainder, and 11 of addition, and 4 received from the Instaurator: total 50 cows and 2 bulls. Of which he counts 1 cow in murrain, hide 2s. 2d.: and 6 delivered to S. le Geldhirde; and 1 bull delivered to the Instaurator: 43 cows and 1 bull remain. Also 3 oxen of addition delivered to Henry Hare. Also 12 yearlings of the remainder: of which 1 sold for 12d.; 3 steers and 8 heifers remain. Also 18 calves of the remainder: of which 1 male and 1 female in tithe; 16 yearlings (6 males) remain. Also 17 calves of the year, and 4 received from the Instaurator; total 21: of which 2 in murrain, hides 1d.; 2 delivered to S. le Geldhirde; and 1 sold for 6d.; 16 calves remain.

3s. 9d.

Total of the cattle remaining in this vaccary: 43 cows, 1 bull, 3 steers, 8 heifers, 16 yearlings (6 males), and 16 calves.

Henry de Reved in place of John de Werbertone renders his compotus of 42 cows and 1 bull of the remainder, and 3 cows and 1 bull of addition: total 45 cows and 2 bulls. Also 1 bull received from the Instaurator. Of which he counts 2 in murrain, hides 4s. 4d.; 2 delivered to S. le Geldhirde, and 2 and 1 bull to the Instaurator: 39 cows and 2 bulls remain. Also 7 oxen of addition, delivered to Henry Hare. Also 13 yearlings of the remainder: of which 1 in murrain, hide 10d.; 5 steers and 7 heifers remain. Also 16 calves of the remainder; of which 2 males in tithe: 14 yearlings (5 males) remain. Also 22 calves of the year: of which 3 in murrain, hides 1½d.; 3 delivered to S. le Geldhirde, and 2 to the Instaurator, 15 calves remain.

5s. 3½d.

Total of the cattle remaining in this vaccary: 32 cows, 1 bull, 5 steers, 7 heifers, 14 yearlings (5 males), and 15 calves.

Robert de Couhope renders his compotus of 37 cows and 1 bull of the remainder, and 5 of addition: total 42 cows and 1 bull. Of which he counts 2 in murrain, hides 4s. 4d.; 3 delivered to S. le Geldhirde, and 5 to the Instaurator: 32 cows and 1 bull remain. Also 2 oxen of addition, delivered

Comitis Lencolnie. 165

5s. 2d.	to Henry Hare. Also 12 yearlings of the remainder: 5 steers and 7 heifers remain. Also 15 calves of the remainder; of which 1 male and 1 female in tithe: 13 yearlings (6 males) remain. Also 23 calves of the year: of which 4 in murrain, hides 2d.; 1 delivered to S. le Geldhirde, and 5 to the Instaurator; and 1 sold for 8d.: 12 calves remain.

Total of the cattle remaining in this vaccary: 32 cows, 1 bull, 5 steers, 7 heifers, 13 yearlings (6 males), and 12 calves.

AKERINGTONE.

	Roger de Catlou renders his compotus of 84 cows of the remainder, and of 16 cows and 2 bulls of addition; total 100 cows and 2 bulls. Of which he counts 2 strangled by the wolf, hides 8s. 9d.; 1 cow sold for 7s. 6d.; 4 delivered to S. le Geldhirde, and 31 to the Instaurator: 62 cows and 2 bulls
Also 1 cow.	remain. Also 11 oxen of addition, delivered to William de Bagestondene. Also 19 yearlings of the remainder; 11 steers, and of them 1 young bull, and 8 heifers remain. Also 25 calves of the remainder, and 18 received from S. le Geldhirde; total 43: of which 1 in murrain, hide 1d.; and 5 in tithe: 36 yearlings (13 males) remain. Also 55 calves of the year and 9 received from Simon le Geldhird; total 64: of which 1 strangled by the wolf, hide nothing; 4 in murrain, hides and flesh 6¼d.; 1 sold with the cow; 2 in tithe; and 30 delivered to the Instaurator: 26 calves remain.
16s. 10½d.	

Total of the cattle remaining in this vaccary: 62 cows, 2 bulls, 11 steers (1 young bull), 8 heifers, 36 yearlings (13 males), and 26 calves.

Also 1 cow.	Mokot de Anteley renders his compotus of 42 cows and 1 bull of the remainder, and 11 cows of addition; total 53 cows and 1 bull. Of which he counts 3 in murrain, hides and flesh 11s. 2d.; 3 delivered to S. le Geldhirde, and 1 to the Instaurator; 46 cows and 1 bull remain. Also 3 oxen of addition, delivered to Henry Hare. Also 13 yearlings of the remainder; of which 1 in murrain, hide 6d.; 5 steers and 7 heifers remain. Also 19 calves of the remainder: of which 2 males in tithe: 17 yearlings (4 males) remain. Also 20 calves of the year: of which 2 in murrain; hides 1½d.; 1 delivered to S. le Geldhirde, and 1 to the Instaurator: 16 calves remain.
11s. 9½d.	

Total of the cattle remaining at the vaccary: 46 cows, 1 bull, 5 steers, 7 heifers, 17 yearlings (4 males), and 16 calves.

Elias de Hayleghes renders his compotus of 24 cows and 1 bull of the remainder, and 14 received from the Instaurator: total 38. Of which he counts 3 delivered to S. le Geldhirde: 36 cows and 1 bull remain. Also 22 calves of the remainder: of which 1 in tithe: 21 yearlings (12 males) remain. Also 5 calves of the year, and 14 received from the Instaurator:

½d. total 19: of which 1 in murrain, hide ½d.: 18 calves remain.

Total of the cattle remaining in this vaccary: 36 cows, 1 bull, 21 yearlings (12 males) and 18 calves.

William de Antelay and Henry Hare, keepers of the oxen, render their compotus of 105 oxen and 1 cow of the remainder, and of 105 oxen received from the cowkeepers as above; total 210 oxen, also 5 received from the Instaurator and 1 cow. Of which they count 2 in murrain, hides 19d.; 126 delivered to S. le Geldhirde, and 77 oxen and 1 cow with a calf

19d. delivered to the Instaurator: total 205 oxen and 1 cow.

10 oxen remain in the keeping of Willliam de Antelay.

William de Bakestonden, keeper of the barren cattle of Akeringtone, renders his compotus of 31 oxen of the remainder, and 11 received from the vaccary of Akeringtone as above, and 33 received from S. le Geldhirde: total 75. Of which he counts 26 delivered to Gilbert de la Lieghe, Instaurator; and 44 delivered to John de Pálden, Instaurator: total 70 oxen.

5 oxen remain in the keeping of the said William.

Simon le Geldhirde, *custos cromii*, renders his compotus of 56 oxen of the remainder, and 126 received from Henry Hare as above: total 182. Of which he counts 33 delivered to William de Bakestondene, and 144 delivered to Gilbert, the Instaurator, and 3 delivered to John de Paldene, Instaurator: total 179: and 2 stolen: and he is quit. Also 69 cows of the remainder, and 79 received from the cowkeepers as above: total 148. Of which he counts 6 in murrain, hides 7s. 2d.; 67 delivered to Gilbert the Instaurator; 74 delivered to John de Paldene the Instaurator; and 1 stolen by robbers: And he is quit. Also 18 calves of the remainder, delivered to the cowkeeper

7s. 3d. of Akeringtone as above. Also 1 calf of the year, and 12 received from the cowkeepers as above: of which two in murrain, hides 1d.; 9 delivered to the cowkeeper of Akeringtone as above; and 2 delivered to John de Paldene the Instaurator; and he is quit.

Gilbert de la Lieghe and John de Paldene, Instaurators, by the testimony of the other Instaurators render their compotus of 23 oxen of the remainder; 147 received from Simon le Geldhirde as above; 70 received from William de Bakestondene as above; and 77 received from William de Antelay as above: total 317. Of which he counts 5 delivered to Henry Hare as above; 213 sold as below; and 1 stolen by robbers: 98 oxen remain. Also he answers for 243 cows and 9 bulls received from the cowkeepers as above; and 1 bought as below: of which 70 cows and 5 bulls delivered to the cowkeepers as above; and 168 cows and 5 bulls sold as below: total 238 cows and 10 bulls: and 5 cows remain. Also 1 young bull steer received from Robert de Penhul as above, delivered to John de Haregreves as above; And he is quit. Also 74 calves received from the cowkeepers as above: of which 1 in murrain, hide of no value; 70 delivered to the cowkeepers as above; and 2 sold as below: 1 calf remains.

Total of the cattle remaining in the keeping of John de Paldene: 98 oxen, 5 cows, and 2 calves, and 1 bull found by John de Paldene.

Money.

The same Gilbert and John as above render their compotus of —

	£	s.	d.
Hides and flesh sold above in the compoti of the cowkeepers and keepers of cattle	7	6	3½
213 oxen sold	105	13	2
168 cows, 5 bulls, and 2 calves sold	67	8	4
From Simon Noel, Receiver of Clitheroe, by 1 tally	3	0	0
From Robert son of Adam, Receiver of Clitheroe, by 1 tally	3	0	0
Total of the Receipt	186	7	9½
From which they count allowance of 5 herds keeping oxen, cows, steers, yearlings and calves in Akerington, Hoddesdene and Penhul from Michaelmas to the feast of St. Elena	2	0	0½
Allowance of 3 herds from the feast of St. Elena to Michaelmas		18	4½
Their wages, yearly		9	0
Mending hedges at Blackay and Haselingwurthe		5	6
A summer lodge made at Okenheved		10	11
Repairing vaccaries in the three forests		8	7
Candles bought for the vaccary of Akerigtone and Bakestondene and for gelding calves		1	7
An iron bought for marking calves and skining cattle		1	1
Expenses of the Instaurator for cattle sold in the markets of Boultone		8	6

168   *Compotus Terrarum Henrici de Lacy*

	£	s.	d.
A bull bought		6	8
Allowed the Instaurator for his expenses in marking calves		8	0
Allowed the Instaurator this year by favour for his labours		16	8
Fee of the Instaurators for the year	3	0	0
Wages of his clerk		5	0
First total of expenses	9	19	11
Allowed to the Instaurator as due to him from the Earl in the last compotus		16	2½
Delivered to Robert son of Adam, Receiver of Cliderhow, who being present acknowledged it	173	1	6
Total of the Delivery	173	17	8
Sum Total of the whole Expense and Delivery	183	17	7½

And so 50s. 2d. are due to the Earl.

AKERINGTONE.

Robert de Rylay, Sergeant of Akeringtone, renders his compotus at Ichtenhil 14 May in the above year before the same and for the same time.

	£	s.	d.
Arrears of the last compotus		16	5½
A curtilage next the manor			3
Herbage sold in various places		1	6
Foldage of cattle and 1 old waggon sold			6
An ox sold		9	0
25 qrs. 4½ bus. of oats sold	2	8	7
From Simon Noel, Receiver of Cliderhou, by 1 tally	4	10	0
From Robert son of Adam, Receiver of Cliderhow, by 1 tally	9	10	0
Total of the Receipt	17	16	3½

From which he counts

	£	s.	d.
Cost of a cart in seedtime			8
Making 2 new waggons and mending other waggons		6	8
Allowance of 1 carter in seed time, who is waggoner during the rest of the year		17	11
Food and wages of one driving a cart in seed time, and of a harrower at the same time.		3	3

Comitis Lencolnie.

	£	s.	d.
His wages		7	0
Cleaning meadows			6
Weeding corn			6
Mowing 80 acres 1 rood of meadow	1	6	9
Spreading grass, gathering hay, carrying and stacking both within and without the grange	1	9	7
Mowing and gathering 20 waggon loads of hay within le Rodes.		6	8
Reaping, gathering and binding 12 acres of oats		8	2
Covering and repairing houses		5	0
Cost of the mill, nothing.			
Making a road through the middle of Akeringtone Wood		2	11
Carrying and spreading dung			10
Making and cleaning hedges and ditches in various places	1	0	10½
An Ox bought		11	0
Threshing and winnowing 41½ qrs of oats		3	1
Wages of the Sergeant fourth year	2	6	8
His stipend		6	9
First total of Expence	10	4	8

Also he counts

	£	s.	d.
Cleaning meadows at Bakestondene			4
Mowing 47½ acres of meadow there, spreading the grass, gathering, stacking and carrying the hay	1	7	11
Covering and repairing houses there		1	3
Cleaning 1 ditch and making hedges there		5	2
Cleaning meadows at Hoddesdene			6
Mowing 72 acres of meadow there, spreading the grass, gathering, carrying and stacking the hay	2	4	0
Covering and repairing house		5	0
Cleaning ditches and making hedges there		3	5
Covering and repairing houses at Rilay and cleaning ditches there, and making hedges in places, with a summer lodge made there anew for the yearlings	1	11	9½
Covering and repairing houses at Antelay and cleaning ditches, and making hedges there, with a summer lodge made anew for the yearlings		11	3
Second Total of Expenses	6	10	7½
Sum Total of the whole Expence	16	15	3½

And so the Sergeant owes the Earl 21s.

Grange of Akeringtone.

The same answers for 44 qr. 3½ bus. of oat grown. Of which he counts 15 qr. in seed; 1 qr. in provender of one workhorse in seedtime; 3 qr. in provender of oxen by estimate; and 25 qr. 4½ bus. sold as above. He is quit.

Workhorses. 1 workhorse of the remainder. 1 male workhorse remains.

Oxen. 16 oxen of the remainder, and 1 bought, total 17. Of which he counts 1 sold as above. 16 oxen remain.

Standene.

William de Brunlay, sergeant of Standene, renders his compotus in the same place and day, before the same, and for the same time as above.

	£	s.	d.
Arrears of the last compotus	5	13	7
9 acres of demesne let		7	4
Grenlache meadow sold this year	1	0	0
26 acres of land in Hulcroftes this year	1	1	8
Herbage sold in places		18	0
Cattle agisted in summer and winter	1	1	7
Profits of 31 animals sold and agisted in the pasture	3	8	0
Foldage this year	1	7	2½
Foldage of the animals of the Abbot of Whalley	2	0	0
Foldage of the animals of Hugh de Cliderhou	2	0	0
1 stray foal sold		3	0
Underwood sold under the Manor		8	7
1 workhorse and 5 oxen sold	4	2	0
Hide of 1 workhorse, and hides and flesh of 4 dead oxen		13	8
4 qrs. 5 bus. of wheat, 1 qr. 7 bus. of barley and 2 bus. of beans	2	3	6¼
83 qrs. 7 bus. of oats sold	7	10	4¼
Total of the whole Receipt	34	18	6¼

From which he counts

	£	s.	d.
Cost of 2 carts for the year with the smiths wages		6	8
Harvest work of 14 carts		2	3
Cost of wagons		1	1
Shoeing horses for the year		2	7½
Allowance of 3 carters for the year	3	16	6
Their wages		17	8

Comitis Lencolnie.

	£	s.	d.
Food and wages of 1 harrowing for 13 weeks		5	4
Food and wages of 2 keeping agisted cattle		16	0
Food and wages of one keeping cattle of foldage		8	9½
Weeding corn		2	6
Mowing 48 acres of meadow		14	0
Spreading grass, gathering and stacking hay		8	3
Food and wages of those reaping, gathering and binding corn in autumn	1	19	4½
Covering and repairing houses		5	3
2 forks, 1 pickaxe bought		1	1
Making ditches and hedges		5	6
2 workhorses and 2 oxen bought	2	0	0
7 qr. of wheat, 3 qr. 5 bus. of barley and 167½ qr. of oats threshed and winnowed		13	4¾
Wages of the Serjeant for the year	2	5	6
His stipend		6	8
Delivered to Simon Noel, Receiver of Cliderhou, as in compotus	2	0	0
Delivered to Robert son of Adam, Receiver of Cliderhou by 1 tally	12	0	0
Keeping the oxen and cows of Hugh de Cliderhou seized for divers distraints		12	7

Total of the whole Expences and Delivery 30 12 1¾
And so the Sergeant owes the Earl 4l. 6s. 5d. of which he says he delivered to Robert de Hephale, Seneschall 22s. in 11 qr. of oats, which he seeks to be allowed to him. .Afterwards 5s. 6d. were allowed to him in 4 bus. of wheat and 4 bus. of barley bought.

GRANGE OF STANDENE.

The same answers for 8 qr. 5 bus. of wheat grown, and 4 bus. bought as above; total 9 qr. 1 bus. Of which he counts 4½ qr. in seed, and 4 qr. 5 bus. sold as above. And he is quit.
Barley.
3 qrs. 3 bus. of barley grown, 4 bus. bought; total 3 qrs. 7 bus. Of which 2 qrs. in seed and 1 qr. 7 bus. sold as above.
Beans.
2 bus. of beans grown. All sold as above.
Oats.
1 qr. 2 bus. of oats of the remainder, and 187 qrs. 3½ bus. [grown]; total 189 qr. 6 bus. Of which he counts 94 qrs. in seed, 5½ qrs.

in provender of oxen, and 83 qrs. 7 bus. sold as above. Total expended as above. And he is quit.

Workhorses.

2 workhorses of the remainder, and 2 bought ; total 4. Of which he counts 1 in murrain, hide sold. And 1 sold as above. And 2 male workhorses remain.

Oxen.

27 oxen of the remainder, and 2 bought; total 29. Of which 4 in murrain, hides accounted for above ; and 5 sold as above. And 20 oxen remain.

ICHTENHIL.

John, parker of Ichtenhil, renders his compotus there, 16 May 1306, before Sir William de Nonny, that is, from 30 Sept 1304 to 30 Sept 1305.

	£	s.	d.
1 ox sold		10	0
Hides of 1 ox, 2 mares and 4 foals		5	8
From Simon Noel, Receiver of Cliderhou	4	10	0
From Robert son of Adam, Receiver of Cliderhou	7	0	0
Total of Receipt	12	5	8

From which he counts

	£	s.	d.
Cost of a cart in seedtime			10
2 new wagons made and other costs for them		4	4
Allowance of 2 carters for the year	1	18	0
Stipend of 2 men for a cart and for waggons for the year		6	6
Mowing 66 acres, 3 roods of meadow	1	3	11
Mowing grass in the Forest		1	10
Spreading the said grass, gathering and stacking the hay		15	9
Watching corn		1	6
Reaping, collecting and binding 7 acres of oats		4	11½
Covering and repairing houses		10	1½
Cleaning ditches and making hedges in places		17	3
Mending paling		2	0½
Felling firewood for the Manor		1	8
Catching and folding mares and colts three times, marking foals, and buying halters for them		7	6
Stipend and food of those keeping colts for 19 weeks		8	2

Keeping mares from Cridelinges, and their provender for one month, that is from the time when they

Comitis Lencolnie.

	£	s.	d.
came from Cridelinges until they were put into the park		5	6
Wages of the parker for the year	2	5	6
His robe		13	4
Allowance of the parker's groom for the year		1	7
His stipend		5	0
Wages of Henry le Hallehyne from 11 Nov. to 29 Sept., by the Earl's letter, and so from year to year until the Earl shall order otherwise, taking 5d. a week		19	2
Allowed the parker, due to him from the Earl in addition to his last compotus		4	4
Total of the whole Expense	12	16	2

And so there is due to the parker 10s. 6d.

GRANGE OF ICHTENHIL.

The same as above renders his compotus of 27 qrs. of oats of the year, of which he counts 11 qrs. in seed and 16 qrs. in supporting the mares, foals, and wild animals.

Oxen. The same answers for 21 oxen of the remainder, of which 1 in murrain, the hide is accounted for, and 1 sold as above. 19 oxen remain.

Horses. The same answers for 35 mares of the remainder and 11 of addition and 4 received from the provost of Cridelinges, total 54. Of which he counts 2 in murrain, hides sold, and 6 sold as in the Compotus of Robert son of Adam Receiver of Cliderhou, total 8. And 46 mares remain.

Runcini. The same answers for 1 iron grey stallion received from the Earls stable and 10 Runcini of addition and 7 received from the horsekeeper at Dynebeghe, total 19 Runcini, of which he counts 17 sold as in the compotus of the Receiver as above. 2 stallions remain.

Foals. The same answers for 15 Foals of the remainder, of which 1 in murrain, hide sold. 6 colts and 8 fillies in the third year remain.

Foals. The same answers for 21 Foals of the remainder, of which 4 in murrain, hides sold, and 2 in tithe. 15 foals over a year remain, of which 10 males.

Foals. The same answers for 26 foals of the year, of which 2 sold as in the Receivers compotus. And 24 foals remain.

Compotus Terrarum Henrici de Lacy

Simon Noel, Receiver of Cliderhou, renders his compotus at Ichtenhil 30 Mar. 1305, before the same as above, that is to say from 30 Sept. 1304 to the above-named day.

	£	s.	d.
Arrears of the last compotus	485	10	0¼
Rent of Rachedale, 11 Nov.	14	7	3
Rent of William le Mara, at the same term	1	5	0
Rent of Adam de Prestwyche in Totingtone, at the same term		4	0
Rent of John Banaster in Penwortham, at the same term		2	0
Rent of Adelingtone and Okesbure, at the same term		3	0
Rent of Standisse and Langtre, at the same term		2	0
Rent of Queltone, at the same term			9
Rent of Baldwynhil at the same term, and 2 Feb.	1	0	3
Thanage of Twyseltone, 11 Nov.		10	0
6 oxen bought as below, sold	3	11	6
The Serjeant of Standene by one tally	2	0	0
Total of the Receipt	508	15	9¾

From which he counts

	£	s.	d.
Covering and repairing houses of Colne, and dressing alders for tables and forms		1	9
2 wheels made anew for Brunley Mill		5	0
Part payment of half a mark to the carpenter for repairing Clevachre Mill		2	0
Covering and repairing houses within the Castle		3	9
Mending a brass pot and a pocinet		1	7
Hay bought for the Castle		10	0
Fee of the Seneschal for three quarters of the year	10	0	0
Fee and robe of the Constable for half a year	3	15	0
Wages of the Porter of the Castle for half a year	1	2	9
Paid to the Abbot of Sallay for finding a lamp there for the soul of Earl John		6	8
Wages of the Warrener keeping the woods of Salthul, Dounum and Worchestone for half a year		13	0
Expences of the Instaurator for selling cattle at Ichtenhil		2	10¾
Expences of hearing the compotus before this compotus	4	1	5¼
Wages of two keeping the Marches of the forest of Penhul and Roscindale for half a year	1	6	0

Comitis Lencolnie. 175

	£	s.	d.
Carrying letters to various places		1	6
Taking 400 marks safely to Pontefract at various times	1	1	5½
Carrying a hind to Burton juxta Lincoln by precept of the Earl		2	9
Carrying alms cloth from Pontefract to Cliderhou		1	6
Repairing folds at Brunlay and Rachedale			6
Expences of the Seneschal in holding Courts during the time of the compotus	4	8	0¾
Expences of the Seneschal to Dynebeghe, London and York, at the mandate of the Earl	2	0	0
First total of expences	30	8	7½
6 oxen bought for carriage of the timber of the Wardrobe, and of stone for lime and for sea coal for burning lime	3	14	0
Felling and dressing timber for the Wardrobe, and breaking freestone for it, and breaking stone for lime, and one kiln for burning lime	2	16	0¾
To carpenters as part of their wages for felling timber and making a paling in part for the park of Alvedene and Musdene. The rest is done by Robert son of Adam, Receiver of Cliderhou, as below	22	10	0
Delivered to Robert, Receiver of Cliderhou, by 1 tally	12	0	0
Delivered to Robert de Rylay, provost of Akerington, by 1 tally	4	10	0
Delivered to John, parker of Ichtenhul, by 1 tally	4	10	0
Delivered to Gilbert de la Lyeghe, Instaurator, by 1 tally	3	0	0
Delivered to Oliver de Stanesfend, Receiver of Pontefract, by 1 tally	266	13	4
Delivered to Robert son of Adam, Receiver of Cliderhou, by 3 tallies as appears below	128	13	8
Second total of expences and delivery	437	8	0¾
Sum total of expences and delivery	477	13	8½

And so the Receiver owes the Earl 30l. 1s. 1½d.

Robert son of Adam, Receiver of Cliderhou, renders his Compotus in the same place and day and before the same as above, that is, from 30 Mar. 1305 to 29 Sep. 1305.

COLNE.

	£	s.	d.
Rent of Colne with its members, and works rented, 1 Sep.	22	13	7½
10½ acres of land approved there, this year being the first		3	6
Rent of the Mill of Colne and Walfredene, deducting tithe	11	2	0
Rent of the fulling mill there	1	4	0
Fines for entering on lands there	4	6	10
Fees of the Court there	2	1	8
Merchet of 5 women		4	6
For Leirwite there, nothing			
Thisteltakes this year		1	0
Impounding cattle in Troudene	1	11	0
Sea coal there		16	0
Winter herbage there		19	2
Summer herbage there		15	2
Hay sold there		3	11
2 yearlings and 1 hog, estrays		7	8
First total of Receipts	46	10	0½

HASELINGDENE.

	£	s.	d.
Rents there, 1 Sept., with the addition made in the preceding year	4	6	8¼
3 acres approved, this year being the first		1	0
Rent of the Mill there		13	4
Winter herbage in Roscindale	3	7	8
Summer herbage there	5	5	10
Herbage of Derplaghe	1	0	0
Herbage of Primerolsykes		1	8
Hay sold there	1	6	5
Ore, nothing			
Second total of Receipts	16	0	7½

TOTINGTON.

	£	s.	d.
Rent there, Whitsuntide. The rest by S. Noel	14	8	11
60 acres 3 roods of land approved there, this year being the first	1	0	3
Rent of Richard de Radecleve for 20 acres of land by the Earl's charter		3	0
His rent for 2½ acres of land at the will of the Earl			10

	£	s.	d.
Rent of Henry de Bury for the land at Schuttleswurthe		1	0
1 lb. of cummin from Geoffrey de Chadertone for Shillingbotham			1½
Rent of the Mills at Totingtone, deducting tithe	3	6	8
Stallage there		6	8
Herbage of Couhope this year		14	0
Herbage of Aldene, Musdene and Ugdene, and not more on account of the park there newly made	3	6	10
Herbage of the forest of Totingtone		17	8
Pannage there		16	3
Old firewood sold there		1	0
Firewood sold for 1 forge for 16 weeks	1	16	8
Fines for entering on lands at Totingtone	4	7	10
Fees of the Court there	6	5	4
Impounding cattle there		6	6
A stray yearling there		2	0
Scutage of 2¼ knights fees in Totingtone for the army of Scotland of the year 1300	4	10	0
Third total of Receipts	42	11	6¼

RACHEDALE.

	£	s.	d.
Eighth part of the Mill of Rachedale		5	0
3 acres 1 rood of land approved, this year being the first		1	1
Rent of the heir of Adam de Balschaghe for the Beadelry	1	6	8
Toll of the fair and market, and stallage there	2	13	4
Fines for entering on lands there	1	7	10
Fees of the Court there	4	12	0
Fourth total of Receipts	10	5	11

ROMMESGREVE.

	£	s.	d.
Winter and summer herbage there	1	13	4
Old firewood sold there		7	6
Rent of Wurchestone, 1 Sept.	4	6	1½

HODDESDENE.

	£	s.	d.
Half an acre of land approved, this year being the first			8
Rent of Adam son of Wyot for 2 collars			2
Domain there let	2	6	9½

A A

Wurchestone.

	£	s.	d.
Rent of the Mill there, deducting tithe	1	1	7½
Fines for entering on lands there	2	18	2
Fees of the Court there	1	0	0

Penhiltone.

	£	s.	d.
Impounding cattle there		3	0
Rent of Penhiltone with the addition of last year	6	4	3
1 plot of waste approved, this year being the first			2

Ichtenhil.

	£	s.	d.
The heir of Henry de Blakeburne for 80 acres of land			1
Fines for entering on lands there		17	11
Fees of the Halmote there		18	8
Merchets of 2 women		1	6
Leyrwite of one woman		1	0
Impounding cattle there		5	6
Rent of Ichtenhil, 1 Sept.	2	13	4
Fines for entering on lands there	14	6	10
Fees of the halmote there	3	16	0
Merchet of two women		3	6
Leyrwite nothing			
Thisteltackes there		2	6
Impounding cattle there	5	6	10
Winter herbage in Penhil	5	13	2
Summer herbage there	6	2	10
Hay sold there		16	8
Old firewood sold there for timber and fuel	1	0	2
Old firewood sold there for ashes		7	4
Stone sold there for roofing houses		1	6
9 ashtrees sold		5	6
3 fillies, 1 colt and 1 mare, estrays		8	0
Fifth total of Receipts	63	10	7½

Habringham.

	£	s.	d.
Rent of Habringham, 1 Sept.	4	14	10
3 acres of land approved, this year being the first		1	0

Padingham.

	£	s.	d.
Rent of Padyham, 1 Sept.	11	1	0
Rent of the Mill there, deducting tithe	4	13	0
Works remitted there		6	8

Comitis Lencolnie.

BRUNLAY.

	£	s.	d.
Rent of Brunlay, 1 Sept.	13	10	1½
Works remitted there		3	4
Rent of the Mill there, deducting tithe	9	8	5
Rent of the Fulling Mill there	1	4	0

BRERECLEVE.

	£	s.	d.
A Measure hired there			10
Rent of Brerecleve, 1 Sept.	5	9	10½
3 roods of land approved, this year being the first			3

LITTLE MERCLESDENE.

	£	s.	d.
Rent of Little Merclesdene, 1 Sept.	4	4	4½
Works remitted there		1	1

CHIRCHE.

	£	s.	d.
Rent of Chirche, 1 Sep.		6	0
Rent of Adam de Simondstone		1	5½
Rent of John de Blakeburne for 28¼ acres in Berdeswurthgrave		14	3
Rent of the same for 5 acres of land found there, and it is ordered that his land shall be measured		2	6
Rent of Burdeswurthe and Ullesbothe		5	6
Rent of Hugh de Cliderhou for land in Salesbury, formerly Thomas de Hiltone's, which Hugh holds in Thanage		13	4
And be it known that the heir of Hugh is to pay 40s. relief for this tenement. And for that formerly John de Salebyry's in others 40s. And also for that formerly held there by John son of Gilbert 40s., when the time of relief shall occur			
From the rent of Adam le Tasker, 11s., for the tenement formerly held by Master Henry de Clayton in Salebyry, nothing, for it was returned to the same Henry by the Earl	0	0	0
Rent of Richard de Tyndyhevede which he used to pay Thomas de Hiltone in Salebyry			1
Sixth total of receipt	57	2	0

PENWURTHAM.

	£	s.	d.
Rent of the assarts and cottars there, for the same terme	2	4	8

Compotus Terrarum Henrici de Lacy

	£	s.	d.
Rent of Adam Ploket for 40 acres there, 29 Sept.	1	0	0
The same for a toft, and half an acre of land, at the Earls will		3	0
The Demesne meadows, and the fishery let, Next year they shall pay 14 marks	8	13	4
A plot between the Priory and Le Moteballe, at will			1
Herbage of Middleford		15	0
Pannage nothing			
Rent of Blacshaghe		6	8
Increase of the same by the Earls charters, this year being the first		19	9
Ward of Lancaster Castle		8	5¼
Fishery of Northmeles	1	6	8
Robert de Northmeles		8	1½
Rent of Galewey landes		1	0
Rent of Henry de Whalley for ¼lb. of pepper			6
Rent of Robert de Eukestone for a tenement in the same			1
Rent of Northmeles		2	0
Rent called Sakepe		18	1½
Rent of William de Mara at Whitsunday	1	5	0
Rent of the tenement formerly belonging to John David atte Halgh		16	0
Thomas de Leyland for the beadelry of Penwortham	1	10	0
Peats sold there		4	0
Fines for entering lands		15	4
Fees of Court there	7	14	4
Custody of the land and heir of Richard de Stokeport, for Birkedale		7	8
Scutage of 2¼ knights fees in Penwortham, for the army of Scotland, for 28 Edw. I., 1300	5	0	0
Seventh Total of Receipt	36	4	9¼

DOUNUM.

	£	s.	d.
Rent of Dounum, 1 Sept. And not more, For 6d. of the rent of Master Henry de Dounum are released to him by the Earl's precept	8	13	0½
Rent of an assart there, 1 Sept.		4	0
Demesne there let	3	13	4
Pasture of Grenhou, and a curtilage there, this year being the first			10
Rent of the Mill there, deducting tithe	2	14	0

Comitis Lencolnie.

	£	s.	d.
Rent of Alexander de Keuerdale		10	0
Rent of Master Henry de Claytone			1
Rent of Walter de Wadingtone		1	0
A pair of gloves of the rent of Richard the Clerk			1½
Fines for entering land there		3 7	0
Fees of the Halmote there	1	11	6
Impoundments of cattle			6
Peat sold there		5	0
Eighth Total of Receipt	21	0	5

AKERIGTONE.

	£	s.	d.
Rent of 60 acres, 1 rood of land there	1	14	11
A plot called Pesecroftes		7	0
Increase from land found there		13	4¼
Rent of the Hall, Grange, and Kitchen, let		4	0
2 acres of land at Akeringtone, let		1	6
Arable land at Antelay let	1	3	3¾
Rent of the Mill there, deducting tithe	1	16	0
Rent of 6 acres 1 rood in Dunschopfal		3	1½
Winter and summer herbage at Akerington	1	4	2
Herbage of Brocholhirstes		6	8
Fines for entering lands there		13	6
Fees of the Halmote there		16	4
Impoundments of cattle there		11	6
12 Ashtrees there		15	0

HODDESDENE.

	£	s.	d.
Cattle agisted in Hoddesdene		6	11

HUNCOTES.

	£	s.	d.
Rent of Huncotes, 1 Sept.	5	0	11

CLIVACHRE.

	£	s.	d.
Rent of tenents, by Charter, in Clivachre	6	17	9
Rent of assarts and cottars there	4	8	7
Rent of Oliver de Stanesfend for 8 acres of land there, and for 12 acres of land in Brunley			6
½lb. of pepper of the rent of Adam son of Matthew de Ormerode			6
2 pairs of gloves and 1 pair of spurs of the rent of Matthew de Berecroftes, John son of Matthew and Adam Smith			5

Compotus Terrarum Henrici de Lacy

	£	s.	d.
Rent of the Mill there, deducting tithe	2	14	0
Cattle agisted in the common pasture there		6	2
Iron ore sold for 10 weeks		6	8
Ninth Total of Receipt	30	2	9¾

CLIDERHOU.

	£	s.	d.
Rent of the Thayns, 1 Sept.	8	10	6
Galfridus de Simonstons for remission of Suit of Court		3	4
Rent of Dyote le Arousmythe and Dinaria his sister for a cottage for life			4
William son of Henry for 2½ acres under Baldwynhil		2	6
A plot under the Hall of Pleas			6
A Herbage of the Castle ditches		2	0
A plot for a forge under the Castle, this year being the first		1	0
Herbage of the garden		6	0
Fruit of the garden, this year		3	4
Entry of 5 prisoners at the Castle gate		1	8
Rent of the Burgesses of Cliderhou, 1 Sept.	6	13	4
Toll of the fair and Market, and stallage	7	6	8
Rent of the Mill, deducting tithe	12	0	0
Rent of John le Arblaster		2	0
Rent of Sandwele and Saltwele		5	0
Rent of David Scoles		6	0
Rent of Thomas le Sureys for the attachment of the pond		4	0
Rent of the demesne lands under Salthul	1	5	8½
Fines for entering lands	6	10	0
Fine of Robert de Holdene for many transgressions of which he was convicted before the Earl	20	0	0
Fine of Nicholas de Holdene his son for a transgression done in the forest against the hunting of the Earl	3	6	8
Fine of Henry Banastre for the same	2	0	0
Fine of Raldulfus de Levesay for the same		3	4
Fees of Cliderhou Court	27	7	9
Chattels of William Hoome, a fugitive	2	11	2
Relief of the heir of Alice de Simondstane for a tenement in the same	1	0	0
Relief of the heir of Henry de Couhope for a tenement in Clivachre		3	3½
Relief of the heir of Peter de Dounum			4

Comitis Lencolnie.

	£	s.	d.
Impoundments of free cattle for escapes in the forests	1	18	0
Adam de Cloghe for the sergeantcy of the free court	3	0	0
Ward of Lancaster Castle	1	11	5
Rent of the Wapentake of Stayncleve	21	6	8
Two parts of a certain tenement in Snelleshou		14	6
Produce of two parts of the land formerly belonging to Adam de Ristone	5	4	7
Rent of Schypen Mill		6	8
White of 29 vaccaries let	87	0	0
From Gilbert de La Leigh and John de Paldene, Instaurators, as in compotus	173	1	6
9 Runcini sold from Ichtenhil	47	3	4
6 Mares sold	6	11	0
8 Runcini of Wales sold	30	4	0
7 cart loads and 36 stone of lead sold	18	18	0
Tenth Total of Receipt	497	19	9
From Simon de Noel, Receiver of Cliderhou, as in his compotus	128	13	8
Scutage of Blakeburneschyre, in part, for the army of Scotland 28 Edw. I., 1300. The remainder will be accounted for in the following compotus	7	13	1
Scutage of Bouland, in part, for the same army. The remainder will be accounted for in the following compotus. The particulars appear in a schedule appended to this	1	19	6
From the sergeant of Standene as in the compotus	12	0	0
From Thomas, Receiver of Dynbeghe by one tally	66	13	4
From the Abbot and Convent of Whalleye for a debt which they owed to the Earl for a Credit given to them by Sir W. de Nony by a bond	85	0	0
From Edmund Talbot, which he had from the Earl as a loan, by the hands of Sir Nicholas de Redinges, Receiver of Household of the Earl, as appears in his compotus	13	6	8
18 oxen sold	8	9	3
Eleventh Total	323	15	6
Sum Total of the whole Receipt	1146	6	6

Also 12l. received from Simon Noel, as in the Compotus.

Expences. From which he counts

	£	s.	d.
Mowing 6 acres of meadow, spreading the grass, gathering, carrying and stacking the hay		5	11
Repairing the head of the Pond of Colne		13	0½
Repairing Mills throughout the country. The remaining repairs are made by the farmers of the Mills		12	11
Covering and repairing houses within the Castle	1	6	4
Repairing the Hall of Penwortham		2	0
Fee of the Seneschal in part. The rest received by Simon Noel, as in the Compotus above	3	6	8
Fee and robe of the Constable for the time of the Compotus	3	15	0
Wages of the Porter of the Castle for the said time	1	1	11½
Making folds for the Master Forester, and cutting down branches for the wild animals		17	8
Expences of the Seneschal and others holding courts, in part	6	2	2¼
Expences of the Seneschal, Instaurator and others for selling foals	1	2	6¼
Expences of Sir William de Norry and Henry de Scrope at Ichtenhil, during four days, for divers affairs of the Earl	3	10	10¼
Wages of the Warrener keeping the wood of Salthil for the time of the Compotus		12	3
Expences of the Instaurator at divers markets, selling stock		6	11
Paid to Walter de Wadington for a yearly rent due to him			6
Paid for Ward of Lancaster Castle	2	10	0
Paid to William de Cathertone for a yearly rent due to him for life from the Manor of Dounum, by the Earls writing	5	0	0
Loss of the rent of Robert de Ormerode for one bovate of land in Clivachre granted to him, by the Earls charter, for life		5	11
Loss of the rent of William de Penhiltone, which he used to pay yearly for 33 acres of land in Habringham, which the Earl released to him for life		11	4
Loss of the rent in Totingtone of one plot of land surrendered to the Prior of Brettone as his right. In future to be effaced from the compotus		5	9½

Comitis Lencolnie.

	£	s.	d.
Loss of the rent of 7 acres of land, which Isabella de Gouildforde held. In future to be effaced from the Compotus of the rents of Ightenhill			10
Loss of rents this year. The particulars appear in a compotus appended to this roll	1	6	5
Canvass and parchment bought for the Compotus and for the Court		4	0
Expences of 4 stallions and one horse, coming from the Earl's Household, remaining at Standen and Ightenhill for a year, with provender, bran, shoeing, farriery, and other things bought for the same, with the wages of the grooms keeping them from the said time, and their stipends	10	2	9¾
Allowed the vaccaries of Rossendale, Penhul and Trawden for young cows, wanting in the vaccaries	1	1	0
First Total	£46	4	1¼

The same counts

	£	s.	d.
Carrying letters to various places		2	4
Expences of the Receiver and others taking money five times to Pontefract	2	3	2
Wages of those keeping the Marches of the Forest of Penhul and Rossendale for five weeks. The rest by Simon Noel		5	0
Salt bought for salting the game, also taking the game		7	9
Carrying 3½ stags and 12 does to Pontefract		7	8
Carrying 7 loads of lead from Baxenden to Bradford		12	2
Carrying a net to Merlande, getting cloth for the poor at Pontefract, and carrying barrels to Altofts		4	7
Expences of 16 hawks at Clitheroe, and of grooms carrying them to London, with cocks bought for them	1	0	5¼
Carrying the Earl's bed to Denbigh		1	8
Making and planting nine hundred, five score and six perches of paling round Musbirry park, with the carriage of the said paling in part from Tottington wood. The rest was done by Simon Noel, as appears in his compotus [page 175]	60	10	5¼
18 oxen bought for the carriage of the paling	8	17	9
Given by the Earl to William le Wainwright and Richard de Helay makers of the paling of Musbirry park, and specially to them, because they worked better and more than the others	1	0	0
Second Total	£75	12	11¾

Compotus Terrarum Henrici de Lacy

The same counts

	£	s.	d.
Delivered to John, Parker of Ightenhill, as in compotus [page 172]	7	0	0
Delivered to the bailiff of Accrington, as in the compotus [page 168]	9	10	0
Delivered to John de Paldene, Stock-Keeper, as in compotus [page 167]	3	0	0
Delivered to Sir Nicholas de Redinges, Receiver of the Earl's Household, as in compotus	35	6	0
Delivered to Oliver, Receiver of Pontefract, as in compotus	732	5	2
Delivered to the same Oliver in lead, as in his compotus [page 183]	18	18	0
Total of Delivery	£805	19	2

Ore. The same counts

	£	s.	d.
91 loads, 6¼ dishes of Ore bought from the miners, 9 dishes make a load, price per load 22d.	8	8	1½
9½ fothers, 7 pieces, 1 stone of lead bought from the same. Of which 6 stone make a piece, and 25 pieces make a fother.	13	13	3
Cutting down and cutting up wood for burning the said Ore		7	5
Carrying the said wood and Ore to le Boole (the Bole)		8	8½
Expenses of burning the said Ore	1	16	6
Making a pair of bellows anew for burning the said Ore		7	8
Making and binding with iron a pair of scales for weighing the lead, and making other necessary utensils		2	6
Making a shed for the lead, and an enclosure for Ore		5	8
Given by the Earl to the miners for making a certain trench underground to draw off the water from the other trenches		13	4
Given to the miners by the Earl		10	0
Wages of Hugh le Welmaker for 24 weeks, besides Ore	1	10	0
Wages of Elyas de Assenhirste, besides the miners, for 42 weeks	2	2	0
Total expenses for Ore	£30	7	2

Comitis Lencolnie.

Sum total of the whole expence and delivery   £958 3 5

And so the Receiver owes the Earl 200l. 2s. 7d., of which 25 Marks are of the fine of Robert de Holedene, with which fine the Receiver is charged above [page 182], and a respite has been granted by the Earl of paying five Marks a year until they are fully paid up.

                                                        £ s. d.

COLNE.

	£	s.	d.
Loss of the rent of Robert son of Gamele for one oxgang of land in Great Marsden		1	0
Loss of the rent of one plot in the same which Richard Sharl held			3

BURNLEY.

	£	s.	d.
Loss of the rent of Adam Caboun		13	0
Loss of the rent of six acres of land, which J. de Leicroft held		2	0

BRERECLIVE.

	£	s.	d.
Loss of the rent of Richard de Wyndhil		18	0

LITTLE MARSDEN.

	£	s.	d.
Loss of the rent of 1 toft, and ½ acre of land, which Galfridus son of Thomas held			9
Loss of the rent of 1 toft, which William Swetemilke held			6
Loss of the rent of 4 acres of land there, which is shown in the payment		1	4

ROCHDALE.

	£	s.	d.
Loss of the rent of one Burgage, which William Galle held		1	0
Loss of the rent of Adam Marchaunt			6

NOTES AND CORRECTIONS.

pp. 5, 120. Alveden (Holden), Musden and Ugden, formed part of the Park of Musbirry. See *posted*, pp. 101, 177; a note below; and *Whalley*, vol. i. p. 316. Couoppe is now Coupe.

pp. 5–7; 120–1, &c. *Hucetum*, or *houcetum*. From the French. It here seems to mean bedding made of dry leaves.

pp. 7, 121. *Ramsgreave*. An indenture of agreement between Henry, Duke of Lancaster, and the Abbot of Whalley, 1361, refers to certain tenements called Rommesgreve in the Duke's Chase near Blackburn. (35*th Rept.*, p. 38; 32*nd Rept.*, p. 343.)

pp. 7, 121. *Collars*. These were greyhounds' or harriers' collars, payable at the feast of St. Oswald. (See the *Inquis.*, p. 6, and *Whalley*, vol. ii. p. 115.)

pp. 7, 121, &c. *Letherwyte* or *Lairwite* was the mulct levied by lords of manors for breaches of the seventh commandment.

pp. 8, 121, &c. *Thistletack*. This was a payment exacted by the lord for depasturing drove beasts upon his commons; or fines for strayed beasts. "It was a custom within the manor of Halton," says Cowell, "that if in driving beasts over the Common, the Driver permits them to graze or *take* but a *thistle*, he shall pay a half-penny a Beast to the Lord of the Fee." (See *Whalley*, vol. ii. p. 306.)

The Inquisition of 1311 describes the Hallmote of Ightenhill with this "perquisite" worth yearly 40*s*.

pp. 9, 122, &c. *Ward* of Lancaster Castle. These payments are connected with the tenure of the Earl's lands in Lancashire. Besides the service of knights' fees, he owed a rent of 105*s*. 8*d*. payable yearly to the *Castle guard* of Lancaster. (*Inquis.*, p. 4.) A *ward-penny* is money contributed to watch and ward: Denarii vicecomiti vel aliis castellanis persoluti ob castrorum præsidium vel excubias agendas. (Cowell.)

pp. 10, 122, &c. *Sac fee*. This old tenure was a part of the Earl's service for his Lancashire lands. (*Inquis.*, p. 4.)

pp. 10, 122. The Earl claimed *wreck of the sea* in his manor of Penwortham in Leylandshire, in North Meols, and Widnes in Derbyshire (*i.e.*, West Derby).

pp. 10, 123. *Richard de Stockport*. The heir of Rd. de S., who died 1292, was his daughter Joan, who afterwards married Sir Nich. de Eton. (Watson's *Earls of Warren*, vol. ii. pp. 233, 244.)

pp. 13, 124. *The Castle Ditches*. The Earl, according to the *Inquis.*, died seised of Clitheroe Castle, with the moat and ditches.

pp. 14, 125, &c. *Instaurator*. The bailiff of the vaccary. (*Cf.* Watson's *Halifax*, p. 240.)

pp. 14, 125. *Peter of Chester*. He was the last Rector of Whalley, and held that post from 1235 to 1294. He was also Rector of Slaidburn. His other preferments will be found in *Whalley*, vol. i. pp. 80–1, where the reference to Sir Peter Leycester in note 1 should be altered to p. 272. The authorities believe that he was "a natural son of Lacy." The Abbot of Whalley mentioned elsewhere was Gregory de North-bury.

pp. 15, 125, &c. The *Abbot of Salley* Abbey, in the county of York, was Hugh, who ruled 1278-1303. The Lacy family were benefactors to the Abbey. John de Lacy, son of "Hell" Lacy, gave them 70 acres of land in 1223, according to an agreement made with the monks when he was in those parts. (Harland's *Salley*, pp. 17, 45.)

pp. 15, 126. *Bolton fair* was at Bolton-le-Moors, a manor of the Earl of Lancaster. *St. Giles's fair* was the great fair at Pontefract, which began on St. Giles's day and lasted eight days. St. Giles was a favourite saint of the Lacies, and his anniversary was their rent-day.

pp. 16, 126. *Buckby.* In Northamptonshire, near Daventry. On 2 November, 1280, the Earl, who had a manor-house there, obtained a grant of a market and two fairs. The Yorkshire *Compotus* enters a large payment for Nony's expenses in carrying money to the Earl up to Buckby.

pp. 18, 127, &c. *Hegham* (now Higham) is another name for Ightenhill.

p. 18, line 15. *Marchancia.* This word is translated *selling* at page 128. It occurs again at p. 114, line 9 from foot, where Mr. Lyons's proof rendered it physic (p. 185)· The word which is probably intended, as Mr. Chancellor Christie suggests, is *Mareschalcia*, derived from the French *Maréchal;* and *ferratura Mareschalcia* (p. 114) would thus indicate the work of the farrier both as smith and surgeon. There are two words in Du Cange, *Marchagium* and *Marescalcia*, connected with the right of lords to provender; but in the present case the services are purchased.

pp. 19, 128, &c. *Horses.* The *jumenta* are not strictly mares, but beasts of labour, pack-horses.—The *Runcini* are the common draught horses. This word is formed from the *rous* or *roux* of the Romance language, and may mean ponies or cart-horses, *i.e.*, horses of inferior quality. The Italian is *roncius*, a nag. The Spanish form is *rosin;* whence the name of Don Quixotte's horse. From pages 95, 173; 112, 183, it seems as if these Welsh ponies were introduced by the Earl from his lordship of Denbigh.

pp. 19, 128. *Wm. de Stopham* often attests the Earl's charters, as in the following (Raines *MSS.*, vol. xiv. p. 53): Henry de Lascy count de linc' and const. cestr. sciat me relax' &c. les frankie hom'es de la suite de n're curte de Cliderhow &c. tesmogneo sires Will' de Bottiler, Rob. Banester, Will' le vavasoure, Johan de hodlestan, Iacob de neville . . . Waterbeck Will' de Stopham, Rob. de Lathum, Wanklin de Arderne, Ada' de hodlestan et Rob. de herford ch'rs. (This Deed penes Dom. Barcroft de Barcroft A° 1659.) This and the other Raines extracts are taken from *Harl. MS.* 2074, containing several Lacy deeds.

pp. 25, 130, &c. *Robbers.* The writ of Trailbâton, issued 6 April, 1305, directed Sheriffs to be more active against murderers, incendiaries, and thieves. The judges appointed for Lancashire, Yorkshire, and eight other counties, were Wm. le Vavasour, Adam de Middleton, and three more. (*Rot. Parl.*, p. 218.)

pp. 41-2, 141-2. *Standen.* (*Cf. Whalley*, vol. i. p. 101.)

pp. 44, 146, &c. The tenure by a service called *breda* or *le brede*, was peculiar to Whitley and Appleton in Cheshire, and Denton in Lancashire. In the Inquisition it is said, p. 23, that "each oxgang of land in Widnes pays yearly at Christmas 3*d.* for a certain service called le Brede ; sum 4*s.*"

pp. 43-8, 142-5. *Halton.* In this account are enumerated all the places belonging to the manor of Halton. Some of the names are miscopied. — *Runcouver Upper and Lower* is now called Runcorn Superior and Inferior.—The fishery of *Budworth*, p. 143, was in the adjoining lake.—Anderbuske is meant for *Comberbach.*— *Cronleycroft* or Cornleycroft we do not identify.— *Northcotes* is Norcot in Over Whitley.— Penre is *Little Peover.* So pages 148, 155.— Aldredley is *Over Alderley.*— Lysenker (perhaps written Lysseker) is *Liscard*, misprinted by Sir Peter Leycester, Listard.—*Byrcheles* is Birtles.—*Hulle and Walmefeld*, in Northwich Hundred, called by Sir Peter Leycester "Hulme at Walfield," is now Hulme Walfield. — *Coten* is Cotton. — Endesbyre and Pexhill is now *Henbury-cum-Pexhull.*— *The Moor* should be More, in Bucklow Hundred.—Fellewell should be *Thelwall.* The other three parts of the fishery at Thelwall belonged to Shrewsbury Abbey.—*Langdendale*, as pointed out elsewhere, is Mottram-in-Longdendale.— *Northwode* was a park belonging to the manor (Orm., vol. iii. p. 36, note *b*).—Netton and Feftone, pp. 48-9, 145, should perhaps be *Stretton.*—Bekewycke should be *Kekwycke.* Some of these corrections apply to the next Compotus for the same fee, pp. 57-61 ; 150-2.

In going over these valuable records of the Halton rents, fines, &c., the reader should have before him the old schedule (dated 1359) of Hugo de Preston, Bayliff of the Serjeanty of Halton, recorded in Sir Peter Leycester, p. 284, and in Ormerod, vol. i. pp. 704-5. The only Cheshire places named in the Earl's Inquisition in the Calendar are Rontere (Runcorn), Whiteleye, Morre, Congleton and Thellewalle.

pp. 50, 146. *Denton Mill. Cf.* pp. 62, 152. This is Denton near Manchester. *Hist. Denton.*, pp. 2-3. The Earl had here a grant of free warren.

pp. 50, 146. *Chevage* was the money paid by villeins to their lords in acknowledgement of their villenage; or the money yearly given for the advancement of a lord as a leader or chieftain.

pp. 53, 147. *Aston.* This is Aston Grange. (*Cf.* Sir Pet. Ley., p. 214.)

pp. 53, 148. *The Knife*, which was out of Millington, was, in Sir Peter Leycester's time, a Manchester knife with a horn haft, p. 284. *Aydrop Mylingtone*, or *Endropa de Millington* at pp. 65, 155, is called by Sir Peter, Aytrop de Millington, p. 315.

pp. 54, 148. *Apples.* The Earl of Lincoln cultivated Apples in his garden at Holborn ; and they are mentioned in Bp. de Swinfield's household expenses.

pp. 62, 152, lines 9-10 from foot, *Hul super Daneno.* Perhaps Hulme Walfield.

p. 62, line 11 from foot, *for* repe silure, *read*, p. 153, reap silver, the money paid for exemption from the customary duty of reaping for the lord.

pp. 91-3, 170-3. *Standen.* (*Cf. Whalley*, vo. i. p. 101.)

pp. 91, 170, &c. *Hugh de Clitheroe* was settled at Salesbury, and held land there

Notes and Corrections.

and Little Penhulton in thanage. (See *Whalley*, vol. ii. pp. 372-5 and ped.) The following deed (Raines *MSS.*, vol. xiv. p. 55) relates to him : O'ib's, &c. Alesia de Lacy salt. in dom. sempt. Sciatis me dedisse &c. Hugo' fil. Hugo' de Cliderhow pro homag' et servic' suo totam illam terram cu' prato et cu' messuag' quæ Robert' del Croslit q'da' de me tenuit in Newton [in Bowland] simul cu' uno acr' et dimid' quæ Will' de Bosco ten' in fœdo hab' libere pacificè &c. Reddendo ann' mihi et hered'b's meis una' libr' piper ad fest. Sci. Mich'is. Testb's Dom. Rog' Tempest, Rad'o de Mitton Mil't's Walter de Waddington Gregor' et Simon fr'ib's suis Eli fil. Ri'ci de Knole Egid. le Fforestar, &c.

pp. 95, 173. *Cridling Stubbs*, near Pontefract, was one of the Earl's manors, and some horses had come thence to Ightenhill Park. (*Cf.* the Yorkshire *Compotus*.)

pp. 101, 177. The *Park newly made* was Musbirry. (*Cf.* pp. 115, 185.) The following charter (Raines *MSS.*, vol. xiv. p. 54) relates to it : Henr. de Lasy Comes Lincoln, &c., dedi co'cessi, &c., Adæ fil Adæ de Holden quadam p'te vasti n'ri in Todington in' apet ad paliu' parci de Mosebury, &c., redd. nobis et hered's n'ris vs. arg' ad festum S'ci Egidii, &c. Dat. xx Junii A° 2 Edwardi fil. R. Edwardi, 1307.

pp. 110, 182. *Robert de Holden* is referred to in the following charters :—
Sciant o'es p'sens &c. Hen' de Lacy concess. Adæ fil. Rob. de Holden tot. illam ter' cu' p'tin's quæ Will. fil. Keelyn ac Will. fil. ejus quond' tenuer' in haslingden et quæ nunc accedit p' felonia d'ci Will.' p' qua suspensus fuit &c. Dat. A° 1272. hijs test'b's Dom Galfr' de Nevile Jo bely Willo. de Vavasoure Willo de Ryther Mil't's Willo. de hackeing Robto de Plessington Henr' de Rischeton Jordan de Clideraou Rob. de Reved et aliis. Dat. apud pontefract die Mercurii pp. fest. S'ci Barnabi ap'li an'o R. R. Henr. fil R. Johis. . . . . (*Raines MSS.*, vol. xiv. p. 54.)

Henr' de Lascy counte de Nicole &c. aver relesse &c. Robto de Holdeno et ses heyres une plase de terr' &c. in Brodeheved, &c. du feoffm. Ada de Bold. A° 32 Edw. I. (*Ibid.*)

p. 112, line 3. *Carratum*. Bailey defines a *charre* of lead as a quantity containing 30 pigs, weighing 6 stone wanting 2 lbs., and every stone weighing 12 lbs. The *charrus, carecta*, or *plaustrata* of lead, says Prof. Rogers, "contained 30 *fontinelli, fotmael, pedes* or pigs. Each *pes* contained 5 *petræ* of 14 lbs. each, and therefore the *pes* was 70 lbs. avoirdupois, and the *charrus* 2,100 lbs. Now, measured by the old hundred, *i.e.*, 108 lbs., the *charrus* contains nearly 19¼ hundreds, *i.e.*, it corresponds to the fodder, or fother, of modern times." (*Cf.* pp. 116, 186; and *Whalley*, vol. ii. p. 98.)

pp. 115, 185. *Altofts* was one of the Earl's manors near Wakefield, co. York.

pp. 115, 185. This *Bradford* was in the county of York, one of the Earl's manors, and part of the dower of Alice, mother of the Earl. It lay in the route of the Earl and his retainers between Clitheroe and Pontefract. The Inquisition refers to the Hall or Manor House, the water mill, and the fulling mill. A charter of John of Gaunt mentions services to be done to him and his heirs "coming to Bradford from Blackburnshire."

p. 115, line 17, *for* l*li.*, *read* (according to the addition) lx*li.*

Notes and Corrections.

p. 118, line 11, *add* 37 qrs. 3 bushels oats sold, 4*l.* 12*s.* 4*d.*; line 23, *add* Repairing houses at Accrington, 12*s.* 4*d.*

p. 119, line 21, *for* marks, *read* works.

p. 121, line 22, *for* 1*l.* 19*s.* 2*d.*, *read* 2*l.* 19*s.* 2*d.*; line 8 from foot, *for* Wild boars, *read* Swine; and so throughout.

p. 126, line 6, *add* Expenses of holding courts throughout the country, 4*l.* 18*s.* 10*d.*

p. 127, line 8 from foot, *for* sold, *read* bought.

p. 128. The feast of the Empress Helen was 3 September.

p. 130, line 14, *for* 1 steer bull, which is tautological, *read* 1 young bull. So also p. 139, line 5 from foot.

p. 132, line 12 from foot, *dele* male.

p. 133, line 4, *after* remainder, *add*: of which 2 in tithe, 14 yearlings remain (5 males). The same accounts for 15 calves of the year. Line 6, *dele* 5 males.

p. 135, line 16, *after* delivered to *insert* S. le Geldhird, and 2 to.

p. 140, line 17, *for* barn, *read* grange; and so elsewhere.

p. 141, line 13 from foot, *for* reaping, *read* weeding.

p. 141, line 9 from foot, *for* seed wheat sold, *read* wheat bought for seed.

p. 143, lines 13, 14, *for* in the same, *read* at the same term.

p. 144, line 1, *for* Hultone, *read* Halton. Line 4 from foot, *Robert de Mascy* of Sale Moor is mentioned by Sir Peter Leycester, page 352.

p. 153, line 24, *for* Dongleton, *read* Congleton.

p. 155, line 3 from foot, *for* grass, *read* herbs; last line, *for* vesture, *read* crop.

p. 156, line 12, *for* £37, *read* £27.

p. 170, line 5 from foot, *for* harvest work, *read* a day's work; and transpose 1*s.* 1*d.* 2*s.* 7½*d.*

p. 172, line 1, after oxen *add*, and 6 qrs. 3 bus. as provender of work-horses. Line 15 from foot, *for* 66, *read* 71.

p. 177, &c., *for* firewood, *read* brushwood (bosca); *for* approved, *read* enclosed; and so throughout. For domain, *read* demesne.

p. 179, *for* measure, *read* measurer; *for* cottars, *read* cottages.

p. 181, &c., *for* impoundments, *read* impounding. *Dunschopfal* is now Dunnishope. (*Whalley*, vol. ii. p. 297.)

p. 182, after line 9, *read*, Rent of a cottage which was Robert le Arrowsmith's 3*s.* 8*d.*; line 11 from foot, *for* hunting, *read* venison.

p. 183, line 9, *for* white (*albo posito*, p. 111), *read* white rent, because it was paid in silver. The white spurs paid for the tenure of Little Peover (pp. 65, 155) may be silver spurs. (*Cf.* Sir Peter Leycester, pp. 284, 341.)

p. 184, after line 18 add, Expenses of the Steward and others inspecting the stock of cattle and letting the vaccaries, £1. 1. 5½; line 21, *for* Norry, *read* Nony; line 13 from foot, add 24 June.

＃ INDEX.

ACCRINGTON, ix., xix., xxv.-vi., 1-3, 118; 11, 123; 16, 126; 83-9, 165-9; 108, 181; 115, 186; Forest, xix.; Grange, 2, 119; 90, 170; Vaccary, 37-9, 138-40.
Adam (baker), 76, 161; (smith), 12, 124; s. of John, 20, 129; s. of Jurdan, 68, 156; s. of Matth., 12, 124; s. of Maulke, 22, 130; s. of Nicholas, 28, 133; 72, 159; s. of Peter, 74, 160; s. of Wyot, 102, 177.
Adlington, 10, 122; 97, 174.
Advowsons, 47, 144.
Affer, xxi., 3, 17, &c.
Agisted Cattle, 41, 141.
Alba Culcaria, 65 bis.; 192.
Alblaster, Walt. de, 13, 124. *See* Arb-.
Albus Vaccariarum, 14, 125; 111, 183; 192.
Albus Vaccarum, 46, 60.
Alcancotes, W. s. of Ad., 4, 119.
Alderley (Aldrededly), 44, 143; 58, 151; 190.
Aldewyke, 60, 151.
Alicia, d. of Wm., 50, 146.
Almonbury, vii.
Altofts, 115, 185; 191.
Alvedene (Aldene), 5, 120; 98, 175; 101, 177; 188.
Amounderness, xi.
Antlay, 90, 169; 108, 181.
Antelay, Makock or Mokot de, 37, 138; 84, 165; Rob. de, 36, 138; Will. de, 37-8, 138-9; 85, 166.
Apples, 54, 148; 190.
Appleton, 49, 145; 62, 152; 190.
Appruviatæ Terræ, xxi., 57, &c.
Arblaster, J. de, 110, 182. *See* Alb-.
Arderne, Sir W. de, 51, 147; 189; Marg., 52, 147.
Arrows, 53, 147-8; 65, 154-5.
Arrowsmith, Dyot and Dinaria le, 109, 182; Robert, 13, 124; 182.
Ashtrees, 103, 178; 108, 181.
Assarts, xxi., 9-10, 122-3; 105-9, 179-81.

Assebroke, W. and Marg. de, 50, 146.
Assenhirste, Elyas de, 116, 186.
Astmore, 60, 152.
Aston, 53, 147; 190.
Attebrigge, Rob., 29, 134.
Aula, 15.
Aura, Arura, 46, 60.

BAGESTONDENE, W. de, 83, 165; 85, 166.
BALDERSTONE, SIMON DE, xxv., 64, 154.
Baldwinhill, 12, 124; 97, 174; 109, 182.
Balshaw, Ad. de, 6, 120; 102, 177.
Banastre, Hen., 110, 182; J., 97, 174; Rob., 189.
Barley, 91-4, 170-3.
Barnoldswick, 16, 126.
Barouford, J. del, 16, 126; 27, 133.
Barton, J. de, 61, 152; T. de, 44, 143; 58, 150.
Baxenden, xxii., 87, 167; 89, 169; 115, 185. *See* Bag-.
Baynel, 62, 153.
Beans, 91, 170.
Bedelria, 6, 120; 10, 123; 14, 125; 102, 177; 106, 180.
Bedewynd, W. de, xviii.
Beer, 61, 152.
Bellows, 116, 186.
Bely, J. de, 191.
Benedict, Ad. s. of Ric., 4, 119.
Bercroft, Matth. de, 12, 124; 109, 181; Ric. de, 28, 133; 33, 136.
Berdeshille, Hen. de, 34, 136; 79, 163.
Berdeworthe, 9, 122; Will. de, 9, 122.
Berdeworthgrene or grave, 9, 122; 104-5, 179.
Birkdale, 107, 180.
Birtles, 45, 143; 58, 151.
Black Death, xxiii.
Blackburn, xix., 188.
Blackburne, Hen. de, 7, 121; 103, 178; J. de, 9, 122; 51, 147; 104, 179.
Blackburnshire, xi., xiv., xvi., xx., xxv.-vi., 68, 156; 112, 183; 191.

C C

Blakay, 40, 140; 87, 167. See *Whalley*, v. i., p. 229.
Blacshaghe, 106, 180.
Bold, Adam de, 191.
Bole, Boole, 116, 186.
Bolton Abbey, xx.–ii.
Bolton-in-Bolland, xxii.
Bolton-le-Moors, xxvi., 15, 126; 87, 167; 189.
Boltone, Hen. de, 14, 125.
Bondheth, 43, 142; 57, 150.
Bondi, 47.
Booth, xx.
Bosca (busca), 7, 60, 101, &c., 192.
Bosco, W. de, 191.
Bothe, John del, 68, 156; Jordan del, 21, 129; Juliana, 69–70, 157; Matilda, 21, 129; 40, 140.
Bottiler, W. de, 189.
Bowland, xii., xiv., xxii., 112, 183; 191.
Boydel, J., 43, 142.
Bradake, J. de, 66, 155.
Bradshae, W. de, 2, 118.
Bradford, co. York., vii.; xxii., 115, 185; 191.
Bradleye (Bradelay), Peter de, 38, 139; Ric. de, 74, 160.
Breda (le Brede), 44, 143; 49, 145; 58, 150; 62, 152; 190. (Qu. *bridde*, a cart-wheel.)
Brettone, *i.e.*, Monk Bretton, co. York., Prior of, 114, 184.
Broadhead, le, 2, 118; 191.
Briercliffe, 8, 122, 104, 179; 117, 187.
Brocklehurst, 12, 123; 108, 181.
Brunghill Moor, xxii.
Brunlay, W. de, xxvi., 91, 170.
Brunschaghe, 14, 125.
Buckby, 16, 126; 189.
Budworth, 44, 143; 58, 150; 190; Vicar, 61, 152.
Burgage, 117, 187.
Burnley, vii., xxvii., 8, 122; 16, 126; 18, 128; 98, 175; 104, 179; 109, 181; 117, 187; Mills, xxii., 8, 122; 15, 125; 97, 174; 104, 179; Cross, xviii., 18, 128.
Burton, nr. Lincoln, 98, 175.
Bury, 5, 120.
Bury, Hen. de, 100, 177.
Busca. See Bos-.
Buter, Simon le, 45, 143.
Butterworth, 6, 120.
Byrchels. *See* Birtles.
Byrchenleye, Ric. de, 23, 131.
Byrun, J. de, 6, 120.

CABOUN, Ad., 117, 187.
Calder (Kelder), v., 18, 128.
Campsall, vii.
Canvass, 16, 126; 114, 185.
Caractata, 60.
Carcatus, 13.
Caratum, 112, 191; 116, 186.
Carecta, 191.
Carlisle, xiii. *seq.*
Carlaverock, xiv.
Cathertone, W. de, 114, 184.
Catlou, Roger de, 83, 165.
Cattle, xx.
Cepes, 44, 58.
Chadertone, Geoff. de, 5, 120, 101, 177.
Charre, xxii., 191.
Chedel, Galf., 48, 145.
Chester, xiv., xviii., xxiv.–v., 45, 143; 53, 147; 58, 151; 64–5, 154; Market, 45, 143.
Chester, Pet. de, 14, 125; 188–9. See *Fasti Ebor.*, i., 321, 331.
Chestershire, xvii.
Chevage, 50, 146; 63, 153; 190.
Church, 9, 122; 104, 179.
Churchfelde, 43, 142; 57, 150.
Clayton, Hen. de, 11, 123; 105, 179; 107, 181.
Cleges, J., 76–7, 161.
Clerks in Cheshire, 51, 147.
Cliftone, Ad. and Marg. de, 47, 144.
Clitheroe, vii., xi., xix., xxiv., 12, 124; 16, 126; 42, 141; 96, 174; 98, 175; 109, 182; 115, 185; 189, 191; Castle, xxvii., 97, 174; 188.
Clitheroe, Hugh de, 91, 170; 93, 171; 105, 179; 190–1; Jordan de, 191.
Cliviger, ix., xxii., xxvi., 12, 124; 109, 181; 111, 182; 114, 184; Mill, 15, 125; 97, 174.
Clivacher, Ivo de, 12, 124.
Cloghe, Ad. del, 111, 183.
Coals (*carbones maris*), xxii., 4, 119; 12, 124; 100, 176.
Cocks, 115, 185.
Cogshull, 60, 151.
Coldcotes, 14, 124.
Collars, 7, 121; 188.
Colne, vii., xix., xxvi., 3, 119; 15, 125; 17, 127; 97, 174; 99, 176; 113, 184; 117, 187; Farm, 4, 119; Mills, xxii., 4, 119.
Comberbach, 44, 143; 58, 150; 60, 151; 190.
Congleton, vii., viii., x., xix., xxv., 50–4, 146–9; 63, 153; 66, 155; 190.
Congleton, Alex., and J. de, 53, 153.

Corbridge, Abp., xxvii.
Cornleycroft (Cronleycroft), 44, 143; 58, 151; 190.
Cotton, 45, 143; 59, 151; 190.
Coupe or Cowhope, 5, 120; 101, 177; 188.
Couhope, Hen. de, 111, 182; Rob. de, 32, 135; 33, 136; 82, 164.
Cridling, 95, 172-3; 191.
Cromii, xxvi., 38-9, 139; 40, 140; 85, 166.
Cronschaghe, W. de, 79, 162; 81, 164.
Croslit, R. del, 191.
Cummin, 5, 120; 53, 147-8; 59, 151; 65, 154-5; 101, 177.
Curtilage, 1, 118; 88, 168.
Cutwulf, Dean, xx.

DANE, River, 62, 152; 190.
Danyel, W., 61, 152.
Danyscales, J. de, 13, 124.
David, J., 106, 180.
Deer, 18, 128.
Denbigh, viii. *seq.*, 96, 173; 98, 175; 112, 183; 115, 185.
Denton, xix., 62, 152; 190 *bis.*; Mill, 50, 146.
Denton, Andrew and J. de, 63, 153; Marg., 50, 146; Ric. de, 49-50, 145-6; 64, 154.
Deresbury, Ran. de, 45, 143; 59, 151.
Deyethalgne, J. de, 10, 123.
Dinaria, 13, 124; 109, 182.
Dirplay (Derplaghe), 4, 120; 100, 176.
Dolle, Rob., 43, 142.
Donington, Ric. de, 49, 145; 62, 153.
Dovecote, 55, 149; 67, 155.
Dower, 1, 118; 52, 147.
Downham, xi., xix., 10, 123; 15, 126; 97, 174; 107, 180; 114, 184; Mill, 15, 125.
Downham, Hen. de, 107, 180; Peter de, 111, 182.
Dunnock, Ric. de, 32, 135; 78, 162.
Dunnishope, 108, 181; 192.
Duttone, Hugh de, 48, 145.
Duxbury, 10, 122; 97, 174.
Dyneley, viii.
Dynley, Ad. de, 14, 125; Christiana, 35, 137; Hen. de, 81, 163; W. de, 35, 137; 76-7, 161.
Dyote (arrowsmith), 13, 124.

EDDA, 50, 146.
Edward I., vi. *seq.*
Edward II., vi., xiii. *seq.*
Elaunde, Hugo de, 6, 120.
Elmeton, x.

Emot, Hen. de, 22, 130.
Endesbyre. *See* Henbury.
Esparvarii, viii., 115, 185.
Estock, Hen. del, 30, 134; 32, 135; 38, 139; Tho. del, 33, 136. *See* Stockes.
Eton, Sir N. de, 188.
Euxton, 10, 122.
Eukestone, Rob. de, 106, 180.

FALDA, 61, 152; 113, 183; 116, 186.
Felon, Felony, 6, 120; 9, 122; 14, 125.
Fernyside, Pet. del, 23, 130; Ran. de, 70, 157.
Ferratura, 114, 185.
FISHEBURNE, THO. DE, xxvii., 1-3, 118-19; 17, 127; 43, 142; 51, 147; 53, 148.
Fishery, 9, 122; 44, 142; 58, 150; 106, 180.
Forester, Giles le, 191.
Forests, xx.
Forges, xxii., 5, 120; 7, 121; 12, 123; 43, 142; 110, 182.
Fother, 116, 186; 191.
Franceys, Alan, 79, 162.
Frekiltone, Ad. de, 10, 123.
Friars Preachers, xviii., 64, 154.
Frodsham, Nic. de, 50, 146; 63, 153.
Fulling Mills, xxii., 3, 119; 8, 122; 15, 125; 16, 126; 191.

GALFRIDUS, s. of Tho., 117, 187.
Galle, W., 117, 187.
Galwey, Galway-lands, 10, 122; 106, 180.
Gamel. *See* Robert.
Geoffrey le Parker, 20, 129; 22, 130; 37, 138.
Gilbert (Instaurator). *See* Legh, de la.
Gilbert (smith), 43, 142.
Giles le Forester, 191.
Gloves, 11, 123; 53, 147-8; 59, 151; 65, 154-5; 107, 181; 109, 181.
Gougge, W., 28, 133.
Grandison, Sir O. de, x., xvii. See *Fasti Ebor.*, i., 337.
Grangia, xx., 11, 40; 42, 192, &c.
Grangia, Ad. de, 72, 159.
Grapenhall, 45, 143; 59, 151.
Grene, Ric. and Alice de la, 47, 144.
Grenhou, 107, 180.
Grenelache, 41, 141.
Guildford, Isabel de, 114, 185.

HABERGHAM, 8, 121; 104, 178; 114, 184.
Hacking, W. de, 191.

Haiæ, 18, 94. See *Whalley*, v. i., p. 283.
Hallehyne, Hen. de, 95, 173.
Hallmote, 4, 119, &c.
Halton, viii., xii., xix., xxiv., 43, 142;
 46-7, 143-4; 51, 147; 53, 148; 55,
 149; 57, 150; 60-1, 152; 188, 190;
 Castle, xxv., 47, 144; 53, 148; Mill,
 64, 154.
Haltonshire, xix., 67, 156.
Haltone, Alan and Marg. de, 47, 144.
Hand-mill, 49, 145.
Hapton, xxvi.
Hare, Hen., 68-72, 156-9; 85, 166.
Haregreaves, J. del, 26, 132; 75, 160;
 86, 167.
Haslingden, xxii., 4, 119; 100, 176.
Haselingwurthe, 87, 167.
Hattone, 48, 145.
Haybote, x.
Healey (Heley, Helay, Heyleghe), Ad de,
 8, 121; Cecilia de, 32, 135; Elias de,
 84, 165; Ric. de, 32, 135; 115, 185.
Henbury, 45, 143; 48, 144; 59, 151;
 190.
Henry, s. of Christiana, 73, 159; s. of
 Kitte, 24, 131; s. of Patric, 6, 120; s.
 of Ric., s. of Hy., 6, 120.
HEPPALE (HEPPEHALE), ROB. DE, xxv.,
 1, 118; 3, 119; 17, 127; 20, 129; 92,
 171.
Herford, Rob. de, 189.
Hesandforth, xxvii.
HESKETH, W. DE, 54, 149; 57, 150; 64,
 154; 66, 155.
Higham, 18, 127; 40, 140; 189.
Hilton, Tho. de, 9, 122; 105, 179 *bis*.
Hoddesdene, 1-2, 118; 7, 121; 16, 126;
 39, 139-140; 87, 167; 90, 169; 102,
 177; 108, 181.
Hoghton, Hen. de, 30, 134; 34, 136.
Holande, Rob. de, 10, 122.
Holcoumbe, Benne de, 26, 132.
Holcome, Rob. de, 71, 158.
Holden. *See* Alveden.
Holden, Adam de, 191; Rob. de, 110,
 182; 117, 186-7; 191 *bis*.
Holford, W. de, 62, 153.
Holme, Rob. de, 81, 164.
Honey, 61, 152.
Horses, xxi., 19, 128, &c.; 189.
Horse-mill, 49-50, 145-6; 62, 153.
Houcetum, 5, 120; 7, 121; 40, 140; 188.
Housbote, x.
Huddelestone, — de, 16, 126; Adam de,
 189; John de, xv., 189.
Hugh, Abbot of Salley, 189.

Hull super Dane, 62, 152; 190.
Hulm, 57, 151.
Hulme Wallfield, 190.
Huncote, ix.; 12, 123; 108, 181.
Hull, 45, 143; 61, 152.

IGHTENHILL, xi., xx., xxi., xxvi.;
 1, 118; 3, 119; 7, 121; 15-20, 125-9;
 41, 141; 88, 168; 93, 172; 96, 174; 98,
 174; 103, 178; 111, 183; 114-15,
 185-6; 188, 191; Grange, 19, 128; 95,
 173.
Instaurator, xx.; 14, 125, &c.; 188.
Instaurum, xx.; 68, 156.
Iron Ore, 109, 182.

*J*ANITOR, 16, 64.
 John, s. of Gilbert, 105, 179; s. of
 Matthew, 12, 124; 109, 181; s. of
 Odousa, 31, 135; (the parker) xxvi., 93,
 172; 99, 175; 111, 186.
Jordan (bailiff), 42, 141.
Jumentum, 3, &c., 189.

KEKEWICK, 48, 145; 190.
 Keuerdale, Alex. de, 11, 123; 107,
 181.
Kirkstall, ix.
Knaresboro', vi.
Knives, 53, 147-8; 65, 154-5.
Knole, Rd. de, 191.
Knottingley, vii.
Kyghley, Hen. de, 17, 127.
Knight's Fees, vii. *seq*., 63, 153; 65, 154.
 See Scutage.

LACY, HENRY DE, Account of, v. *seq*.;
 5, 120; 10, 123; 94, 184; 115-17,
 185-7; his Inquisition, xvii., xxii. *seq*.;
 Edmund and John de, sons of Hy., xi.;
 Alice de, mother of Hy., vi., 191 *bis*;
 Alice de, dau. of Hy., vi., xi.-xii.;
 16, 126; "Hell" Lacy, vi., 189; John
 de, 1st Earl, vi., 15, 125; 97, 174; 189;
 pedigree, vi.
Lancashire levies, xiii., xvi.
Lancaster, xi., xxv.; Castle, 9, 122; 14-
 15, 125-6; 106, 180; 111, 183; 114,
 184; 188.
Lancaster, Edmund, E. of, vi. *seq*., 64,
 154; Thomas, E. of, vi., xi.-xii.; John
 de, xv.; Henry, Duke of, 188; John of
 Gaunt, 191.
Lances, 53, 147-8; 65, 154-5.
Langdendale. *See* Longdendale.
Langtre, 10, 122; 97, 174.

Latham, Rob. de, 189.
Lawnds, xxi.
Lead, xxii., 115-16, 185-6. *See* Ore.
LEIGH, GILB. DE LA, xxvi., 14, 125; 38, 40; 139, 140; 85, 166-7; 99, 175; 111, 183; Mich. de la, 38-9, 139; Ph. de la, 49, 145.
Leicroft, J. de, 117, 187.
Lenke, Ad. and Marg., 47, 144.
Letherwyte (Leirwite), 7, 121; 99, 176; 103, 178 *bis*; 188.
Leyburne, Sir Nich. and Sir Rob. de, 55, 149.
LEYCESTER, NICH. DE, xxv., 53, 148; Rog. de, xxvi., 65, 155.
Levesay, Ran. de, 111, 182.
Leyland Hund., xi., xxv.
Leyland, Tho. de, 106, 180.
Lille, Alice, 61, 152.
Lincoln's Inn, xvii.
Liscard, 44, 143; 190.
London, 98, 175; 115, 185.
Longdendale, xxiv-v., 45, 143; 59, 151; 190. *See* Mottram.
Longdendale, Rob. de, xxiv.
Longspee, W. de, v-vi.
Lothresdene, Godf. de, 70, 157.
Lovell, Sir W., xxiv.

MABOTA, 16, 126.
Macclesfield, Tho. de, 45, 143; 59, 151.
Magge, J., 50, 146.
Manchester, xxii., 190.
Mara, W. de, 96, 174; 106, 180. *See* Mere.
Marchancia, 18, 114; 189.
Marchagium, 189.
Marchiæ, 16, 126; 98, 174; 115, 185.
Marchaunt, Ad., 117, 187.
Marchet. *See* Merchat.
Mareschalcia & Marescalcia, 189.
Mariscus, 46.
Market-galt, 46, 144; 60, 152.
Marsden, Gt. and Little, 9, 122; 73, 159; 117, 187; 104, 179; 117, 187. *Cf.* Beamont's *Halton*, p. 33.
Mascy, Rob. de, 48, 144-5; 192.
Maulke, Ad., s. of, 22, 130.
Meols (Meles), 9-10, 122. *See* N. Meols.
Meles, Rob. de, 10, 122. *See* N. Meols.
Mercer, Alex., 53-4, 148-9; 66, 155; Ric. le, 61, 152.
Merchats (*Mulierum*), xxiii., 4, 119; 7, 121; 8, 121; 17, 127; 50, 146; 61, 152; 63, 153.
Mere, 190.

Mere, W. de la, 10, 122.
Merlande, near Rochdale, 115, 185.
Mersey Fisheries, 44, 142.
Middleford, 9, 122; 106, 180.
Middleton, Adam de, 189.
Midgelay, W. de, 64, 154.
Millington, Aydrop de, 53, 148; 65, 155; 190. *Cf. Arley Charters*, pp. 1-2.
Millstones, 15, 125; 51, 146; 66, 155.
Minera, 5, 120. *See* Ore.
Mitton, 13, 124.
Mitton, Ran. de, 13, 124; 191.
Molyneus, Ric. de, 62, 153.
Monk Bretton. *See* Bretton.
Monkerode, Emma del, 21, 130.
Moore (More), 53, 147; 58, 151; 60-1, 152; 190.
More, Alan de, 62, 153.
Motoun, H., 10, 123.
Mottram in Longdendale, xix., xxiv.
Murrain, 19, 128 *seq.*
Musbirry Park, viii., xx., 101, 177; 115, 185; 188, 191.
Musdene, 5, 120; 98, 175; 101, 177; 188.
Mustone, Ric. de, 48, 144.
Mutuum, 112.

NANTWICH, ix.
Narrator, 64, 154.
Nativus, 47, 49, &c.
Neville, G. de, 191; J. de, 189.
Newton, J. de, 10, 123.
Nichole, v., xv., 191.
NOEL (LE NOEL), SIMON, xxvii., 1-3, 118-19; 17-18, 127-8; 87-8, 167-8; 92, 171; 94, 172; 96, 174; 112-13, 183-4; 115, 185.
NONY, SIR W. DE, xxvii., 1-3, 118-19; 17, 127; 43, 142; 53, 148; 57, 150; 68, 156; 93, 172; 113, 184; 189.
Norcot (Northcotes), 44, 143; 58, 151; 190.
Noreys, Rob. Le, 50, 146.
Northbury, Greg. de, 188. *See* Whalley, Abbot of.
Northmeles, 106, 180; 188; Fishery, 9-10, 122. *See* Meols.
Northmeles, Rob. de, 106, 180.
Northwich, 45, 143; 59, 151.
Northwode, 46-7, 143-4; 60, 151-2; 190.
Norton, Prior of, 53, 147; 65, 154.

OATS, xxi., xxv., 88-9, 168-9; 90, 170.
Ogdene, 5, 120; 101, 177; 185.
Okenheved, 87, 167.

Olla, 97.
Oliver. *See* Stansfield.
Ore (Iron), 5, 120; 12, 123; Lead, 116, 186.
Ormerode, Matth. and Ad. de, 109, 181; Rob. de, 114, 184.
Ox-galt, 49, 145.

PADIHAM, 8, 121; 104, 178; Mill, 15, 125.
PALDEN, J. DE, 68, 156; 85-6, 166-7; 111, 183; 115, 186.
Pannage, 6, 120; 50, 146.
Pannus, 98, 175.
Parchment, 16, 126; 114, 185.
Peat, 11, 123; 49, 145; 62, 183; 106, 180; 108, 181.
Pendle, xx., 8, 121; 23, 131; 30, 134; 38-9, 139; 71, 158; 87, 167; 98, 174; 115, 185.
Pendleton, 7, 121; 102, 178.
Penhulton, Will. de, 25, 132; 75, 160; 114, 184; 191.
Penhul, Rob. de, 86, 167.
Penwortham, xiv., 9-10, 122-3; 15, 125; 97, 174; 105-6, 179-80; 113, 184; 188; Priory, 9, 122; 106, 180.
Peover, 44, 143; 53, 148; 58, 151; 65, 155; 190, 192.
Pepper, 10, 121; 12, 124; 53, 147-8; 59, 151; 65, 154-5; 106, 180; 109, 181.
Pes, 116, 186; 191.
Pocinet, 97.
Pexhill, 45, 143; 48, 144; 59, 151; 190.
Plessington, R. de, 191.
Ploket, Ad., 106, 180; Hugh, 9, 122.
Pontefract, v. *seq.*, xxvi.-vii., 16, 126; 18, 128 *bis*; 51-2, 147; 64-5, 154; 98-9, 175; 114-15, 185; Fair, 189, 191.
Porci Silvestres, 8, &c., 192.
Præpositus, 98, 175.
Precaria, 92, 170; 192.
Prestwich, Ad. de, 96, 174.
Preston, Hugh de, xxv., 190.
Primerol-sykes, 5, 120; 100, 176.
Pycoppe, J. de, 30, 134.

RADECLEVE, Ric. de, 5, 120; 100, 176.
Ralph, s. of Luke, 42, 141.
Ramsgreave, 7, 121; 101-2, 177; 188.
Ranulph, br. of Hen., 6, 120.
Rayneville, Tho. de, 16, 126.
Reading (Redings), Sir Nich. de, xvii., 65, 154; 112, 183; 115, 186.

Reap silver, 49, 145; 62, 153; 190.
Redecima, 46, 60.
Rediker, Elene, dau. of W., xxiii., 4, 119.
Reved, R. de, 191.
Reyl-aker, 1, 118.
Richard the clerk, Instaurator of Pendle, 38, 139; clerk of Halton, 43, 142; of Downham, 11, 123; 107, 181.
Richard, s. of Benedict, 24, 131; 71, 158; s. of Hen., 50, 146.
Ridings, royds, xxi.
Rimmington, xxii.
Rishton, x.
Rishton, Ad. de, x., 111, 183; Hen. de, 191.
Roads, xxiv., 45, 143; 60, 151; 89, 169.
Robbers, 25, 131; 30, 134; 86, 166; 189.
ROBERT, SON OF ADAM, xxvii., 87-8, 167-8; 92, 171; 94-5, 172-3; 98, 175; s. of Gamelle, 17, 187; s. of John, 69, 157.
Robert (miller), 4, 119; (parker) 43, 142; (smith) 8, 122.
Rochdale, vii., xi., xix., 6, 120; 96, 174; 98, 175; 101, 177; 117, 187; forest, 16, 126; mill, 6, 120.
Rocheleye, W. de (Instaurator of Trawden), 38, 139.
Roclif, Alan de, 35, 137.
Roger (smith), 59, 150.
Roof-stones, 103, 178.
Rossendale, xx., 4, 120; 15, 125; 30, 134; 32, 135; 38-9, 139; 40, 140; 76, 161; 98, 174; 100, 176; 114-15, 185.
Roter, Ran. de, 59, 151; Sim. le, 53, 147; 65, 154.
Roundhey, le, x.
Royle (Rohill), 17-18, 127-8.
Ruddeby, Pet. de, xxv.-vi., 16, 17, 126-7.
Rufford, x.
Rughley, 40, 140. See *Whalley*, v. i., pp. 219, 299; v. ii. p. 390.
Runcini, 95-6, 173; 111-12, 183; 189.
Runcorn, 43, 142; 46-7, 144; 49, 145; 57, 150; 61-2, 153; 190 *bis*.
Ryley, 90, 162.
Ryley, Rob. de, xxv., 1-2, 118-19; 88, 168; 98, 175; 115, 186.
Ryther, W. de, 191.

SABDEN, 40, 140.
Sac fee, 10, 122; 49, 145; 62, 153; 106, 180; 188.
Sale, 48, 145; 192.
Salewelle (Clitheroe), 13, 124; 110, 182.
Salesbury, 105, 179; 190.

Salesbury, J. de., 105, 179.
Salfordshire, xi.
Salley, Abbot of, xviii., 15, 125; 97, 174; 189.
Salthille, 13, 124; 15, 126; 97, 174; 110, 182; 113, 184.
Salt, Saltwork, 1, 118; 45, 145; 59, 151; 115, 185.
Sandale, John de, xvii.
Sandwelle (Clitheroe), 13, 124; 110, 182.
Schypen mill, 111, 183.
Scoles, David, 110, 182.
Scotland, army of, xi. *seq.*, 63, 153; 64, 154; 101, 177; 107, 180; 112, 183.
Scrope, Sir Hen. le, xvii., 113, 184.
Scutage, xiv., 101, 177; 107, 180; 112, 183.
Secroft, x.
Segersteyn (?), J., 44, 143; 58, 150.
Serviens, 2, &c.
Shadwell, x.
Sharl, Ric., 117, 187.
Sheep, xx.-xxi.
Shillingbothim, 5, 120.
Shippewelbothym, Ad. de, 40, 140.
Shuttleworth, 5, 120; 100, 177.
Silkstone, Rob. de, xvii., xxvii., 16, 126; 57, 150.
SIMON LE GELDHIRDE, keeper, xxvi., 20, 129; 22, 130; 23, 131 *seq.*; 38, 139; 192.
Simondestone, Ad. de, 9, 122; 104, 179; Alice de, 111, 182; Galf. de, 13, 124; 109, 182.
Skipton, xvi.
Slaidburn, xii., xxii., xxvii.; 188.
Smith, Ad., 109, 181.
Snaith, xii.
Snelleshowe, 14, 125; 111, 183.
Snodworth, 14, 124.
Sproscroft (Spronthescrofte), 53, 147; 65, 154.
Spurs, 12, 124; 53, 148; 65, 154-5; 192.
Staincliff, Wapentake, vi., 14, 125; 111, 183.
Stallage, 59, 151; 101, 177.
Standen, 14, 125; 40-2, 140-2; 91-2, 170-1; 97, 174; 112, 183; 114, 185; 190 *bis*.
Stanlaw Abbey, v.-vii.
STANSFIELD, OLIVER DE, xxvii., 12, 124; 15-16, 125-6; 52, 147; 99, 175; 109, 181; 116, 186.
Standish, 10, 122; 97, 174.
Starky, Ran. de, 48, 145; 52, 147; Ric., 61, 152.

Stockes, Hen. del, 78, 162-3; Tho. del, 80. *See* Estock.
Stockport, Ric. de, 10, 123; 107, 180; 188.
Stopham, W. de, 19, 128; 189.
Strete, Tho, del, 61, 152.
Streteward, 46, 60.
Stretton, 48-9, 145; 52, 147; 60, 151; 190.
Sureys, Tho. le, 110, 182.
Sutton, in Prescot par., xii.
Swetemilke, W., 117, 187.
Swine, 8, 121, &c.

TALBOT, SIR EDM., x., xxv., 68, 156; 112, 183.
Tallage, 47, 144, &c.
Tanshelf, 19, 128.
Tasker, Ad. le, 105, 179.
Tempest, Rog. 191.
Thanage, 105, 179. *Cf. Whalley*, v. i., pp. 231-2.
Thanes (of Clitheroe), 13, 124; 109, 182.
Thayn, Elias, 14, 125.
Thelwall, 45, 143; 53, 147; 59, 151; 65, 154; 190.
Thisteltack, 8, 121; 60, 152; 63, 153; 99, 176; 103, 178; 188.
Thomas, s. of Alan, 27, 133.
Thomas of Dynbeghe, 112, 183.
Thomas, Serg. of Standen, xxvi., 14, 125; 41, 141-2; the Parker of Halton, 43, 144; 59, 150.
Tockholes, Ad. de, 14, 125.
Toft, 8, 122; 13, 124; 45, 143; 59, 151; 106, 180; 117, 187.
Torale, 43.
Tottington, viii., xiv., xix., 5, 120; 96, 174; 100-1, 176-7; 114-15, 184-5; 191; Mill, 5, 120; 15, 125; 101, 177.
Townley, 14, 124.
Townley, Ric. de, 14, 124; fam., xxv.-vi.
Trailbâton Writ, 189.
Trafford, Hen. and W. de, 61, 152.
Trawden, xx., xxii., 20, 129; 23, 130; 36, 138; 38-40, 139-40; 68, 156; 99, 176; 114, 185.
Tudor ap Carwar, xiii, 51, 147.
Tyndehevyd, Ric. del, 14, 125; 105, 179.
Twyselton, 97, 174.

UGDEN. *See* Ogden.
Ulvesboth (Ullesbothe), 9, 122; 105, 179.
Upton, 49, 145; 62, 152.
Upton, Amabella and Dobbe de, 50, 146; Matilda, 63, 153; Will. de, 62-3, 153.

V ACCARIA, xx., 11, 123, &c.
Vavasour, W. de, 189 bis, 191.

W ADDINGTON, Greg. and Sim., 191; Walt. de, 11, 123; 15, 125; 107, 181; 113, 184; 191.
Wainwright, W. le, 115, 185.
Waleys, Hen. de, 49, 145.
Waleton, 45, 143; 48, 144-5.
Waleton, Tho. de, 48, 145.
Walley, Rog. de, 10, 122.
Walmesfelde, 45, 143.
Walter, Bp. Chester, xv., xviii.
Walton (Nether), 59, 152.
WAMBWELLE, W. DE, 43, 143; 53, 148; 56, 149; 57, 150.
Warburton, J. de, 81, 164.
Wardrobe, 98, 175.
Wardship, 48, 145, &c.
Warren, E. of, xv.
Warrener, 15, 126; 97, 174.
Waste lands, xxi.
Waterback, —, 189.
Wax, 61, 152.
Wellmaker, Hugh le, 116, 186.
Welsh Ponies, 19, 128.
Weltone (*i.e.*, Walton), 10, 122; 97, 174.
West Derby, xi., 188.
Whalley, vii.-viii., xvii., xix.; 10-11, 123.
Whalley, Abbot of, 4-6, 120; 91, 170; 112, 183; 188, 189.
Whalley, Hen. de, 106, 180.
Whitacre, 18, 128.
Whitaker's *Whalley*, xxiii.
Whiteley, 44-7, 143-4; 58, 150; 61, 152; 190.

Whitteley, Ric. de, 47, 144; and Amabilia, 48, 145.
Widnes, xiii.-xiv., xix.; 49-50, 145-6; 62, 152; 188, 190.
Widness, Ran. de, 50, 146; 63, 153; Rog. de, 50, 146.
William, s. of Andrew, 36, 138; s. of Edde, 50, 146; s. of Gryffry, 26, 132; s. of Hawysia, 26, 132; 72, 158; s. of Hen., 13, 124; 109, 182; s. of Keelyn, 191; s. of Margery, 14, 125; 17, 127; 19, 128.
Windle (Wyndhil), Rd. de, 117, 187.
Winewall, 40, 140.
Wode, Will. del, 75, 160.
Wodehouses de, Christiana, dau. of Ad., xxiii., 4, 119.
Wolf, xx.-xxi.; 20, 129; 23, 130; 30-1, 134-5; 77, 161; 80, 163; 84, 165. (Cf. *Loidis*, p. 177.)
Wolfreden, xx., 4, 119; 99, 176.
Wool, xxi.
Wordhille, Ad. de, 31, 135.
Worsthorn, near Burnley, xxvii.
Worston, near Clitheroe, xi., 7, 121; 15, 125-6; 97, 174; 102, 177-8.
Wreckage, 10, 123; 188.
Wulnet, Alan, 62, 153.
Wymondeshouses, 7, 121.
Wyot, Ad. de, 7, 121.
Wythns, 5, 120.
Wyrisbanke, W. de, 60, 151.

Y ORK Prebends, x., xviii.
Yorkshire Estates of E. of Lincoln, xix.

CHARLES SIMMS & Co., Printers, 53, King Street, Manchester.

www.ingramcontent.com/pod-product-compliance
Lightning Source LLC
Chambersburg PA
CBHW021830230426
43669CB00008B/923